ROCKY MOUNTAIN
WALKS

ROCKY MOUNTAIN
WALKS

Gary Ferguson

Research Coordinated by Jane Ferguson
Illustrations and maps by Kent Humphreys

Fulcrum Publishing
Golden, Colorado

Rocky Mountain Walks provides safety tips about weather and travel, but good
decision making and sound judgment are the responsibility of the individual.

Library of Congress Cataloging-in-Publication Data
Ferguson, Gary.
    Rocky mountain walks / Gary Ferguson.
        p.   cm.
    Includes bibliographical reference and index.
    ISBN 1-55591-120-X
    1. Hiking—Rocky Mountains—Guidebooks. 2. Rocky Mountains—
Guidebooks. I. Title.
GV199.42.R62F45 1993
917.8—dc20   92-74515
                                                      CIP

Printed in the United States of America
    0   9   8   7   6   5   4   3   2

Fulcrum Publishing
350 Indiana Street, Suite 350
Golden, Colorado 80401-5093

To Mom—for the love, for the lessons

▪ Contents ▪

Contents

• Introduction •

I'm not exactly sure how the notion of the Rocky Mountain West drifted across half a continent to take hold of me, an eight-year-old boy, sitting in the corn fields of Indiana. Maybe it seeped from the musty pages of an old *Writers Project* tour guide, or poured out into the living room one Sunday night, when The Wonderful World of Disney was airing "Bear Country," or some such True Life Adventure. But take hold it did. Two years later I got my first glimpse of the Colorado Front Range from the back seat of a '64 Impala, and I knew it was true love. I went home, sent in my subscription to *Rocky Mountain West* magazine, and announced to my parents that, if it was all the same to them, the Rockies was the place for me. Like my heroes the trappers, explorers, naturalists and wagon-train guides, at the ripe age of 10 I had come to a conclusion similar to that of William Blake, 150 years earlier. "Great things are done," he said, "when men and mountains meet."

It was not until I had lived here for some time that I began to catch on to the fact that there was far more to be found in these Rocky Mountain states than just mountains. There were forests—great, wet cathedrals of ancient red cedars in the northwest corner of Montana, and lonely pockets of piñon and juniper huddled in New Mexico along the old Santa Fe Trail. Deserts were here too. I found windswept tablelands in Wyoming where wild horses still poured from the mouths of sagebrush draws, and ruts along the Texas border from the wheels of John Butterfield's stage. And perhaps most surprising of all, I found beautiful prairie—places where June grass and bluestem still rippled at the feet of wooden windmills, and the great swells of land and sky held lean, fleet herds of pronghorn, and great flocks of south-bound birds.

The majority of these walks are not meant to take you to any particular destination; indeed, many of the turnaround points are quite arbitrary. I've tried only to point you down the quietest, most-gentle paths possible, introduce you to a few of the neighbors, and leave the rest to you and Mother Nature.

Each walk in this book will highlight one of four general environments, or ecosystems: desert, forest, prairie and mountain. Within each of these environments you'll find levels of adaptation and diversity sufficient to stretch the imagination of even the most jaded explorer. Before we head down that first trail, let's take a closer look at each of these landscapes—these worlds within worlds, thick with beauty and intrigue.

"No one else looks out on the world so kindly and charitably as a pedestrian," said John Burroughs. "No one else gives and takes so much from the country as he passes through." It's my hope that in your saunters down these gentle, brown paths, you'll discover he was right.

Mountains

Although over half of the landscape of the Rocky Mountain states is composed of plains, plateaus and deserts, it is the mountains we dream about most, the mountains that we remember best. These soaring parapets of granite and gneiss, limestone and shale, form a world like no other on earth—a bold, astonishing place, a sacred marriage of earth and sky. More than a few miners who came here in the 19th century looking for gold seemed unable to get enough of the Rockies, routinely selling out promising claims for the chance to roam even deeper into these dense forests, even farther along some icy braid of mountain water.

The geologic story of the Rockies is a complex one, not fully understood even today. While the oldest rocks in these states can be dated back more than two billion years—fully half as old as the earth itself—the rise of land that would become the Rockies we know today began much later, perhaps 50 to 60 million years ago. (These mountains are actually very young when compared to those of the eastern United States.) The ridge of Rocky Mountains through New Mexico, Colorado, Wyoming and Montana is located in the center of a large tectonic plate, one of more than a dozen gargantuan land masses that encircle the globe. It is the ability of such plates to actually move, to drift across a broth of molten rock deep within the earth, that 200 million years ago allowed the entire North American continent to break from Europe and drift 1,500 miles to the west. This plate eventually rode up and over the Pacific Plate, submerging it, causing an abundance of turmoils deep within the earth—turmoils that would cause great, slow uplifts, or "orogenies," to occur throughout the Rocky Mountain states. In many areas, this was followed by periods of intense volcanism.

Yet much of what we find most exciting about the high Rockies—the great rock amphitheaters, cobalt-colored lakes and waterfalls making dramatic plunges into enormous, U-shaped valleys—is the result of the chilling scour of glacial ice. Over the past two million years there have been at least four periods when great sheets of ice ground their way out of the high country, where it often surrounded all but the highest peaks, carving the land-scapes as effectively as hot metal scoops in a carton of ice cream. Small snowfield remnants of the last active glacial period, which ended many thousands of years ago, can still be seen in the high folds of the Rocky Mountains.

More delicate, though no less spectacular touches occurred thanks to the erosional power of wind and water. It was the incessant beating of raindrops, the splitting power of ice freezing and thawing between cracks in the rock surfaces, that gave many of the Rocky Mountain peaks their rugged, dramatic profiles—a sculpting process that continues to this day. It's also important to remember that as the land uplifted, it raised the streams and rivers with it, giving them extraordinary strength. It was this "power of descent" that allowed the Colorado, the San Juan and the Clarks Fork of the Yellowstone to create such magnificent canyons. Inch by inch these rivers cut, exposing layer after layer of rock. As a result, today we are left with a canyon compendium of earth history that geologists can read as one might flip through the pages of a book.

By sending the landscape ever so slowly skyward, the forces that created the Rocky Mountains also determined what kind of plants (and therefore, animals) would one day be able to live here. As you've undoubtedly noticed on your visits to the mountains, the air becomes colder the higher you go. Add to this the fact that cool air cannot hold as much moisture as can warm air, and you've got the key that unlocks a good portion of the Rocky Mountain climate mystery. Air coming in from the west will rise up the western flanks of the Rockies (after having already done the same above the Cascades or Sierras), losing most of its precipitation in the cold air of the high country. By the time that it descends again over the eastern side of the range these air masses have very little moisture left to give. This is why there is a great belt of dry prairie running up the east side of each of the Rocky Mountain states. Such uplifts are also, incidentally, what cause the summer thunderstorms that are so common to the Rockies. Air lying next to the sun-warmed earth begins to rise in the early afternoon, invariably dropping its load of rain on surprised backpackers trekking the high-mountain trails. (Be aware of this phenomenon, and the fact that such thunderstorms are often accompanied by lightning, when you walk the mountain paths of this book.)

This well-regulated moisture-release system has created fairly predictable zones of vegetation. Depending on where you begin your trek up the mountains, you may pass first through a piñon pine and juniper woodland, most often growing in lower areas that receive 10 to 20 inches of precipitation per year. Rabbitbrush, mountain mahogany, Mormon tea and bunches of rice grass and blue grama are typical companions. As you move up, the "p-j" forest gives way to ponderosa or Douglas fir, which in turn gives way to lodgepole pine and aspen. Finally there are the great, sweeping blankets of subalpine fir and Engelmann spruce, both of which will typically battle their way up to the very limits of tree-growth, shrinking in the process to little more than ragged flag trees and creeping mats, their branches sheared by the raw, stinging fingers of the winds.

Beyond this trees do not stray. Temperatures which usually average no more than 45 degrees even in summer create a growing season too short for trees to maintain their cells, let alone repair damage wrought by the winter winds blowing in excess of a hundred miles per hour. At this level you'll find relatively few species of wildlife. White-crowned sparrows, horned larks and brown-capped rosy finches nest in dwarf timber, grassy meadows and along high cliffs. Elk and mule deer show up here and there to feed on the tundra grasses, while bighorn sheep can be seen dancing on dizzying stages that have been chiseled from the steep sides of the mountains. Coyotes, bobcats and weasels meander through the rock gardens. As winter is pulled across the landscape, all but the truly hardy drift down to the protection of the timber below. Plump yellow-bellied marmots settle into their burrows for a long winter's nap, not to emerge again until the onset of the breeding season in the spring. Pikas, on the other hand, remain active throughout the winter, existing on larders of grass that were cut and dried on flat rocks during the previous summer. White-tailed ptarmigans are the sole bird to brave this long, bitter season, nestling into snow banks out of the wind, feeding on the tender buds of willow to survive.

The Rocky Mountains are not a forgiving landscape. Their storms can rise as if from beneath a magician's cape, turning a pleasant summer ramble into a frantic dance with spears of lightning. Autumn can dawn sunny and still, and by late morning be cloaked with great curtains of gray clouds bulging with ice and snow. Yet men have always relished the mystery loosed in these rocky folds, the raw, unfettered complexion of the place. They came for the adventure, the thrills or, as one refugee explorer from a well-to-do 19th-century family put it, for "freedom from conventionalities and a disregard of those social amenities to which I was accustomed." It was once said that the wild country of the Rocky Mountains never judged a person according to his past accomplishments or failures, but rather on the state of his character at that particular moment. Indeed, to anyone standing atop one of its wind-scoured peaks for the first time, the Rockies could hardly offer anything but the present moment: a long, lovely eternity, stretching past the gentle curve of the far horizon.

Deserts

Though not particularly expansive, the fingers of desert that reach into the Rocky Mountain states are perfect places to wander on foot. Bypassed by the moisture-laden air systems that loose their cool, liquid cargo on the nearby mountains, life and landscape here have a striking clarity, a clean, crisp look that stays with you long after you leave these lonely, windswept soils. The fact that most of these desert pockets are fringed by high plateaus or even expansive mountain ranges makes them all the more irresistible. The contrast between high and low, hot and cold, and wet and dry makes for a truly enchanted landscape, where you can trace a long line of life tumbling across highlands thick with timber, down through cottonwood-lined canyons, finally arriving at the rock and scrub of the desert floor. In parts of New Mexico, the dance of mountains and desert is so extreme that you can be skiing in the morning, and drop down for a warm sun bath among the yucca and greasewood by mid-afternoon.

The four great desert systems of the United States lie between two massive lines of mountain peaks—the Rockies in the east, and the Sierra Nevada to the west. Only two of these systems, however, the Chihuahuan Desert to the south and the Great Basin Desert to the north, actually lay claim to portions of the Rocky Mountain states.

The Chihuahuan is the desert of southern New Mexico, and perhaps the most classic of any you will tramp through in the pages of this book. Here is 175,000 square miles (more than a third of the continent's total desert land), stretching almost from the center of the "Enchantment State" to the Sierra Madres of Mexico. In New Mexico it occurs as a series of tongues lying between north-south mountain ranges and high plateaus. The common vegetative fabric on this pastel landscape consists of greasewood, tarbush, lechuguilla, yucca, prickly pear and cholla cactus. Yet this hardly completes the picture, as any nook, cranny or mountain slope will have its own particular signature of shrubs, grasses and forbs, depending on altitude and exposure to the sun. The sight of spindly ocotillo branches sprouting brilliant scarlet flowers, the fluttering cottonwood canopies that line the major washes here, and the rich mats of sunflowers, marigolds, groundsel and primrose are visual delicacies not soon forgotten.

The elevation, and therefore the moisture content in many regions of the Chihuahuan Desert, are high when compared to other dry-land areas, a trait that tends to produce an above-average amount of plant material. This, in turn, results in high concentrations of small mammals such as antelope, squirrels, pocket mice and black-tailed jackrabbits. These animals, in turn, lead to healthy populations of predators, including foxes, coyotes, mountain lions and various birds of prey. While the actual numbers of species, especially bird populations, come nowhere near to equaling those of the forests and mountains, the open, spacious quality of desert flora can make many of them easier to see. Because more than a few of these creatures tend to be nocturnal, serious wildlife watchers would do well to spend a moonlit night hidden above some Chihuahuan Desert water hole.

The other desert arm, this one reaching into western Colorado and Wyoming, is that of the Great Basin. Besides being the second largest of the American deserts, this is by far the highest and coldest of the lot. It was given its name by the frontier explorer John C. Frémont, who, during an exploration of the region in the 1840s, became convinced that the entire region was completely without drainage to the ocean; hence, he dubbed it the "Great Basin" of the West. Actually there are scores of different basins in the region, spiked with more than 150 separate mountain ranges; it's this almost endless rise and fall of landscape that led geographers to dub the region the "Basin and Range" province.

You'll find that the Great Basin Desert lacks the variety of large plants visible in the Chihuahuan provinces far to the south. The land is woven primarily with big sagebrush, along with healthy collections of saltbush, Mormon tea, rice grass, galleta and wheat-grass. Despite the lack of variety, the increased elevation of this particular section of the Great Basin creates larger plants, and they occur in somewhat greater concentrations than can be found in the lower reaches of the same desert in Nevada and western Utah.

As you may have guessed, fewer plant species, which means fewer seeds and opportunities for browse, tend to result in fewer birds and mammals. But there are indeed special attractions waiting here. Many of our walks, for example, provide excellent opportunities to see that fleetest of all the North American mammals, the pronghorn. Also here are coyotes, badgers and foxes. A wide variety of raptors soar above the Wyoming basins and the Colorado Plateau, including kestrels, golden eagles and Swainson's, ferruginous and red-tailed hawks.

Whether in the high, cold fingers of the northeastern Great Basin, or the low, hot sands of the northern Chihuahuan, the problem of surviving in these climates is one that has been met with remarkable evolutionary solutions. Ord kangaroo rats, for instance, receive all the moisture they need from the plants they eat. Daylight hours are spent in a network of burrows in which holes can be plugged to regulate both temperature and humidity. Likewise, pronghorn are able to exist quite well without water, some researchers suggesting that certain herds may never take a single drink. Also in the pronghorn's favor is its wide-ranging appetite, being able to gain sustenance from cacti and sagebrush, both of which many animals will not touch.

Plants, rooted to their environment, are even more remarkable in their abilities to survive the extremes of desert life. Ocotillo will drop its leaves under conditions of drought, and then sprout an entirely new crop after the next good rain. The lechuguilla patiently waits through the roll of seasons—often for decades—storing up nutrients from the desert soil. Then, in one remarkable spurt of growth a towering stalk 6 feet high and laden with creamy yellow flowers will appear; later, the seeds are offered to the ground, and the plant withers and dies. Globemallow, on the other hand, will increase its chances for propagation by flowering once in the spring, and then, if there are sufficient rains, again during the summer.

When walking the desert, allow your attention to focus more on the nooks and crannies lying at your feet than on the lilt of distant peaks and valleys. The bottom of a small wash, a hillside shaded from the blast of the summer sun, a thin draw split by a seep of fresh water—these are the magic places of the desert. It's here that you'll discover some of the most startling of life's miracles, all the more unforgettable when held against the desert's vast, shimmering stillness, the long, rugged swell of rock and sky.

Forests

One can hardly speak of forests in the Rocky Mountain states without talking about mountains, as well. The fact is that the rise of the Rockies, and later the Cascades and Sierras, has altered the climate in ways that would change the face of the landscape across much of the continent. These soaring peaks forced storm systems upward, where, in the cooler air they dumped their moisture on the flanks of the mountains, often leaving lands to the east high and dry. Whereas the forest belt once stretched across the entire northern reach of America in one long melting pot of deciduous trees and conifers, the drying effect of the Rockies helped split it into two parts, divided by a great sea of grass. Afterward, any areas of the West that were warm enough to support trees now lacked the moisture they required. On the other hand, the higher reaches that did receive sufficient moisture for tree growth were too cool for deciduous trees to survive.

Much of the mountain West, therefore, would become a land ruled by conifers, a dizzying plunge of landscape blanketed with thick quilts of spruce, fir, juniper and pine. Everything about a conifer—which, by the way, was among the first plants to colonize the earth—fits well into the climate parameters of the Rocky Mountains. By keeping their leaves (needles) year-round, these trees have the option of growing during warm spells of winter and spring, when the moisture content in the mountains is at its peak. Special waxy coatings on the needles keep water loss at a minimum, while the sticky resin that they produce freezes at temperatures far below that of water. Even the shape of a conifer is appropriate to this environment. Their spire-like appearance, a phenomenon especially pronounced in species growing at high altitudes, is perfect for shedding heavy snows; what's more, most conifers have slender, flexible branches that can "give" beneath the weight of ice and snow.

Just as lower, drier areas of the Rocky Mountain states are not suitable growing sites for most trees, so there are upper limits to timber growth, as well. These are the frigid, howling places that beat normally stately trees into cowering mats that crawl on their knees across forlorn reaches of the high country. Growth in such places is extremely slow; a 500-year-old tree may measure only 2 inches across.

Given these two extremes, then, you'll find that most of the timber of this region grows in a distinct belt, neither too high and cold nor too low and dry. Because moisture and cold tend to increase as you go north, this timber belt tends to become lower as you move in that direction. In the central Rockies, it lies roughly between 5,000 and 11,000 feet.

While each of the four Rocky Mountain states covered in this book has its own special blend of forest, there are certainly great overlappings. Douglas fir, for example, which is found at relatively low elevations in northwest Montana, can also be found in the peaks of central New Mexico. Ponderosa pine peppers many of the dry slopes along the entire Rocky Mountain range. This mixing is the result of the fact that the Rockies form a nearly continuous north-south high line over which species can easily migrate into other appropriate regions. Spruce and fir species typically poured out of the Canadian boreal forest, while the long-needled pines worked their way up from Mexico.

There are, of course, exceptions to the conifer monopoly in the Rocky Mountains. Gambel oak, for instance, is especially common throughout the drier slopes of the southern range, while a great many stream banks support alder, mountain maple or red-osier dogwood. But perhaps the most noticeable exception of all is the aspen, a member of the willow family and the most widely distributed tree on the North American continent. To see this tree set fire to an entire mountainside each autumn with a blanket of gold is one of the most unforgettable experiences in the West. Similarly appealing is the sight of milky-white aspen trunks, flying soft, shimmering, green canopies against a deep blue wash of summer sky.

New aspen often sprout from the rootstems of existing trees, a fact which creates large clone groups. This tendency is a decided advantage to a tree whose existence depends heavily on exposure to light. When new clearings are created in the forest by fire, disease or avalanche, the aspen can send up a new crop of trees from the undamaged root system, virtually guaranteeing themselves a place in the sun. On the other hand, it is precisely because of their love for sun that, barring a disturbance of some kind, the aspen is ultimately doomed to be replaced by shade-tolerant conifers.

Certainly the forests of the Rocky Mountain states do not live by trees alone. There are literally thousands of species of flowers, ferns, grasses and shrubs here. Succulent berries splash the trails with reds, purples and even whites. Wildflowers with names as delightful as their blooms—shooting stars, monkeyflowers, yellow bells and paintbrush—turn cool stream banks and sun-drenched rips in the forest canopy into splendid gardens of color. Like the trees themselves, the plants that spread along the floor of the forest have a certain range of tastes that must be met in order for them to survive. Some, like the paintbrush, are amazingly adaptable, perfectly able to sponge off the nutrients in the root systems of other plants, across a wide variety of settings and exposures. Others, like marsh marigold, are limited to rather narrowly defined environments.

It is much the same for the birds and mammals of the forests. For example, you will typically spot golden-crowned kinglets, mountain chickadees, gray jays, pine grosbeaks or Williamson's sapsuckers only in conifer forests. Birds such as redstarts, northern orioles or warbling vireos, on the other hand, are much more likely to be seen in deciduous woods. Some feathered residents of the Rocky Mountain states can switch between deciduous and coniferous forest at will, even ranging into grassland or desert areas, while others are so specialized that they will feed and nest only in particular parts of a certain type of tree! Some have developed physical traits that complement the environment. Crossbills, for instance, have bills that are perfectly suited to opening pine cones to retrieve the nuts. Seen in this way, evolution is much less a vicious survival of the fittest than it is an attempt by each species to minimize competition by becoming particularly adept in a specific niche.

Animals survive by utilizing a similar strategy. It is the amazing acrobatic ability of the marten that allows him to catch his limit of squirrels in the tops of tree canopies. The porcupine has developed a strong, easily manipulated tail which allows him to steady himself while stripping a bark dinner from the trunks of ponderosa pine. Deer mice, which live along grassy edges of the forest, suffer enormous casualties in the clutches of hawks and coyotes. Their survival as a species depends almost entirely on their ability to reproduce; during the warm months of the year, the adult female goes through continuous 23- to 30-day gestation periods.

The niches defined by animals and the plants they use form a marvelously complex web of life, each strand being dependent on many others. This systems lesson, where the whole is seen as more than just the sum of its parts, is just now beginning to sink in. Scientists have hardly begun to trace all of the intricate crossings and anchor points of a Rocky Mountain forest, let alone its place in the larger web of the planet. While our technology has given us new tools to understand these worlds, it has also allowed us to impact them to degrees which were absolutely unfathomable just a century ago.

Today we are still bound to promoting the preservation ethic as a purely pragmatic philosophy. No ecologist worth his salt fails to mention the fact that we may yet discover a myriad of forest plants that have valuable medical applications, or that the destruction of forest cover might severely deplete our groundwater supplies. I can't help but wonder, though, if we will ever grow enough to fit the notion that the forest is valuable in and of itself—that beyond the nurturing and sustenance it offers to us, it represents a sacred life song, one that deserves to be sung whether or not the music ever falls upon human ears.

Prairies

The eternal illimitable sweep of the undulating prairie impressed on me a sense of vastness quite overwhelming. ... I know not when I have felt so forcibly conscious of my own insignificance, as when struggling through this immense waste, and feeling as though I were suddenly carried backward into some remote and long past age, and as though I were encroaching on the territories of the Mammoth and the Mastodon.

—*John Palliser*
1853

While a great many people have learned to enjoy the subtle beauty of the deserts—their quiet vastness, their pockets of colored blossoms and textured sandstones—the lands that make up our prairies have for the most part gone unnoticed. Indeed, a hundred years ago these great expanses of grass were themselves known as deserts. They were areas that would never be settled, places to endure on the way to the rich valleys of Oregon and California or the gold fields of Colorado and western Montana. The elk, pronghorn, bison and birds supported by these rich mats of grasses and forbs were no more than curiosities. Hundreds of thousands were shot for sport from passing trains, and by dudes on horseback looking for nothing more than the thrill of the kill.

In the mid-19th century, cattle were driven to the northern prairies from Texas to get fat on the lush grasses here. Fifty years later, eager to fill the last empty spaces of the West, people swarmed to the prairies to homestead. Unfortunately, homestead laws required that a certain number of acres of each parcel be put into crops, and so for the first time, many of America's most fragile grasslands felt the sting of the plow. A particular problem was the size of the homestead grants. Settlers were at first given 160 acres, which was later increased to 320. Still, this was hardly enough in a land that required 40 acres to manage a single cow. Overgrazing soon became not the exception, but the norm.

Meanwhile, the Native Americans who had lived in these rich grasslands for thousands of years watched civilization roll west, angry at those who would engineer such a conquering of Grandmother Earth. Of all the earth's bounties, the Plains Indians held in special reverence the grasses. It was the grasses, after all, that regularly brought bison, pronghorn, deer and birds. Despite relentless efforts to turn reservation Plains Indians into farmers, many would have none of it, believing it sheer madness to tear into the living skin of a land that had sustained them for so many generations.

The retribution that many tribes believed would happen to those who took the land for granted did, in fact, occur. In the 1930s, a fatal mixture of overgrazing, plowing and drought conditions turned living carpets of prairie grasses into millions of acres of blowing dust and hummocks of sand. Street lights burned all day long in the darkened streets. Layer after layer of Colorado dust settled not only onto the capitol building in Washington, D.C., but onto decks of ships 300 miles out in the Atlantic Ocean.

In themselves, the fantastic storms of the dust bowl days were not unprecedented. The prairie was, in fact, built by wind-borne soil, which over countless millennia accumulated in the central plains to depths of several hundred feet. What had changed at the hand of man, however, was the conditions under which such events would occur. Removing the plants that covered the prairie was like turning up the volume of the already mighty wind. Instead of conquering the West, we suddenly found ourselves more vulnerable than ever to one of its greatest forces.

When Resettlement Association agents arrived to buy up the worst of the homesteaders' lands, they found that many had already left, totally abandoning their homes and goods. Some were seen driving cars or trucks piled high with possessions west to California; others, either without cars or money to fuel them, walked by the sides of the roads, hoping for a ride to anywhere. The government appropriated moneys to acquire these lands, either by outright purchase—typically $2.00 per acre—or simple payment of delinquent taxes. (By 1930, almost 70 percent of the plains homesteaders were delinquent on their taxes.) The lands were slowly restored by the Soil Conservation Service through the seeding of crested wheatgrass, along with wind-break and erosion-control projects. These land-utilization projects, or, as they were later known, national grasslands, remained in the hands of the government, which today manages them primarily for grazing and energy development.

Belts of grassland, or former grasslands, actually cover a good portion of the United States. One stretches from Illinois to the eastern sections of the Rocky Mountain states. Another is found between the Rockies and the Sierras and Cascades, and yet another occupies the central and certain coastal sections of California. For the purposes of this book, however, we'll confine ourselves to discussions of the shortgrass and, to a lesser extent, the mixed-grass prairies of the Rocky Mountain states. As a plant type, grasses began to evolve more than 75 million years ago. They developed in intriguing ways, bringing into the world new methods of dealing with the problems that plague all plants growing in this type of environment. For one thing, the root systems of grasses, especially perennials, tend to make up a very large portion of their total biomass—more, in fact, than a comparable area of forest. These roots allow the plant to tap into water resources lying far below the ground. In addition, since these roots store large amounts of energy, they can easily send up new growth once they've been clipped by grazing animals. Having relatively small leaves reduces the amount of moisture lost through transpiration, and their long, narrow shape allows the strong winds here to flow through without damaging them.

The mix of grasses on the prairie is surprisingly complex. Some are perennials (lasting several years with deep root systems), while others are shallow-rooted annuals. Annuals, which conduct their business and set seed all in one season, have been able to increase their numbers as the land continues to suffer from erosion and overgrazing. Some grasses, such as blue grama, put out runners, which form sod, a trait that tends to keep other species from invading their territory. Others, especially in drier areas, grow in well-spaced bunches. Some prairie grasses conduct photosynthesis in the spring and fall, while their neighbors do most of their work through the heat of summer.

Shortly after grasses arrived in the world, animals evolved to take advantage of the bounty they offered. A quick look around the prairie will give you good clues as to what attributes are most appropriate for survival here. Hard to miss is the fact that grasslands offer few places to hide. Thus, if you are a ground bird, an appropriate amount of camouflage will come in handy, as the prairie chicken or savannah sparrow so aptly demonstrates. If you can't blend in, then head underground, like prairie dogs, moles and ground squirrels. If even that is not an option, then be prepared to run, as the pronghorn that range these vast expanses are able to do. Pronghorn are also armed with extremely good eyesight; if you can get a close look at one through a pair of binoculars, you'll notice that the eye sockets form the highest part of their skeletal frames—a trait that allows them to see the farthest distance possible.

Although prairies have been ravaged as completely as any environment in the West, those who take the time to tramp the last of the remaining prairies will find them to be a rich, fascinating environment. Like the great herds of bison that pushed their way across these lonely lands, life here still seems to ebb and flow in great, unfettered waves. Light washes over the land in blankets of blue and rose, fading at last to darkness; birds rise and fall in clatters of beating wings, and are gone.

▪ MONTANA ▪

MONTANA

■ ■ ■

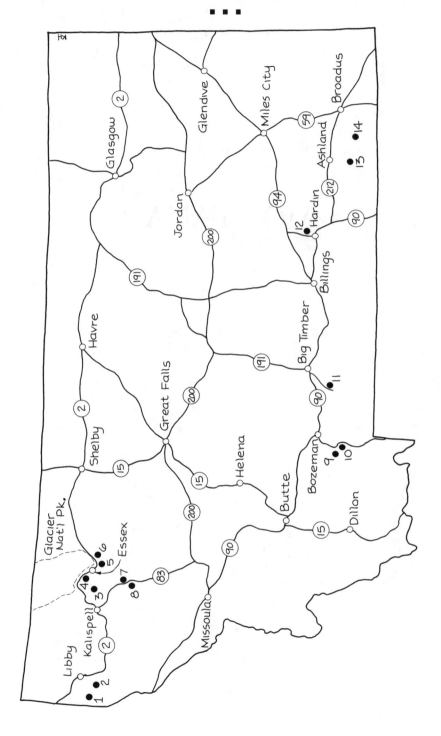

Northwestern Montana

WALK #1—ROSS CREEK

DISTANCE: 2.4 miles

ENVIRONMENT: Forest

LOCATION: Kootenai National Forest. Located south of Troy on Montana Route 56, about 18.5 miles south of the junction with U.S. Highway 2. Turn west off of Montana 56 between mile markers 16 and 17, and follow this road for 4 miles, following signs for Ross Creek Cedars. *Note:* Trailers are not allowed beyond a point roughly 0.75 mile west of Montana 56. Those with trailers may want to park them just east of this closure point, or leave them near Bad Medicine Campground, located 1 mile to the north.

It would be hard to think of another pocket of forest anywhere in the Rockies that offers the sense of mystery and enchantment of these thousand-year-old red cedars. Here it's easy to feel close to a time when Kootenai Indians passed through these groves, bound for clearings thick with juicy berries, or crept on hide moccasins through the grassy fringes of lower Ross Creek, looking for white-tailed deer.

To find a collection of western red cedars this old is rare, most having been lost long ago to fire, or more commonly, to the teeth of the loggers' saws. It's astonishing to consider that some of these trees were just starting life when Peter the Hermit was busy leading half-a-million peasants on the epic first Crusade to the Holy Land.

Besides red cedar, another fairly common tree you'll see here is the western hemlock. But while hemlocks may grow in profusion in wet soils like these, red cedars have the edge when it comes to drier environments, because they're better able to absorb water from the surrounding soil. As you walk this trail, take a close look at the growth patterns that occur in different habitats. How do sunny sites compare to shady ones, or rocky sites to those with deeper layers of soil? Part of the path we'll be following, incidentally, is along the Ross Creek Nature Trail, a pleasant loop walk with interpretive signs to help you identify a few of the more common plants.

Near the beginning of the nature trail, an interpretive sign mentions the fact that the path you're walking is part of an old pack trail used by miners and prospectors. As in much of the Rocky Mountain West, the 1860s and '70s saw swarms of determined men sweeping through the valleys of the Cabinet Mountains looking for silver and gold. Strangely, many who did stumble across fairly promising sites sold their claims and moved on before they could really be developed, a fact that gave rise to the notion that it was as much the roaming as the lure of riches that pushed these adventurers from one slice of mountainscape to the next.

While there were a few small, mildly successful placer operations in the Cabinets, the closest thing to a bonanza in the immediate area occurred near the turn of the century about 13 miles east of here as the hawk flies, at a site called the Snowshoe Mine. Before the ore wagons stopped rolling, this mine had loosed from the earth over a million dollars' worth of silver, gold and lead. Descendants of these early Montana miners can be found today in the nearby towns of Libby and Troy. As you walk through this forest, besides

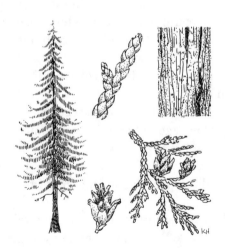

Western Red Cedar

Western Hemlock

towering red cedars and hemlocks you'll see Engelmann spruce, mountain maple, western white pine and grand fir. The ground itself is covered with a rich weave of queencup beadlily, wild ginger, violet, showy devil's club, lady fern, fragrant bedstraw, oak fern, foamflower, Solomonseal and trillium. The trillium's beautiful three-petaled white flower is considered by many outdoor lovers to be the first assurance that spring has really arrived. One species of this plant (ovatum) was widely used by Indian peoples to ease pain during childbirth, hence one of the plant's other names, "birthroot." Trillium roots are firmly anchored in a myth that claims they produce a wonderful love potion.

A short distance past a wooden bridge crossing Ross Creek is a fork in the nature trail. Take the right branch, and watch for Trail No. 142, which also takes off to the right. We'll follow this more rugged, far less-used path for about 0.75 mile, meandering through grand red cedar stands and lush pockets of groundcover, finally joining up with the Middle Fork of Ross Creek.

About 0.25 mile after leaving the nature trail, notice the abundance of exposed tree roots woven across the path. Many of the trees in this forest actually have very shallow roots, a fact which comes as somewhat of a surprise, considering how much weight they have to support. But the soil here is not particularly rich; instead, the trees of these environments have evolved the technique of gathering their nutrients from the constant supply of plant material decaying on the forest floor.

Just before our turnaround point beside the Middle Fork of Ross Creek, you'll pass through an open area supporting an amazing collection of ground plants. Compare the growth here to that beneath the canopy of the nearby forest. Survival is largely a matter of finding a place in the sun. The strategies that plants have developed to capitalize on openings in the forest canopy are remarkable. Some conifers, for example, have cones that will open to release their seeds only if exposed to intense heat. This way, when a fire comes through and "clears the competition," they will get a significant jump on colonizing the newly opened sun space.

When you reach the nature trail again on your return trip, take a right to complete the loop. Try to really slow down in this forest. Smell its smells, listen to its bird song, throw back your head and note the overwhelming size of these great trees. It's hard not to agree with the famous explorer David Thompson, who was struck at the difference between the great forests of western Montana and the smaller trees that grew a week's ride away on the eastern slope of the Continental Divide. "There we were men," he wrote in the early 1800s, "but on the west side we were pygmies."

Devil's Club

WALK #2—EAST FORK, BULL RIVER

DISTANCE: 3.25 miles
ENVIRONMENT: Forest
LOCATION: Kootenai National Forest. From Montana Route 56, head east for 4.5 miles on Forest Road 407. A sign along the highway reads "East Fork Bull River." This turn off of Montana 56 is about 8 miles north of the junction with Montana Highway 200. The trail we'll be following is the one to St. Paul Lake.

The East Fork of the Bull River begins its westward roll from beneath the shadows of St. Paul Peak, high in the Cabinet Mountains Wilderness. (Some say these mountains got the name "Cabinet" from a steamboat by the same name that operated on the Clark Fork of the Columbia River during the 1860s.)

Driving to the trailhead on Forest Road 407 will offer you a tempting glimpse into the rugged beauty of this mountain range. These vertical walls and serrated ridge lines are a definite contrast to the more gentle, rounded peaks visible elsewhere in this part of Montana. When glaciers inched their way southward out of Canada 75,000 to 100,000 years ago, most of the mountains, such as the Purcells north of Libby, were covered completely by ice. But the taller peaks in the more southerly Cabinets stayed above the level of advancing ice. They stood as grand sentinels through the long, relentless winters, their faces splitting into rugged ridges and headwalls under the pounding of the weather, while great rivers of glacial ice carved U-shaped valleys at their feet.

After a few short climbs during the first 0.25 mile of trail, the pathway along the Bull River's East Fork becomes a gentle, relaxing meander through a quiet, soothing forest of old-growth red cedar, hemlock, fir and spruce. Because of the abundant moisture here, and therefore increased decay, much of the path lies on a soft, plush surface that is an absolute delight to walk on. After 0.25 mile you'll begin a slow amble along a forested bench perhaps 40 feet above the East Fork valley bottom. From this slightly elevated perch you can look down into an absolutely magical interplay of light and shadow, where shafts of sun seem to float down for soft landings on rich, green carpets of thimbleberry and bracken fern.

You may notice that you can't begin to compare in lushness the forest ground immediately surrounding you with that visible below. These dramatic differences are the result of several conditions, a key one being sunlight. Because many species of trees cannot grow well if their roots are submerged in water, a saturated bottomland adjacent to a stream will usually not be as heavily forested as the surrounding hillsides. Fewer trees means a more

Thimbleberry

Bracken Fern

Marten

open tree canopy, which means more sunlight will reach the floor of the forest to support the growth of ground plants.

You'll see a particularly striking example of how a rip in the forest canopy can affect groundcover at 1 mile into the walk. Here the trail suddenly emerges into a large opening thick with fireweed, thimbleberry, cow parsnip, ferns and paintbrush. After 30 yards the path ducks back into a thick conifer forest with almost no groundcover, and finally into a more open forest supporting a modest growth of wild ginger, violets, bracken fern and false Solomonseal. While we tend to view a forest as a fairly stable environment, a simple event like a large tree blowing over in a windstorm can have a profound effect on what plant life will grow there. This, in turn, influences the number of grazing and browsing animals like deer and elk.

Approximately 1.6 miles into the walk, just past another open area, the trail will come very close to the East Fork of Bull River. This is our turnaround spot. Plan to spend some time here watching this lovely stream fast-dancing through what can best be described as a great cathedral of old-growth red cedars, many of which have been guarding this lush pocket of wilderness for over 400 years. For those who wish to keep walking, it's slightly less than 2.5 miles to beautiful St. Paul Lake, high in the Cabinet Mountains Wilderness.

If you haven't already noticed them, on the way back to the trailhead look for fairly large, triangular holes that have been cut in several of the trees lining the trail. These are trap sites used to catch the marten, a beautiful weasel-like creature that spends much of its time hunting squirrels in the conifers. Typically, a small log is set against the trunk, with its upper point placed in the opening that has been carved in the side of the tree. A baited trap is inserted, luring the unsuspecting marten up the pole and into its steel jaws. This method of trapping results in a slow, cruel death to the marten, not to mention causing unnecessary destruction to the tree. If you see such trap sites in the national forests, report them to the Forest Service.

WALK #3—BLAINE MOUNTAIN

DISTANCE:	8 miles
ENVIRONMENT:	Mountain
LOCATION:	Flathead National Forest. From the town of Hungry Horse, head south on the West Side Reservoir Road (Forest Road 895). Then turn right on Forest Road 895A, leaving near the Doris Boat Landing, and continue west for about 5 miles to Forest Road 1602. Begin your walk along this road.

The trail to Blaine Mountain is located roughly 2 miles down Forest Road 1602. In the recent past this route was open to cars, but now it has been blocked off, thus making our walk substantially longer than it used to be. Rest assured, however, that the road walking here is very pleasant, some of it along a clear, tumbling mountain stream, with grand views of the high peaks of the Great Bear Wilderness to the east. Even if you never make it to the summit of Blaine Mountain, this is still a route well worth your consideration.

After you gain the actual trail (again, about 2 miles from where you parked your car), you'll find yourself in lush gardens of cow parsnip, leafy aster, twinberry, alder, fireweed and the fine, delicate purple hoods of the harebell. The harebell is also quite common in Scotland, where it has been known by the names "bluebell of Scotland" or "witches' thimble." This latter reference to witches, by the way, may give a clue to the origin of the name harebell. In the Scottish Highlands, witches were once thought to be able to change into hares at will. Thus it was considered a very bad omen to have a hare cross your path as you were out walking the countryside. Don't worry, though; the only bunny you're likely to see on this walk is the mountain cottontail, and it really isn't a true hare at all.

As the trail climbs gradually along a series of switchbacks, you'll have fantastic views of the Flathead Range to the east, between Hungry Horse Reservoir and Glacier National Park. These peaks, as well as the striking block formations of Glacier, were carved from a great slab of billion-year-old rock that migrated to its present location from the west some 65 million years ago. It was this transported assemblage of Precambrian sedimentary rock that was eventually eroded by ice, rain and snow to form the ragged crest of the Continental Divide.

While the importance of conservationists' efforts to protect the wilderness before you cannot be overestimated, the truth is

Peregrine Falcon

that most of these areas, in particular Glacier National Park, were originally protected because they were not considered to be good for much else. The Hudson Bay Company's fur harvest had long since come and gone by the time the national park bill first came up in 1907, as had a minor mining boom along the Continental Divide. Promises of oil around the turn of the century were, thankfully, short-lived, and much of the park didn't contain a great amount of valuable timber. In addition, some legislators were swayed by the argument that this area could be used to grab a lucrative tourist trade that was spending too much time and money in the Alps of Switzerland. On the third try, in 1909, the bill to establish Glacier National Park passed. Other wildernesses in the region followed much later, with the last of these, the Great Bear, created in 1974.

Interestingly, at the hearings for establishing Glacier National Park, one congressman objected to the whole idea, claiming that the area was so remote and inaccessible that it could never be exploited anyway. Less than 75 years later, in 1980, a report to Congress on the state of the national parks identified Glacier as the most beleaguered national park in the country, with 56 separate threats to its integrity, primarily from energy-development proposals around its perimeter. Even with current protections, it will take a considerable effort to save the wild essence of this region in the years ahead. The biggest problem is that national parks were established according to political, rather than ecological, boundaries. A grizzly bear wandering her territory has no way of knowing that she's just crossed the line into an area slated for mining development or summer homes. It would seem an easy solution to simply add buffer zones in the national forests that would better ensure that the needs of the wild residents of the region will be met; unfortunately, there continues to be tremendous pressure to develop extractive industry along the park perimeter.

Climbing higher and higher, you'll find yourself in a thicker and thicker quilt of high-country sights and smells—a whiff of balsam fir, the sway of lavender wildflowers dancing in the winds. You can turn around at any point along this gradual climb, or follow the path a total of 2 miles to a quiet meadow where it meets the Alpine 7 Trail. The Alpine 7 is a spectacular footpath, running along a high ridge just south of Columbia Falls into the beautiful Swan Range, east of Flathead Lake.

WALK #4—STANTON LAKE

DISTANCE: 2.5 miles

ENVIRONMENT: Mountain

LOCATION: Flathead National Forest. Located east of Hungry Horse, on the south side of U.S. Highway 2, and 0.25 mile west of mile marker 170. A sign is next to the turnoff which reads "Stanton Lake Trail 146." Because there is only a small parking area at the trailhead, you may want to park along the power-line corridor next to Highway 2 and walk the extra 50 yards to the trail. *Note:* This is bear country; please take appropriate precautions.

Just as an old adage warns us not to judge books by their covers, we must be careful of shunning trails because of what happens in the first few steps. If you haven't already guessed, I'm talking about a climb. Standing at the bottom of the Stanton Lake Trail looking up, you may be tempted to scrap this walk entirely, or at least sit down in the path and hope for a lift from a south-bound mountain goat. In fact, the toughest section of the walk is over rather quickly, and virtually all climbing will have come to an end before a half mile of trail has passed under your feet. If you need more convincing, there is plenty of great plant life to study during rest stops, and the view waiting for you at the end of the walk is truly something to write home about.

If you've spent much time in other forests of the Rocky Mountain states, you may be surprised at how incredibly lush this corner of the Rockies is. Fir, spruce, birch and larch grow thick here, while the open ground is covered with green carpets of bracken fern, fireweed, thimbleberry, cow parsnip, red twinberry and false Solomonseal. To the native people of this region these wild gardens were pantries, medicine cabinets and general stores all rolled into one. Thimbleberries, as well as the young shoots and leaves of the fireweed (so named for its ability to colonize burned areas), made very tasty eating, while cow parsnip and the sap of the western larch had significant medicinal values. Sewing thread could be obtained from the stringy outer layers of larch-tree roots,

Douglas Fir

while birch bark provided an excellent covering for canoes. Despite this bounty, most of us shudder to think how much time and energy it took to harvest and prepare each of these plants so that they could be used to sustain everyday life. On the other hand, it is perhaps no less amazing to consider how much time modern man spends making money, only to trade it in for the food and shelter that was once his for free.

In 0.5 mile the trail flattens out onto a bench, with beautiful views over your left shoulder of the majestic mountains in the southern tip of Glacier National Park. The landscape of the Glacier region is truly spectacular, a great story board of geologic history. Here one can see thick, multi-colored layers of rocks that are at least a billion years old. This congregation of stone formed a block nearly 2 miles thick, and actually migrated here from the west over what is known as an overthrust belt. During the ice ages, tremendous rivers of glacial ice, some thousands of feet thick, carved the peaks into a collage of horns, cirques and long, U-shaped valleys. In fact, the stream you hear below (Stanton Creek) actually gets its start at the foot of a remnant glacier lying 8 miles to the southwest.

A hundred yards after entering the Great Bear Wilderness you'll come to an open spot along the trail offering a wonderful view to the southwest of Great Northern Mountain and Mount Grant, 8,705 feet and 8,790 feet high, respectively. Near here you'll also get your first glimpse of Stanton Lake. Shortly after this view the trail will begin to make a descent, most of which is far more gradual than the fast climb you made at the beginning of the walk. The outlet stream of Stanton Lake is a wide, meandering ribbon of crystal framed on either side by the dark green of fir trees—the classic hiker's fantasy of an alpine wonderland. Just after crossing a wooden footpath over a wet area you'll come to a trail on the left in the middle of an incredibly lush garden of cow parsnip, ferns, fireweed and paintbrush. This small path will take you to the north shore of the lake, where a few old logs serve as perches from which to drink in the view.

Sitting here gazing down this long, blue line of mountain water, it's easy to imagine that time has hardly budged since great fur trappers like Thomas Fitzpatrick and David Jackson plied the streams of this region in the 1820s looking for beaver. Reading the diaries of these early explorers one gets the sense that, just as much as the promise of riches, it was the adventure, a love for the sheer brilliance of these mountains, that kept them roaming the wilds season after season, year after incredible year.

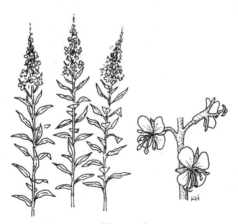

Fireweed

WALK #5—MIDDLE FORK, FLATHEAD RIVER

DISTANCE: 1 mile
ENVIRONMENT: Forest
LOCATION: Flathead National Forest. Located on U.S. Highway 2 mile at marker 185, about 5 miles southeast of Essex. The parking area is located on the south side of the highway, next to Bear Creek. Our walk begins by crossing Bear Creek on a wooden bridge located approximately 50 yards west of the parking area. *Note:* This is bear country; please take appropriate precautions.

The Middle Fork of the Flathead River begins in the womb of one of the largest, wildest mountainscapes to be found anywhere in the continental United States. Near its birthplace along the high peaks of the Continental Divide it is little more than an icy finger of snowmelt. But as it makes its way to the northwest it quickly gathers heart, dancing through the Bob Marshall and Great Bear wildernesses, then along the southern border of Glacier National Park, finally joining its equally dazzling sisters—the North and South forks of the Flathead—near the town of West Glacier. Fortunately, large sections of each of the three forks of the Flathead have been designated by Congress as National Wild and Scenic Rivers, a special type of protection that will keep their spirits from ever dissolving into the slackwaters of a reservoir.

The term *Flathead,* by the way, refers to a great Indian nation whose homeland once stretched across much of western Montana. There are two accepted stories as to the naming of these Indians. The first, and perhaps most popular, puts responsibility for the title in the laps of Lewis and Clark, who apparently made the bestowal after hearing secondhand stories that the Indians used special cradle boards to flatten the heads of their young. Many tribal members, however, both past and present, deny that their people ever engaged in this practice. The other version claims that the name was given by 19th-century trappers and missionaries because of the fact that these people made their homes along the "flat head" of the South Fork.

As you cross Bear Creek on the wooden bridge, just west of the parking area, take a look at the tall western larch trees to the south, towering above the rest of the forest canopy like feathered lances piercing a cloak of tattered green cloth. The first 0.25 mile of the trail will take you through the shady heart of this forest, the ground dressed in a rich collection of thimbleberry, queencup and lichen. Here, too, you'll spot birch, easily recognized by its lovely thin layers of light-colored bark. Several northwest Indian tribes used birch bark as a sort of drawing paper, as, on occasion, did the famous western artist Charles M. Russell.

After a short climb the path will turn south to parallel the Middle Fork of the Flathead River, which for the time being will remain out of sight. Here you'll enter a rather thick, homogeneous forest of lodgepole pines. The somewhat somber mood of this lodgepole forest is broken up nicely by a profusion of thimble-berry, a ground plant with large, maple-like leaves. You'll also see a few tall spikes of beargrass here, their bundles of white flowers resting on tall, green stems like tiny puffs of cloud.

The lodgepole pines along this stretch of trail are actually the most common pine species of the region. They're especially adept at getting things growing on a site that has been disturbed by fire or logging. (This area was in fact burned many years ago.) Lewis and Clark were probably the first to call these trees "lodgepole," a title they came up with after noticing that many Indian tribes used young trees of this species as framing poles for their lodges.

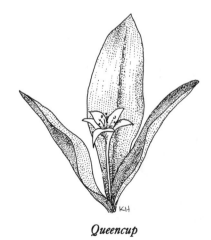

Queencup

In 0.5 mile the trail makes a sharp horseshoe turn to the left. At this turn you'll see a faint path continuing on to the south. Trail crews may have blocked off this south-bound path with a small pile of logs, since a short distance from here a rockslide has made it impassable. But if you walk this faint path for about 80 yards, you'll come to an open area offering sweeping views of the Middle Fork of the Flathead River. (Our turnaround is located beside an old, wooden pole, the last remnant of a telephone system that once led to a Forest Service ranger station a short distance up the river.) The U-shaped valley visible from this perch was formed during the last ice age, when mighty glaciers ground northward, rounding the sharp edges of this rocky landscape.

To the south lies the Great Bear Wilderness, drained by the Middle Fork of the Flathead River. This region is a stunning collection of spruce-fir forests, glacier-scoured valleys and endless braids of mountain water, not to mention the great bear herself— the grizzly—for which the wilderness was named. Combined with the Bob Marshall Wilderness to the south and Glacier National Park to the north, this federally protected area is a virtual master-piece of unspoiled nature—one of only about two such ecosystems in the Rocky Mountains that still contain significant populations of the birds and mammals that made their homes here a century ago. Here at the feet of Spruce Point, Java and Vinegar mountains is a rare opportunity to experience wilderness on a grand scale, a last chance to touch the very spirits that gave form and color to those first visions of the American West.

WALK #6—SKYLAND

DISTANCE: 4 miles

ENVIRONMENT: Mountain

LOCATION: Flathead National Forest. From the town of Essex, head east on U.S. Highway 2. Just past mile marker 195, turn south onto Forest Road 569 and follow it for 3.9 miles. Here you'll see a sign on the left side of the road for Trail No. 382 to Elkcalf Mountain. Our walk takes off about 20 yards past this sign, on the other side of the road. (You'll find parking roughly 0.75 mile past where our trail leaves the road.) *Note:* The first mile of this trail can be muddy; wear appropriate shoes. Also, this is bear country. Please take appropriate precautions.

After a steep, but short, climb our trail heads northwest along a high bench, offering fine glimpses of Elkcalf and Flattop mountains to the northeast, near the Continental Divide. There is a very definite feeling of wildness here, a great deal of it born of the thick spruce-fir forests that mark so much of the high, lonesome reaches of the northern Rockies. This is the land of grizzly and black bear, of elk, deer and moose; here are the twitters and squawks of Steller's jays and Clark's nutcrackers, and the silent wings of golden eagles soaring on the mountain winds.

Along the first mile of trail you'll be in a forest dominated by subalpine fir, underlain with queencup lily, twinberry, Canada violet, thimbleberry and asters, as well as the beautiful yellow columbine. This latter flower, by the way, derives its name from the Latin word for "dove," since the bloom somewhat resembles a cluster of five doves, their heads formed by the bloom's trailing spurs.

At a point just under a mile the path tops a small knoll and then continues along a faint roadway. Just past this point another trail takes off to the left, heading into a northern arm of the Great Bear Wilderness; we'll keep to the right. From this intersection on you'll notice the forest becoming a bit less congested. Alder thickets and the 7-foot-tall rustyleaf menziesia give way to open areas dotted with plants more common to better-drained soils. The tufts of thin, needle-shaped grass you'll see along much of this route belong to beargrass. This is the same plant that produces a large cluster of beautiful white flowers on a green stalk 2 to 3 feet tall. Beargrass sends up these large blooms only once every four to seven years, so in any given season there will only be a portion of the plants actually flowering. While the grassy base may look like it would provide good forage, running one through your hand will give you an idea of how tough these leaves really are. In fact, with the exception of the Rocky Mountain goat, few animals will eat them. Northwest Indians used the dried leaves to weave very durable clothing and baskets, hence the plant's common name "basket grass."

At about 1.3 miles into the walk, along a climbing section of trail, you'll pass a beautiful collection of wildflowers on the right, set against a grand view of both the mountains to the northeast along the Continental Divide, as well as the Blacktail Hills in the southern reaches of Glacier National Park. Besides lupine, paintbrush, beargrass and stonecrop, in June and early July there will be the delicate, three-petaled flowers of the mariposa lily. This plant has a bulb-shaped root that tastes a great deal like a potato. Native Americans used it widely as a food source, as did thousands of hungry Mormon settlers in Utah, who were so thankful for its presence in those early years that they ended up making it the Utah state flower.

Clark's Nutcracker

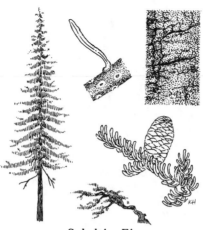

Subalpine Fir

It's often been written that the area before you, in particular the rugged mountainscape of Glacier National Park, formed a region that was generally avoided by the Indians who called this area home. This simply isn't so. The Blackfoot especially regarded many sites in these mountains as sources of great spiritual power, and not only used them regularly for religious ceremonies, but lost a number of their best warriors defending the place from intruders.

At 2 miles you'll reach our turnaround point—a flat section of trail with a sweeping view of the high country to the north and east. As you look north at the peaks of Glacier, much of the forest before you is made up of subalpine fir, certainly the most abundant fir in the American West. The tall, green spires of this tree lend a bold, dramatic beauty to the Rocky Mountain high country, marking one of the last belts of protective vegetation before reaching the wind-blasted rock above timberline. At the base of a couple of these firs you can see small semi-circles of young, shrubby-looking trees. When branches of the subalpine fir are held down by heavy winter snows, they will often take root, thus creating these clusters of small growths, sometimes referred to as "snowmats." The other tree near to you (primarily behind you) on this perch is the lodgepole pine, the only type of pine in the area to bear its needles in clusters of two.

Sitting atop a high, wild slice of mountain such as this one seems to somehow shorten the span between the present and the days when Blackfoot warriors roamed these rocky folds. The

Beargrass

Blackfoot drifted into this country in the early part of the 17th century, during their famous "dog days," when great packs of dogs carried their meager possessions across the land, following the seasonal movements of the buffalo. Comparing them to other tribes of the region, one writer called them "the most independent and happy people." Throughout most of the 19th century they were able to remain strong and confident, taking the best of European culture—horses, guns, metal arrow points, etc.—and adding them to their traditional lifestyles. Only when they were forced off of this rugged, windswept land, the true source of their inspiration and power, did their struggle begin to keep their bold, unfettered spirits from waning.

WALK #7—BOND CREEK

DISTANCE: 3.5 miles
ENVIRONMENT: Forest
LOCATION: Flathead National Forest. Our walk heads east off of Highway 83, just south of mile marker 70, near the town of Swan Lake. A sign along the highway identifies the Bond Creek Trail. There is enough parking here for a couple of cars, but make sure that you don't block the dirt road that runs past the trailhead.

The walk to Bond Creek is a gentle, soothing meander through the forest—the perfect trek for walkers wishing to lose themselves in a thick, green cloak of solitude. Here you'll find rich carpets of wildflowers, grasses and shrubs, along with a pleasant sprinkling of birches and mountain maples. This latter tree, by the way, forms the northernmost maple on the continent, extending from here all the way up through western Canada to southeast Alaska. Stop for a moment and look at the tips of the branches on the mountain maple. More than likely you'll see places where a hungry white-tailed deer has made a meal of the soft, nearly hairless leaves.

The sheer variety and density of plant life in this forest is far different from that found on the other side of the Continental Divide, just 40 miles east as the eagle flies. The reason for this, as you might have already guessed, comes down to a matter of moisture. Great storm clouds from the Pacific Ocean routinely roll into Montana, herded like sheep by the prevailing westerly winds. When these storms finally reach the Rocky Mountains, there is nowhere for them to go but up. And, as you may already know if you've spent any time in the mountains, the higher up you go, the cooler the temperature becomes. Since cool air cannot hold as much moisture as warm air, any cloud working its way up the peaks will end up dumping most of its moisture before it can get across the high line of the Continental Divide. The forest you are walking through right now may receive 7 to 10 inches more precipitation each year than regions immediately to the east.

It will be hard to miss the lacy strings of dark-colored lichen hanging from the branches of the conifers surrounding much of this walk. This is known as black tree lichen, and was a common source of food for Flathead, Nez Perce and Kootenai Indians. It was usually soaked in water first, and then baked in fire pits for one to two days. Far from being "survival food," it was considered to be quite delicious. Some Native Americans, in fact, continue to enjoy black tree lichen even today.

If you are here during midsummer, 0.75 mile into the walk you'll see an abundance of small, golden flowers lining the path-way. These are, in fact, an introduced species of clover, perhaps first brought into the area on some hiker's shoe or pant leg. In the same area, look for a shrub that has oval-shaped, olive green leaves with small brown spots on the underside, and attractive, reddish orange berries. This is buffaloberry, and it was relished by Indians

Western Tanager

and early settlers alike. In fact, when it was mixed with water and beaten with a stick to which grass fronds had been tied, the buffaloberry foamed into a tasty concoction known as "Indian ice cream." These plants still provide many a meal for the occasional black bear, as well as for a host of birds.

You'll find this stretch of trail to be a good place to spot (or at least hear) several of the common feathered residents of this low-lying woodland. Look for hermit thrushes and dark-eyed juncos foraging on the ground and in the lower branches of shrubs, while crossbills, evening grosbeaks and the beautiful yellow body and red head of the western tanager may be seen flitting through the more open stands of conifers.

At about 1.25 miles you'll reach a junction where the trail forms a "T" intersection with a faint roadway. Here you'll turn left, and pick up the trail again in about 25 yards. Shortly after this intersection is a gradual descent into the Bond Creek drainage, which sports a great variety of plant life. Just before you make this descent, keep an eye out for the prickly leafed groundcover known as Oregon grape. The plant's purple berries, which follow beautiful clusters of yellow flowers, are enjoyed by humans as well as wildlife, the former using them for everything from jelly to wine.

Pay particularly close attention to the stretch of trail about 1.5 miles into the walk, which occurs after the previously described descent, and just after crossing a small stream. On both sides of the path the forest has become suddenly somber, so thick with middle-aged conifers that no light can penetrate the canopy. Consequently, the ground is almost devoid of vegetation. But where trees have been cleared for the trail, sunlight pours in like honey, giving rise to a virtual garden of bracken fern, thimbleberry, twinflower and pathfinder. There could be no better place than this to get an idea of what a little sunshine can really do.

Our turnaround point is at Bond Creek, which is reached in about 1.7 miles. This beautiful little watercourse empties into Swan Lake after a delightful run down the mountains high in the northern reaches of the Swan Range. The path you've been on continues along the creek for 4.5 miles to Bond Lake, turns north to Trinkus Lake, and finally joins the beautiful ridge-running trail known as the Alpine 7, roughly 7.5 miles from our parking spot along Highway 83. Those who elect to continue on won't regret a single step.

WALK #8—POINT PLEASANT NATURE TRAIL

DISTANCE: 0.6 mile

ENVIRONMENT: Forest

LOCATION: Swan River State Forest. North of Condon on Montana Route 83, and just south of mile marker 64. If you're traveling from the south, you'll see a small, wooden sign on the east side of the road, which reads "Point Pleasant Campground"; from the north, however, there is no sign. The campground road heads west from the highway for a short distance, then makes a sharp left turn before reaching the trailhead. (The trailhead is just before the campground.)

Though only slightly over a half mile in length, this trail, developed by the Montana Department of State Lands for the Swan River State Forest, serves as a wonderful introduction to the plethora of plants that grow on the moist western flanks of the Rocky Mountains. A small interpretive brochure can be picked up at the beginning of the walk, which should then be deposited at the end of the trail in the box provided. Rather than duplicate what the Department of Forestry has already covered, we'll take a closer look at some of the plants along the trail that have been merely identified with signs.

Before we start talking plants, however, be sure not to miss interpretive stop 1, a collection of nesting cavities in an old larch snag that, at least for the time being, has a family of flying squirrels living in it. Flying squirrels should really be called gliding squirrels, since they use the two large folds of skin between their front and back legs not to fly as birds, but to glide from the branch of one tree to the trunk of another. Nonetheless, the grace they exhibit while soaring through the air—controlling their flight paths carefully with tail and skin flaps—is remarkable.

These handsome animals mate during late winter, and have litters of two to five young during the spring. Flying squirrels are quite common in the forests of northwestern Montana, but, because their airborne missions to round up pine nuts are almost always conducted under the cloak of darkness, they are seldom seen by people.

About 0.1 mile into the walk is a sign identifying lodgepole pine. Try to become familiar with the look of this tree, since it is one of the most widespread pines in the area. It is the only one which bears its needles in bundles of two. Besides using the straight trunks of young lodgepoles to support their tipis, some

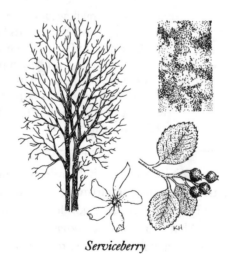

Serviceberry

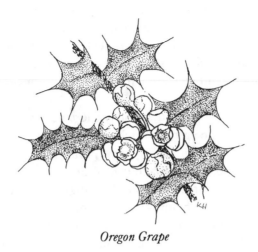

Oregon Grape

Indian people chewed the sap or sweet inner bark, and used the pitch in the treatment of burns and minor skin irritations.

The trail continues to wind through a fine forest, dominated by grand, old-growth stands of western larch. While man uses this tree for little besides lumber, Flathead Indians of the area used to gather a sweet syrup from the larch, and Nez Perce tribes drank a tea made from the bark to help cure colds and coughs. If you're here late in the fall you'll notice that the needles of the larch have turned gold, perhaps causing you to wonder whether or not they are the victims of some terrible insect invasion. In fact, unlike other conifers, each autumn the needles of the larch lose their green color and drop off.

Near interpretive stop 12 you'll see a small sign identifying Oregon grape. Perhaps you're familiar with the use of this plant in jams and jellies, but throughout history it has had enough health uses to fill a medicine chest. Flathead people, for example, used the roots of Oregon grape for everything from antiseptics and contraceptives to treatments for syphilis and gonorrhea. Early settlers made a tea from the roots which was widely used for kidney problems. (If you're confused as to which of the plants around this sign is the Oregon grape, simply look for a creeping ground plant with dull green leaves 2 inches to 3 inches long, each of which sports small spines on the tips, giving them a look somewhat like a holly.)

The overlook of the Swan River at stop 16 is truly beautiful. It may, however, leave you somewhat melancholy about how heavily logged this area has become, a process that began almost from the time that settlers first moved into the area during the latter part of the 19th century. What a magical experience it must have been to be one of the first to see this clear, meandering watercourse flowing through giant western larch trees, white swans floating in the morning mist.

This is not to suggest that had settlers not come, this region would have been one vast, untouched forest. Roughly 80 percent of this landscape was burned by light ground fires that occurred every 20 years or so, and fully a fourth of the trees were completely consumed by major fires that roared through the area about once every four decades. Such burns not only helped control insects and disease, but also provided a mosaic of habitats that served a wide variety of wildlife. This dynamic was most seriously altered beginning about 1900, when the state adopted an aggressive fire-suppression policy—a policy that soon resulted in less than 1 percent of the forest being burned each year.

To a certain extent, then, timbering can help re-create some of the diversity that nature once managed by fire. But such activity must be done in a manner that keeps soil erosion and wildlife disturbance to a minimum. What's more, revegetation efforts have to focus not just on the trees that are best for the sawmill, but on plants that closely resemble the natural diversity of the forest. "Tree farms," after all, not only offer less opportunity for wildlife, but are far more susceptible to devastation by insects and disease.

Southwestern Montana

WALK #9—SOUTH FORK, SPANISH CREEK

DISTANCE:	2.5 miles
ENVIRONMENT:	Mountain
LOCATION:	Gallatin National Forest. From Highway 191, south of Bozeman, head west on Spanish Creek Road (Forest Road 982). This road is approximately 1.5 miles south of mile marker 70. The trailhead is located at the end of Spanish Creek Road, 9.5 miles from Highway 191.

The trailhead of this walk is so beautiful that you may well find yourself intoxicated before you even take the first steps down the path. The stream before you comes laughing out of a high country thick with great stands of timber, fringed for much of its northward flow by olive green willows, and to the distant south, by the great, granite domes of the Spanish Peaks. This mountainscape is home for an amazing variety of wildlife, including bighorn sheep, Rocky Mountain goat, black bear, mountain lion, elk and mule deer. From an ecological point of view, the land here is considered to be part of the Greater Yellowstone Ecosystem—one of only two large, relatively intact environments left in the lower Rocky Mountains.

The peaks visible at the head of the South Fork of Spanish Creek are part of the Madison Range, a name first given by Lewis and Clark to the fine river running west of here along Highway 287. The Madison these two explorers were referring to is James Madison, who at the time was serving as Secretary of State. After Lewis and Clark passed from this country on their return to the east in 1806, the Madison country remained fairly untouched by outsiders until half a century later, when gold strikes at the town of

Bannack brought hopeful prospectors pouring through these valleys like ants to a picnic.

Bannack went on to become Montana's first territorial capital in 1864, although such status was hardly a guarantee of future stability. As soon as rumors of other gold strikes came in, the fickle citizens of Bannack hit the trail at first light to start life anew at the infamous Virginia City, just 35 air miles to the east (10,000 people streamed into Virginia City in a single year!). As it turned out, Virginia City lay beside the largest collection of placer gold in the Rocky Mountains. In fact, of the $65 million in minerals that Montana produced in the 1860s, nearly half came from this area.

Bighorn Sheep

Nevertheless, Virginia City proved hardly more successful than other towns at holding its citizenry, especially when rumors started to fly of even better finds to the north.

After crossing the South Fork of Spanish Creek near the trailhead, turn left, following the footpath upstream through a beautiful forest of lodgepole pine and Engelmann spruce. I've long treasured the fragrance of riparian environments in the central and northern Rockies, a luscious blend of willow and conifers, stirred on occasion by breezes laden with whiffs of damp earth from nearby meadows.

At 0.5 mile you'll enter the Spanish Peaks unit of the Lee Metcalf Wilderness. This unit alone contains more than 50,000 acres of land, nearly all of which is perfect for anyone seeking aimless wanderings up and down nameless folds of rock, sky and water. After passing a side trail on the left (stay right), the path will climb up on a small bench overlooking the stream, now coursing through a maze of willow-lined passages.

The generic scientific name assigned to the class of plants known as willows is *Salix*, an old-world combination of "sal," which means near, and "lis," a word meaning water. In North America alone there are over 150 species of willow, 29 of which occur in Montana. The inner bark of willow contains an acid related to common aspirin, and has been used in similar fashion as a healing compound for headache and fever for over 300 years. In addition, many Montana Indian peoples have used willow preparations to stop cuts from bleeding, as well as to treat various ailments of the stomach and upper intestine. As if all this were not enough, the humble streamside willow has for centuries served as building material for making animal traps, snowshoes, baskets, drum and sweat-lodge frames and fish traps. Indeed, it would be hard to think of a plant with a longer or more varied history of human use.

Roughly 0.3 mile after the previously mentioned fork in the path, a side trail once again joins the main footpath. This is our turnaround point. For a bit of variety, take the other fork back, passing through the thick, lush, willow environment you were looking down on just a few minutes earlier. Incidentally, such streamside vegetation, especially when combined with nearby stands of timber, is a favorite environment of the mighty moose. These grand animals, which should always be given a wide berth, can stand more than 6 feet tall at the shoulder and weigh in at over

1,200 pounds! Incidentally, the rather bizarre-looking posture of this animal is largely due to the construction of its rear legs. They are formed in a way that allows the moose to pull the lower portion of its leg straight up. While this may sound like a strange attribute to have, you'd understand the advantages immediately if you spent much of your day up to your kneecaps in sticky mud.

Mountain Goat

WALK #10—CASCADE CREEK

DISTANCE: 6 miles (round-trip to Lava Lake)
ENVIRONMENT: Forest
LOCATION: Gallatin National Forest. U.S. Highway 191, between Bozeman and West Yellowstone, Montana. The turnoff is located on the west side of the highway, 0.3–0.4 mile north of mile marker 61, and just north of a bridge crossing the Gallatin River. Follow this small roadway a hundred yards or so to the signed trailhead on the right.

Before you take your first steps along this trail, turn around for a moment and enjoy the magnificent river running just to the east. The Gallatin was named in 1905 by Captain William Clark (of the famous Lewis and Clark expedition) for then–Secretary of the Treasury Albert Gallatin. To the Indians of the region, however, much of the watercourse was known as the "Valley of Flowers," a name which walkers along Cascade Creek will also find appropriate. Besides finding favor with the likes of John Colter and Jim Bridger, the stretch of the Gallatin to the north of here was most impressive to those who came with an eye toward feeding cattle. "Such a wealth of grass I had never before seen," wrote one early visitor. "Silence reigned everywhere, broken only by the startled bird, antelope or deer, many of which I disturbed as I came upon them unawares, hidden as they were by the tall, waving grass." The Gallatin Valley was to many as close to a high-country paradise as they would ever see.

There is no getting around the fact that this trail is an uphill affair. The grades are quite variable, however, with short huff-n-puff sections broken up nicely by climbs of a much more mellow nature. What's more, there is no shortage of beautiful scenery along the way. The walk makes a nice all-day affair, ideally broken up by a long, lazy lunch on the cool, green shores of Lava Lake.

The path begins in a classic lodgepole-pine forest, a tree whose name refers to the fact that many Native Americans of the region used this species to build their tipis. A typical tipi, or lodge, required poles approximately 20 to 25 feet in length. The lodgepole is the dominant tree from this point south, where they form endless blankets of dull green across the broad, wild shoulders of Yellowstone's Central Plateau. (Some historians have suggested that it was the dominance of this commercially worthless tree that enabled Yellowstone National Park to be established in the face of a strong 19th-century timber lobby.) The lodgepole is, in fact, one of the most widely distributed conifers in North America, and the only pine growing naturally in both Mexico and Alaska. As you walk through this forest, keep ears and eyes peeled for brown creepers, pine grosbeaks, Steller's jays, pine siskins, calliope hummingbirds and hairy woodpeckers.

You'll become partners with Cascade Creek at a point about 0.3 mile up the trail. This is a beautiful, frothing flow of water that supports an incredibly rich variety of plant life. During the first part of your walk, notice how much more lush the stream bottom is compared to that of the forest floor to your right. Besides having more water nearby, plants growing along streamsides also tend to have more sunlight available to them, since few Rocky Mountain conifers (and perhaps least of all lodgepoles) grow very well with their feet planted in saturated soil.

Lining the trail at 0.5 mile will be white clover, spirea and, at just over 0.75 mile, lots of thimbleberries, with their distinctive maple-like leaves and beautiful white flowers. This plant derives its name from the delicious red, thimble-shaped fruit it produces, which is an important food source for many birds and mammals.

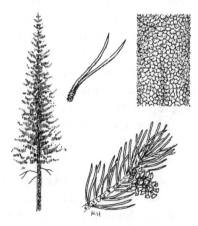

Lodgepole Pine

Pine Siskin

Wild Rose

At 1.5 to 1.7 miles into the walk, keep your eye on the foaming waters of Cascade Creek. Here you'll find several large rocks in the stream sporting wonderful islands of lush moss and plant life on their upper surfaces. This is a wonderful testimony to the fact that a little water can greatly speed up the rate at which plants break down solid rock into new soil. From here on, largely because you've gained elevation, you'll notice a much different kind of forest than that which you left behind along the Gallatin River. At higher elevations the air is cooler, meaning that it cannot hold as much moisture. Clouds routinely rise from the lowlands and drop their liquid cargo up on these high-mountain flanks, giving rise to thick huddles of grasses and wildflowers, as well as to Engelmann spruce and Douglas fir.

By the time you cross Cascade Creek at 2.4 miles, the land will have exploded into a rush of willow, cow parsnip, columbine, wild rose, fireweed and sticky geranium—each lending splashes of lavender, scarlet, lemon or cream to the rich, green carpets that grow at the feet of the great trees.

Lava Lake itself is a geologic splendor, carved out of 2,500-million-year-old Precambrian "basement" rock. The peaks before you are part of the eastern fringe of the Spanish Peaks mountains, which rise dramatically from the larger Madison Range to the west. The northern shore of the lake is lined with willow and rose, as well as thick mats of common juniper.

WALK #11—NATURAL BRIDGE STATE PARK

DISTANCE:	1 mile
ENVIRONMENT:	Mountain
LOCATION:	Natural Bridge State Park. From downtown Big Timber, head south on Montana Route 298 for approximately 28 miles. Natural Bridge State Park is located on the east side of the road, just past the boundary sign for Gallatin National Forest.

Although the 25-foot natural bridge that was once a key part of this monument collapsed in July 1988, the area still has no shortage of splendid natural beauty. Here flows the lovely Boulder River, fresh out of the rugged high country of the Absaroka-Beartooth Wilderness. (The main fork of the Boulder is considered the divide between the Absaroka Range to the west, and the Beartooth Range to the east.) At a point just below the park footbridge, the slow, relatively gentle waters found a short distance upstream change dramatically as the water spills over a magnificent 105-foot precipice. In low water, the stream completely disappears into an underground channel 200 feet upstream from the precipice, and then emerges with a rush from a hole it has bored in the limestone wall near the main falls.

Add to this liquid magic the surroundings in general— sedimentary cliffs, and rugged mountain ridges draped with lodgepole pine and Douglas fir, and it's easy to see why this place has become such a weekend favorite for local Montanans. (Interestingly, though, in the late 1970s at least one local resident was less than thrilled with the whole notion of opening this area to the public; at one point attempts were made to blow up the footbridge across the river, and boulders were rolled off the cliffs onto the trail below.)

Perhaps the best way to approach this area is to first walk the 500-yard interpretive loop trail, which is reached by taking the left branch of a footpath that takes off from the main parking area. The interpretive signs on this short loop offer information about everything from geology to fossils; when you've finished with this trail, then try the walk discussed in this book—a 0.5-mile pathway that begins by crossing the Boulder River on a large wooden footbridge. (Please note that the paved interpretive trail does have abrupt edges; handicapped visitors and those with children should use caution.)

One of the most common trees you'll see along this walk is Douglas fir. You can readily identify Douglas fir by its cones, which have thin, pitchfork-shaped bracts sticking out from between the scales. While here in the Rockies this tree is often rather modest in size, in the Pacific Northwest it reaches colossal proportions; it is, in fact, the third largest tree on the continent, taking a back seat only to the redwood and sequoia. The botanist for which this tree is named, David Douglas, found a Douglas fir in 1825 that measured 227 feet tall and was 48 feet around. Though much of the old growth has since been cut, there are a few thousand-year-old trees still growing in Oregon, Washington and British Columbia. It's astonishing to consider that a tree this age would have been a sapling when Macbeth murdered the king of Scotland!

In spring and early summer these loosely forested slopes are also where you'll see, or more likely hear, the territorial drumming of the male ruffed grouse. This is the strange noise that sounds like someone beating on a hollow log or wooden drum, slow at first, growing faster and faster until individual beats are no longer distinguishable. The ruffed grouse creates this sound by first standing up very straight and leaning back on its tail, and then beating the air with cupped wings. Most of the time a ruffed grouse will perform his ritual each day from atop the exact same log, always facing in the same direction. When a female finally arrives, the drumming suddenly stops; at that point the male will first fan his tail and raise his neck feathers, and then begin a rather slow, hypnotic-looking dance with his neck and head.

Continue following the Boulder River downstream past mats of snowberry, currant, silver sage and squawbush. Squawbush is a 3- to 4-foot-tall shrub, the branches sporting lobed leaflets in clusters of three—one main leaflet, and two on either side. The dark red, somewhat hairy berries that appear on squawbush during the summer have a distinctly sour but still pleasant taste, an attribute that has led to the plant sometimes being called lemonadeberry. (The leaves, however, are not so pleasant; crushed, they smell somewhat like a skunk, thus creating another common name for the plant, skunkbush.) Squawbush takes its most widely used common name from the fact that in some parts of the country Indian women showed a strong preference for using the stems in making baskets, claiming them to be second in quality only to willow.

The well-traveled path ends at an interpretive sign at about 0.5 mile. From here you can simply retrace your steps back to your car.

You may be interested to know that the Main Fork of the Boulder played a small part in the epic flight of Chief Joseph and 200 Nez Perce warriors, 500 old men, women and children and nearly 2,000 horses. Having eluded and, when necessary, fought off the soldiers who were relentlessly pursuing them across the panhandle of Idaho, through the Big Hole Valley and across much of the most rugged terrain in Yellowstone National Park, the army believed that Joseph and his people would come out of the mountains heading north down the Main Fork of the Boulder. In anticipation of this, they built rock breastworks south of here to hide behind, several of which are still visible today. Joseph, instead, headed down the Clarks Fork of the Yellowstone.

In the end, the Nez Perce were finally stopped almost within sight of the Canadian border. Some historians feel that if the government had not set up forts in eastern Montana some years earlier to fight the Sioux, it's doubtful that the manpower would have been available to stop these courageous people before they landed on Canadian soil.

Southeastern Montana

WALK #12—GRANT MARSH

DISTANCE: 1.2 miles
ENVIRONMENT: Prairie
LOCATION: Lower Bighorn River. Head north out of Hardin, Montana, on Montana Highway 47 for approximately 7 miles. At 0.5 mile north of mile marker 7, turn right (east) at a road signed for Grant Marsh. In 1 mile you'll come to a small, two-track road taking off to the right (south). Turn here, and at the first fork, stay left. In a hundred yards you'll come to a "T" intersection in a large grove of cottonwoods. Park here. The walk begins by heading west along the dirt road. *Note:* Just after the first fork, the road passes through a low spot in the road, which might have water from the marsh lying across it. Get out and check the depth before driving through.

This is one of those little surprises in the middle of nowhere that the road-weary nature buff dreams of finding after a hard day on the asphalt. Framed during much of the year by the cool, swift waters of the Bighorn River, this is an especially fine place to come to during the fall, a pit stop for south-bound birds pushed out of the north by the arrival of winter. The network of shallow pools that exist here, many with thick curtains of reed and cattail spikes drawn across their perimeters, also makes this a good waterfowl breeding area.

The area takes its name from the man who is unquestionably the most famous steamship captain of the 19th century, Grant Marsh. Marsh began his steamboat career at the age of 12 as a cabin boy on the Ohio River, taking his skill ever farther west as the years went by. By age 24 he was a first mate on a ship out of St. Louis, his assistant a witty young man who would one day write about his times on the Mississippi under the name of Mark Twain. After the Civil War Marsh moved on to the upper Missouri trade, eventually becoming a captain on a ship owned by "Slippery Dan" Coulson. It was in late June 1876, while he was piloting Coulson's Far West as a troop transport on the Yellowstone River, that Marsh would turn into a national hero. For it was then that a haggard messenger stumbled down to the Yellowstone and told of Custer's crushing defeat in the Battle of the Little Bighorn.

Grant Marsh moved immediately. Of the treacherous, previously unnavigated 64 miles of Bighorn River that lie between the Yellowstone River and the mouth of the Little Bighorn, he managed to push the Far West almost 50 of them. This was not only a feat of amazing skill but also of courage, since to strand the boat in the Bighorn's shallow waters would have meant almost certain death at the hands of the Sioux. By two o'clock in the morning of June 28, the wounded men under General Reno's command had been loaded onto the Far West, and Marsh was steaming for Bismarck, where, along with the wounded, he would give to the world the first report of Custer's shocking defeat. Marsh made this approximately 900-mile run in a mere 54 hours—an absolutely incredible feat, never again equalled in the history of Missouri River navigation. As if that wasn't enough, Marsh went on to make a second hurried trip to rescue more wounded, and then a third to bring supplies for General Terry.

Our walk begins in a lovely grove of plains cottonwood trees. The lives of cottonwoods are bound to watercourses and their active floodplains, a fact that results in the formation not of deep woods, but of long, shimmering green lines of woodland painted across the canvas of the prairie. Curiously, these groves were rarely mentioned by early explorers of the prairie West, many of whom were assessing lands for commercial timber potential. Part of the reason for this may have been that cottonwood just didn't fit what they were looking for. It may also have to do with the fact that with millions of buffalo using the stream-bank corridors, many of these fabulous groves probably didn't exist.

Cottonwoods are famous for their ability to grow rapidly, and during the early stage of their lives they may rise several feet each year. Not in the cottonwood's favor, however, is the fact that its seeds have rather stringent requirements in order to take root, and may remain viable only for a couple weeks after being launched from the tree. (Compare this to lodgepole pine seeds. Locked tightly away in cones that rarely open except during a fire, they may be viable for 40 years!)

Besides providing a great deal of beauty to the prairie rivers they commune with, cottonwoods were very important to the Indians of the northern plains. Among the Cheyenne people, for example, an honored warrior was chosen to select one of these beautiful trees to form the center pole of the lodge used in the sacred Sun Dance ceremony. Most people familiar with this ritual remember it only for its grueling feats of endurance, in particular, how warriors would hang from poles by strips of rawhide laced into the muscles of their backs and chests. But the "medicine," or visions, that these ceremonies produced were taken very seriously. In fact, it was during the Sun Dance ceremony of 1876 that Sitting Bull foresaw many dead soldiers "falling right into our camp." Only weeks later, a group of more than 200 U.S. Cavalry men led by General George Custer did indeed ride right into a large Indian village where Sitting Bull's people were camped, not far to the south of where you now stand.

Many Indian peoples ate the sweet sap and inner bark of the cottonwood, scraping the latter from the trees with the rib bone of a bison. The buds of the trees produced a beautiful yellow dye which was painted on various articles of clothing, and poultices and teas were made from the leaves, bark and buds for treating everything from sore muscles to coughs and colds. Warriors of some tribes would rub the sap of the cottonwood on their bodies to mask their scent when stealing horses from enemy camps.

Soon you'll join the Bighorn River, its fast waters running quietly northward to rendezvous with the Yellowstone. (It was at this river junction that General Gibbon crossed the Yellowstone in a rush to aid Custer, only to find Custer and his men already several days dead on the battlefield.) Lewis and Clark actually named the Bighorn River, as well as the mountains from which it flows, after the regal bighorn sheep, which fascinated them to no end with the graceful way it clambered up and down precipitous slopes.

The roadway turns to the right, and crosses a marsh. Approach this area quietly, and you may see green-winged teals floating in the quiet waters, or a red-winged blackbird clutching a cattail spike. Also commonly seen here are migratory American coots, snipes, black terns, mallard and wood ducks, Canada geese, bald eagles and even pelicans. Beaver, mink, red fox, white-tailed deer and fox squirrels can also be found nearby.

Just past this marsh is a "T" intersection. Take a left here, and continue along a road lined with kochia. Kochia, sometimes known by locals as fireweed (not the fireweed of the Rocky Mountains), is a tenacious resident of this part of the country. A pest to some, there are ranchers who claim that, used as hay, it offers more nutrition than alfalfa.

In 0.4 mile from this last junction in the road you'll reach our turnaround point, on the banks of the Bighorn in a quiet pocket of cottonwoods. This is an especially secluded little nook, a perfect place to cast your troubles out onto the cool, roiling waters of the river, to be lulled into daydreams by the sound of the wind stroking the leaves high overhead. To make a loop out of this walk, continue straight when you reach the road intersection near the marsh, and then take a right at the junction near the entrance to the wildlife area. Keep in mind that this may require a barefoot fording of any water you might have driven through on your way in. Those who prefer to stay on terra firma should return the same way they came.

WALK #13—POKER JIM LOOKOUT

DISTANCE: 2.5 miles
ENVIRONMENT: Forest/Prairie
LOCATION: Custer National Forest. From Ashland, Montana, head east on U.S. Highway 212 for 4 miles. Turn right onto County Road 484 (Otter Creek Road). Continue south for about 20 miles, turning right (west) onto Forest Road 95. (This is 0.5 mile south of the Fort Howes Ranger Station.) After 10 miles, turn right onto Forest Road 801. Continue to follow signs for Poker Jim, which is reached 3 miles from this last intersection.

Even if you never make it past the parking lot, this fire lookout and picnic area, perched atop a high, rolling quilt of ponderosa pine and mixed prairie grasses, will be well worth the trip. According to legend, it was during a fall roundup in the late 1800s that two cowboys, one named Jim, decided to stop chasing doggies long enough to play a game or two of poker. Unfortunately, the boss rode up on the game and fired them both. The place has been known as "Poker Jim" ever since.

There are a number of things in this forest—two-track campground roads, old corrals and wood-frame fire lookouts like this one—that remind me of being a kid in the back seat of a station wagon in the mid-1960s, reveling in the warm, almost timeless feeling that seemed to pervade the national forests of the West. For most of the summer this is a true small-town recreation area, a place where you'll see a few families scattered here and there riding horses or enjoying picnic lunches. On one particular summer weekend, however, usually in mid-July, the site becomes much more crowded. It's then that a theatrical touring group arrives on this cool ridge to perform Shakespeare for the locals—a happy mix of lawn chairs, Budweiser and Hamlet unfolding beneath the wide Montana skies. I was told that these productions were greatly appreciated by area residents; seeing cow punchers at the Ashland hardware store wearing "Shakespeare in the Park" t-shirts convinced me that it must be true.

Little Bluestem

On a clear day, the view from Poker Jim Lookout is splendid. To the northwest lies a fascinating maze of badlands. The Tongue River and its surrounding feeder streams have made thousands of graceful slices through the soft mudstone and Tongue River Sandstone, leaving a strange collage of towers and buttresses and fluted columns. Most of the formations in this area are protected by brittle caps of scoria, or "clinker." Scoria is a beautiful brick-red rock that's common throughout much of the region, hardened to the point of brittleness by fires burning beneath the surface of the earth. These fires begin when dry, underground coal seams ignite, either through lightning, prairie fire or spontaneous combustion; how long they burn will vary, but some will continue to smolder for hundreds of years. The heat generated by such burns rises into the stone layers above, baking them in much the same way as if they had been placed in a giant kiln. Since scoria is a dead giveaway for those looking for coal seams, it comes as little surprise that this region is on the threshold of major coal development.

Unfortunately, in this case such development may mean sacrificing one of the best prairie rivers in the entire West. The Tongue, in its slow, serpentine flow to the Yellowstone, is a gentle, unspoiled floating stream that hums through a line of canyons and grasslands overflowing with deer, fox, fish and birds, including nesting double-breasted cormorants and migrating sandhill cranes. Current coal-development plans would not only shatter the silence of this special river, but perhaps even jeopardize its flow. As you might expect, reductions in flow would have dire consequences for many of the furred and feathered creatures who live along its banks.

In the other direction from this perch, 70 to 80 air miles to the southwest, lie the beautiful Bighorn Mountains, named by Lewis and Clark for the bighorn sheep. It was this particular mountain massif that caused so many headaches for prospectors looking for a shorter route from the Oregon Trail to the gold fields of Montana. Among the many men who set out to pioneer such a route, the efforts of John Bozeman and John Jacobs in 1863 were by far the most noteworthy. Their first outing took them along the northern and western edge of the Bighorns, during which time they were robbed by Crow Indians and forced to eat grasshoppers in order to survive long enough to reach their destination on the North Platte River. Even with such an auspicious beginning, the route was destined to become the major path for northwest-bound pioneers; in fact, some evidence suggests that as many as 85 percent of all those heading to the Montana gold fields did so on this trail. For their part, the Indians remained determined to protect the Bighorns, which was one of their last unspoiled hunting grounds. The bitter fighting that ensued led to the wagon road being dubbed the "Bloody Bozeman."

Begin your walk by descending the hill road you just came up on, passing through lovely folds of grass and ponderosa, spiced with the orange, white, yellow and lavender of mallow, phlox, coneflowers and horsemint. These "pine breaks," as they're sometimes called, are a feature that pepper much of the northern plains. In some ways they are a subdued version of the Black Hills, similarly populated with white-tailed deer, porcupine and a wide variety of magnificent raptors. As you make your way down the hill, notice the shrub growing along the road with the three-part, lobed leaves and, in summer and fall, red, hairy berries. This is commonly known as squawbush, a name that arose from the fact that its supple stems were frequently used by Indian women to weave baskets. Two other common names suggest additional characteristics of the shrub: "skunkbush," because some find the crushed leaves to smell like skunk, and "lemonadeberry," because the tart berries were often mixed with water for a drink that tastes remarkably like lemonade. Rabbits, pronghorn and deer are fond of squawbush twigs and foliage.

In 0.3 mile you'll reach the intersection you passed on the way up. Take a right this time, heading west. Notice the rather large pocket of dead timber off to your left. This was the result of a 300-acre fire that burned here in the summer of 1980.

The walk continues westward and, at 1 mile, the road begins a descent toward our turnaround point, in a mixed-prairie parkland of wheat grasses, Idaho fescue and little bluestem. In places where the soil is somewhat sandy watch for narrowleaf yuccas, which add a splash of desert feel to these cool green mats of Montana grassland.

WALK #14—DIAMOND BUTTE LOOKOUT

DISTANCE: 1.8 miles
ENVIRONMENT: Prairie
LOCATION: Custer National Forest. From Ashland, Montana, head east on U.S. Highway 212 for 4 miles. Turn right on County Road 484 (Otter Creek Road). Continue south for about 20 miles, turning left (east) onto Forest Road 127. (This is 0.5 mile south of the Fort Howes Ranger Station.) Approximately 15.75 miles from County Road 484, a fork takes off to the right of Forest Road 127 toward Powder River. Continue straight. The walking road to Diamond Butte Lookout is 2.3 miles past this junction, and the tower is clearly visible from Forest Road 127. Park along Forest Road 127.

If ever you find yourself looking for a job far, far removed from the madding crowd, in a place where the empty land rolls away in a vast sea of grassy swells and ponderosa islands, where wind and sky offer the only communion, then being a fire lookout at Diamond Butte might be well worth your consideration.

The lookout itself is visible from the very beginning of this walk, standing as a lonely sentinel atop a thumb-shaped headland at the brink of the prairie sea. Look for kochia (locally called fireweed) along the edge of the road, as well as a smattering of wild roses and squawbush, the latter sporting in summer clusters of red, hairy berries. These tart berries stimulate the flow of saliva, and many a pioneer crossing these vast expanses chewed them to help alleviate thirst. Beyond the roadside fringe lie vast mats of grasses—wheatgrass, Idaho fescue, little bluestem and blue grama—rippling under the fingers of the wind. Depending on what time of year you're here, scarlet mallow, phlox, prairie coneflowers and horsemint lend delicate splashes of color to the scene.

Though to some this land may look harsh and barren, it is in fact one of the most productive regions on earth, having been a cradle of civilization for Indian peoples for thousands of years.

During the ice ages, this particular area did not feel the cold tongues of glacial ice that ground south out of Canada into much of the northern United States. It thus became a protected home for large populations of humans. Hundreds of archaeological sites have been found here, some of which date back more than 9,000 years. There was also, as you might expect, a regular Noah's Ark of animals. Millions and millions of bison, pronghorn, elk, bear and coyotes roamed these swells, while flocks of migratory birds were so extensive that their passing actually darkened the prairie sky. For sheer numbers of life forms, this region actually rivaled, and may well have surpassed, Africa's great Serengeti Plain.

These grasslands came into being in large part because of the creation of the Rocky Mountains. The high peaks of the Rockies pushed moisture-laden, east-bound air upward, causing it to drop most of its liquid cargo in the cool air of the high country. As a result, those lands lying to the east, in what is known as the "rain shadow," became drier. This dryness, as well as a general cooling of the climate, turned the region from a place of wet forests and ferns into one marked by great expanses of drought-tolerant grasses and forbs capable of supporting enormous populations of grazing animals. Evidence that a very different type of climate once existed here is found in the region's expansive coal seams, which are really just layers of dead plant material that accumulated from ancient swamps. This plant material first existed as peat, and later, under enormous pressure, turned into coal. It is estimated that a billion tons of coal may exist in this immediate area, along what is known as the Knoblock seam.

About 0.5 mile into the walk you'll be able to look down to the left and right into a pair of small draws. Notice how deciduous plants such as willow are seen nowhere else but in these ravines, their lives tied to the thin tether of water that courses down these drainages from the surrounding plateaus. As you make your way toward the lookout watch these draws for meadowlarks, ruby-crowned kinglets and loggerhead shrikes.

When you reach the fire lookout itself, take a minute to sit on the edge of this promontory and fly a few fantasies on the ever-present wind. Though you may not think of it as a critical part of the landscape, the wind has a great deal of influence on what you see before you. Each year it propels Russian thistle (tumbleweed) across the land, allowing each plant to scatter hundreds of thousands of seeds, thus ensuring that the species will be around next year. In winter, wind scours the ridges and hilltops clean of snow, allowing the pronghorn to reach the sagebrush they need to stay alive until the return of spring. It is wind, of course, that also strokes the blades of old Aeromotor windmills, filling water tanks, allowing thousands of Angus and Hereford cattle to survive.

For Sioux and Cheyenne warriors that lived here in the late 1870s, however, the wind, armed with the cold sting of winter, was no friend. Knowing this, the American army, enraged by the defeat of Custer and his men on the Little Bighorn, waited until winter to strike the Sioux and Cheyenne in earnest. Clothing, tipis and food supplies were burned, allowing the icy blasts to drive the people to quick defeat. A great many froze to death. After one such winter attack on a Cheyenne village in the Bighorns, a dozen babies were found frozen at their mothers' breasts. Finally, weary with winter warfare, and indeed, with a lifetime of fighting, most of the last of the free Plains Indians laid down their weapons, and made their way to area forts.

■ WYOMING ■

WYOMING

...

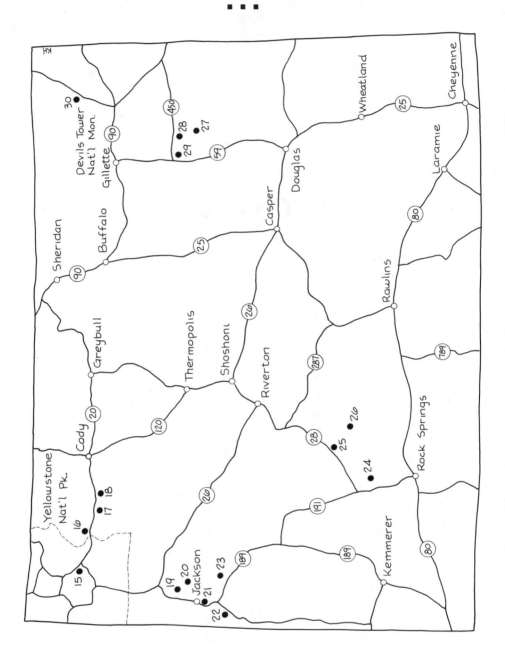

Northwestern Wyoming

WALK #15—ELEPHANT BACK LOOP TRAIL

DISTANCE: 3 miles

ENVIRONMENT: Forest

LOCATION: Yellowstone National Park. From the intersection of the East Entrance Road (the route from Cody) and the West Thumb–Canyon Road, head toward West Thumb. In 1.1 miles from this intersection is a small parking area on the right (north) side of the road; our trail begins here.

Never mind that this pine-covered ridge really looks nothing at all like an elephant's back. Or that the man who gave it this name, the great explorer-geologist Ferdinand Hayden, lifted it from a map of W. F. Raynolds, who had applied it not to this ridge at all, but to Mount Washburn to the north. When it's all said and done, sitting on this perch high above Lake Lodge, the rich blue waters of the lake spreading before you like a great sweep of sapphire, names really don't seem to matter at all.

Our trail begins in a beautiful forest of Englemann spruce, subalpine fir, whitebark pine and most notably, lodgepole pine. Now this is not the infamous "dog hair" lodgepole found in certain pockets of the central plateau, where the trees grow as tight and straight as a good crewcut. Here the lodgepole literally tower over an open, spacious forest floor sprinkled with whortleberry, Oregon grape and common juniper, the trees growing just far enough apart to create a wonderful interplay of light and shadow. Those who go slowly through these woods will find them to be remarkably beautiful—a clear way, as John Muir said of the forest wilderness, into the depths of the universe.

Of several kinds of "fire pines" in America, so named because many of the cones open up only in the presence of fire, lodgepole is perhaps the most notable. In fact, a large proportion of this tree's seeds remain locked up for years; only when the intense heat of a burn roars through the forest does the thick layer of resin melt from between the cone scales, finally releasing the precious cargo to start life anew in the midst of the ashes. And start anew it does. Under the right conditions, as many as a hundred thousand lodgepole seedlings can sprout on a single acre of burned forest! After about a mile of easy walking, the trail will split into a loop; stay left, following the loop up and across the Elephant Back in a clockwise direction. While you'll of course have to do a little uphill shuffling to reach the top of the Elephant Back, for the most part this is relatively pleasant walking, made even more so by the tantalizing views of the lake that begin to appear as you hit the first switchbacks. Once on top, it's a short stroll to a fine sitting area; from here you can survey an absolutely magnificent wash of wild country, the scene dominated by the shimmering waters and dusky green islands of Yellowstone Lake.

Speaking of islands, the large one lying farthest to the north (closest to the outlet) is called Stevenson Island. It was named for James Stevenson, assistant to the same explorer, Ferdinand Hayden, who applied the name Elephant Back to the ridge where you now stand. In 1871 Hayden and Stevenson rowed out to the island in a 12-foot boat covered with tarred canvas, the first recorded boat launch into the chilly waters of Yellowstone Lake. (The lake was actually "discovered," however, 45 years earlier by trapper William Sublette.) Once the island was reached and explored, the party felt confident enough of the boat's seaworthiness to put it to work making depth readings of the lake. Yellowstone Lake is more than 300 feet deep, has 110 miles of shoreline and covers nearly 140 square miles. It is one of the largest freshwater natural lakes in the world, and contains the largest inland population of wild cutthroat trout in North America.

Directly to the south of Stevenson Island are two other islands. The smallest of these is Dot Island, and it was here in 1896 that E. C. Waters received permission to place a population of non-park wildlife as an attraction for passengers on his steamboats. For a while the bison and elk were well cared for, brought to shore each fall and fed on good, rich hay cut in the Hayden Valley. Sadly, as

Waters began to experience serious financial problems, the first to suffer were his animals. By 1907 letters began appearing on the superintendent's desk in protest of the miserable conditions the elk and bison faced both on the mainland and the island. Already thoroughly disgusted with Waters' operation, the superintendent finally ordered that all animals be removed, thus ending Yellowstone's first and last island zoo.

Finally, the island lying farthest to the south—the largest of the three in Yellowstone Lake—is called Frank Island. Like Stevenson Island, this too was named during the Hayden expedition of 1871; Henry Wood Elliot, artist for the expedition, named it for his brother Frank, who to this day remains thoroughly unknown.

WALK #16—PAHASKA SUNLIGHT TRAIL

DISTANCE: 2.5 miles
ENVIRONMENT: Forest
LOCATION: Shoshone National Forest. This trail is located on the north side of the Cody-Yellowstone Highway, approximately 2.5 miles east of Yellowstone National Park. The turnoff, which is marked by a sign reading "Pahaska Sunlight Trail," takes off to the north, just east of a bridge crossing the North Fork of the Shoshone River. The trailhead lies 0.2 mile down this road, on the right. *Note:* This is bear country; please take appropriate precautions.

During the extraordinary fires of 1988, the upper reaches of the North Fork of the Shoshone were severely burned, much of the area experiencing far greater than average levels of heat. One of the reasons for this is that this was a spruce-fir forest with a significant number of downed, highly flammable trees—a condition that was in large part due to our having aggressively suppressed fires throughout the 20th century. Also, spruce and fir are unlike lodgepole pine in that they do not self-prune their lower branches.

When a lodgepole falls to the forest floor there is relatively little branch material to serve as a fuel bed; when a spruce or fir topples over, however, it lies almost totally wrapped in flammable twigs and branches.

While you may not appreciate this forest the way you would have when it lay thick and green and filled with wildlife, this walk is nonetheless a wonderful opportunity to see how new life comes to the most savagely burned land, how pioneer plants like fireweed, elk sedge, heartleaf arnica and dandelions slowly begin to cover the ground, one day to be followed by a young forest of lodgepole and Engelmann spruce.

A century ago, this stretch of the North Fork of the Shoshone River was known by the not-so-beautiful Indian name of Stinkingwater. It was at the headwaters of this river, little more than a day's walk from here, that one of the more dramatic events took place in the epic tale of Chief Joseph's flight for Canada. In 1863, the United States handed a treaty to the peaceful Nez Perce Indians of eastern Oregon and Washington, calling on them to give up nearly all of their Wallowa Mountain homeland so it could be opened for exploration by the rush of gold miners scouring the mountain West. Chief Joseph, representing a band of about 700 Nez Perce, mostly women, children and old men, had refused to sign the treaty, thereby insisting (quite correctly) that rights to the land still belonged to them. Unfortunately, most whites in the area thought otherwise.

Several miners repeatedly harassed the band, until, in the summer of 1877, a few Nez Perce braves finally retaliated. Quick

Sticky Geranium

Black Bear

Grizzly Bear

as a messenger could gallop, cries went out to the U.S. Cavalry, calling on the boys in U.S. blue to come in and take care of the Nez Perce problem once and for all. But the Nez Perce refused to fight. Instead, Chief Joseph rounded up his people and approximately 2,000 horses, and set out on a twisted, 1,700-mile run through some of the most rugged country in the West, ultimately bound for the free turf of Canada.

On urgent request from General Howard, hot on Chief Joseph's trail as he headed east toward the Yellowstone country, the War Department dispatched General Sturgis and about 360 men to intercept the Nez Perce a short distance north of where you now stand. Smelling a trap, Joseph sent a small band of braves riding ahead pulling brush behind them, raising such a dust that Sturgis couldn't help but think that the distant commotion was made by the entire band. As he doggedly pursued the decoy, Joseph and his people doubled back and escaped northward through a wild maze of narrow canyons thick with timber.

Chief Joseph and his people were eventually caught by the Cavalry almost within sight of the Canadian border. Thinking they had already reached their destination, Joseph had called a rest for his tired people, most of whom had been marching day and night. Despite surrender terms that guaranteed the Nez Perce would reside on a reservation in their northwest homeland, the government gave in to pressures from settlers to send them elsewhere. Tired, their spirits broken, more than 200 perished in a matter of months. It was a sad, sad ending to one of the most unfortunate tales of the Indian campaigns.

Before the fires, this path ran through the thick of a mature mountain forest, composed primarily of Douglas fir and Engelmann spruce, with a lush understory dappled with lavender splashes of sticky geranium, lupine and harebell. In 0.6 mile you'll reach the southern boundary of the Absaroka Wilderness. Absaroka, or more correctly Absarokee, is a combination of Hidatsa Indian words that formed the original name of the people we now know as the Crow. *Absa* means large-billed bird, and *rokee* is best translated as offspring, or children. European explorers combined this description with the sign language used to describe these people—a flapping of arms—to arrive at the name "Crow."

Even with the land laid open by fire, there is still a certain wild feeling to this place. Elk and bear can still be found here, as can several birds and a host of smaller mammals. The Shoshone, incidentally, is the only national forest in the entire state of Wyoming that contains elk, mule and white-tailed deer, grizzly and black bear, bighorn sheep, mountain goat, antelope, moose and mountain lion.

Our turnaround point is at about 1.25 miles, along a bench that overlooks a grassy area framing the North Fork of the Shoshone. For a dose of almost haunting tranquility, walk down into this park and sit by the river for a while. Between the sound of your own slow breathing and the sound of mountain water, you may hear the hooves of Nez Perce horses echoing up the canyon, the whisper of moccasins shuffling quickly toward the north.

WALK #17—BLACKWATER CREEK

DISTANCE:	3.8 miles
ENVIRONMENT:	Forest
LOCATION:	Shoshone National Forest. This walk leaves from the Blackwater Pond Picnic Ground, east of Yellowstone National Park on the Yellowstone-Cody Highway. This picnic ground is located on the south side of the road, 0.5 mile west of the Rex Hale Campground. Park in the lot provided; the walk takes off on a bridge across the North Fork of the Shoshone River. *Note:* This is bear country; please take appropriate precautions.

Even if you don't make it very far up the walking road, this riverside picnic ground, complete with a lovely little rush-lined pond, is certainly worth a stop on your way to or from Yellowstone Park. The landscape is a beautiful mix of wet and dry. Cool streams flow under thick quilts of mature conifers, many perched in the most precarious positions on high, sun-baked shoulders of 40-million-year-old volcanic rock. In addition, some of the volcanic gravels surrounding the picnic area contain petrified trees.

This region is also rich with wildlife. Moose routinely amble along the North Fork of the Shoshone on early morning browsing forays while, as evening shadows begin to roll across the landscape, deer begin drifting along the grassy fringes of the conifers. Elk, black bear and an occasional grizzly also call these woods home. Although this can be a harsh land during winter, there is no doubt that it was an important place to countless generations of Native Americans. In fact, just north of the highway is a cave that some archaeologists feel was occupied off and on from 7280 B.C. to A.D. 1580—a span of almost 9,000 years! This shelter is known as Mummy Cave, so named for the mummified body of a man found here who is thought to have lived in the latter part of the seventh century.

Begin your walk by crossing the North Fork of the Shoshone River on a wooden bridge. You may notice that this stretch of valley is defined by a rather narrow "V" shape, instead of the broader, "U" shape common to many other canyon systems in the region. More rounded features are the result of massive glaciers grinding their way down the valleys during the last ice age; this stretch of the Shoshone, however, saw no such activity.

After crossing the Shoshone, Blackwater Lodge will be on your left, and, shortly afterward you'll pass through a Forest Service gate. From here the dirt road makes a sharp huff-n-puff climb for about 0.25 mile, after which it continues to rise along Blackwater Creek at a far more gentle rate. By 0.3 mile into the walk you'll be wrapped in a beautiful forest environment—tall, thick conifers with common juniper, buckwheat and balsamroot gathered at their feet, broken here and there by patches of grass

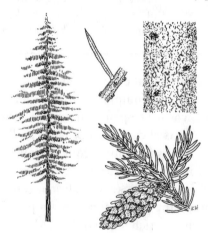

Blue Spruce

and clusters of aspen. The balsamroot you see was a popular source of food for many early residents of the region. The inner portion of young flower stems was frequently eaten, as were the seeds, which are very similar in taste to those of the sunflower. A few tribes ate the woody roots, which would have been an almost impossible feat had they not first baked them in a hot fire pit for several days. The arrow-shaped leaves of this plant were also quite effective as a poultice for treating burns. If you leave the road occasionally and wander over to Blackwater Creek, you'll be treated to gardens of other mountain wildflowers throughout much of the summer.

By the time you go 0.75 mile you'll catch several glimpses of Coxcomb Mountain to the south. This is part of a long, wild finger of land protruding northward out of the Washakie Wilderness. (Washakie was the name of a great chief of the Shoshone Indians.) This is a massive, broad-shouldered country, where the edges of flat-topped volcanic plateaus make dizzying plunges into untrammeled mazes of stone and timber. The rugged nature of this land is often reflected in the names of area peaks: Sleeping Giant, Citadel, Giant Castle and Fortress mountains, to name a few.

Both the lushness and age of the forest continue to increase as you climb southward. Old, stately Engelmann spruce and Douglas fir are joined by ponderosa, as well as mats of thimbleberry, harebell and wild rose. Our turnaround point is at 1.9 miles, at a point where the road ends and the footpath portion of the Blackwater Fire Memorial Trail begins. This trail eventually climbs up to the high, windswept shoulders of Clayton Mountain. It traverses a battleground of sorts, the site of a heroic fight against a forest fire that raged through this country half a century ago, a fire as tragic as any that has burned through the forests of the Rocky Mountains.

The fighting men, a combination of Forest Service employees and a band of Civilian Conservation Corps workers from Company 1811, first hit the line of the Blackwater burn on August 20, 1937. The forest was hot and dry, and it didn't take long to realize that a major fire was close at hand. Then, on August 21, a windstorm roared across the land, whipping flames up the forested gulches and flanks of Clayton Mountain, where a number of firefighters were cutting lines to keep the blaze in check. Paul Greever, delivering the address at the dedication of the fire memorial located near where you parked for this walk, described the scene: "These boys for hours fought the raging blaze. They cut timber, and fought the fire in every way known; cut, bruised and injured by fierce, scorching blasts as the walls of fire closed in upon them. Some were suffocated, some were burned."

By the end of that fateful summer day, 15 young men were dead and 39 were injured. A shocked crew of survivors fought on for three more days, finally bringing the Blackwater Fire to rest after it had consumed more than 1,200 acres of national forest. "To those families," Paul Greever went on to say, "who mourn here today the loss of a son, brother, husband or father, may there come a solace in the promise of immortality which is held in every beautiful thing—in the trees, the mountains, the streams, and the flowers." Today in these woods you can still find a few charred remains from the Blackwater Fire. But the other components of the forest—the flowers and trees, the birds and the animals—have returned, carrying with them that special promise of immortality.

WALK #18—ELK FORK CREEK

DISTANCE: 3 miles
ENVIRONMENT: Mountain
LOCATION: Shoshone National Forest. This trail takes off from the south end of Elk Fork Campground, which is located on the south side of the Cody-Yellowstone Highway, just east of mile marker 22. The campground is approximately 1 mile west of the Wapiti Ranger Station.

Besides offering healthy doses of incredible mountain scenery, this trail, along with the two Shoshone National Forest walks just west of here, offer some interesting history. The Shoshone National Forest was the first national forest in the United States. It was created by congressional mandate in 1907, after having been known for 16 years as the Yellowstone Park Timberland Reserve. The Wapiti Ranger Station, just 1 mile east of here, served as the first ranger station ever built with federally appropriated moneys.

(*Wapiti*, incidentally, is the name that Algonquin Indians gave to the elk; the literal translation of the word is "light colored.")

The life of the first forest rangers here was certainly colorful, if not downright exciting. During the early years rangers received little direction from Washington other than to "manage the resource." A new guardian of the nation's forests might find himself building trail during the day, pulling a rancher's wagon out of the mud before supper, and coming to blows with a gang of timber thieves in the evening—finally bedding down under a sheet of wagon canvas about the time summer twilight sank into a black sky shot full of stars. His efforts earned him a salary of about $25 a week.

Standing at the trailhead for this walk, you'll see a road going off to the right and a trail going up a small hill to the left. We'll stick to the trail, which makes a flat, beautiful meander along the hills that rise gently above the eastern flank of Elk Fork Creek. The first part of our walk is through healthy mats of sage and paintbrush. More often than not, paintbrush sticks its tendrils into the roots of other nearby plants, in this case the sagebrush, thereby stealing nutrients for its own survival. Another common resident you'll see in this area is rabbitbrush, a thin-leaved plant with soft golden flower heads. While rabbitbrush is an important food source for deer, rabbit and elk, the fact that it grows on nutrient-poor soil has made it an important index for assessing the condition of the land. Widespread growth of rabbitbrush is often an indication that overgrazing has occurred.

One of the finest features of this walk is the dramatic rock formations visible on the other side of Elk Fork Creek. Dry, windswept shoulders give way to fantastic spires of eroded volcanic conglomerate rock. These rocks erupted from the depths of the earth more than 40 million years ago, spewing through a series of volcanic vents scattered throughout much of the Yellowstone country. The pinnacle effect you see is the result of ice and rain eroding the fairly soft rock along large vertical cracks. The strangest formations of all are the tall, lone spires topped by large cap stones. The hard cap stone actually protects the rock column beneath from the eroding effects of the weather; the resulting spires are referred to by geologists as "hoodoos."

Far ahead are equally dramatic views of huge, flat-top mountains, some composed of 300-million-year-old rock that actually slid to this point along a great fault. Up the canyon you'll also see a series of east-west drainages that have been carved into the landscape by water pouring out of the high country over thousands of years.

A short distance into the walk the trail forks. Follow the left branch, which will fork again into several smaller paths. Your goal is simply to wind around a small, wooded draw and head back out again to the bench overlooking Elk Fork. Common in this draw are huddles of Rocky Mountain juniper, a hardy, beautiful tree sporting dull blue fruits, which are not really fruits at all, but cones. This was a sacred tree to many Native Americans throughout the Rockies; the sweet-smelling incense it produced, for example, was used in many purification ceremonies. Interestingly, this particular use of juniper was common in cultures totally removed from each other, from the Pueblo people of the southwestern United States, to early nomads in the far reaches of China. American Indians also used the wood to construct fine bows, and teas made from the boughs and branches were consumed regularly to relieve colds and flu.

As you continue up the canyon, at about 1.1 miles, look once again to the other side of the creek and notice how, in many places, tree growth is completely limited to the deep draws cut into the mountain by running water. In this arid country, such draws are often the only places where rain or snowmelt concentrates in sufficient amounts to support tree growth. The far richer slice of life visible along the creek corridor below—from fine stands of cottonwood to pockets of tall meadow grass—is an even more dramatic example of the difference that soil moisture can make on the face of the western landscape.

Of course, changes in vegetation also bring changes in the kinds of animals and birds that frequent an area. The stream corridor below you is rich enough to support a wide range of wildlife, including moose. Those who sit patiently and scan the cottonwood groves or willows that fringe the creek stand a good chance of seeing one of these great creatures.

About 1.5 miles into the walk you'll reach our turnaround point, opposite another fine collection of eroded volcanic rock pinnacles on the far side of Elk Fork Creek. If you wish to continue on, however, rest assured that you'll be rewarded with an increasingly spectacular collage of rugged mountains, mesas, cliffs and canyons.

WALK #19—SHADOW MOUNTAIN

DISTANCE:	1.2 miles
ENVIRONMENT:	Mountain
LOCATION:	Bridger-Teton National Forest. Take U.S. Highway 89/191 north out of Jackson, Wyoming, for 7 miles to the Gros Ventre Road, and turn right. Continue through Kelly. Several miles north of Kelly you'll pass an intersection with Antelope Flats Road. Continue straight. At 1.6 miles past this intersection turn left, following a Park Service sign pointing toward Bridger-Teton National Forest. In 0.7 mile from this point make a right turn, and head up a hill through a grove of aspen. Our trailhead is on this road, 3.7 miles from that last right turn. (You'll join a fence at 2.7 miles. Past this fence the road continues to climb, eventually reaching a level section with a small road turning off to the right; the trail takes off to the west, opposite this side road.)

Far below these soft, green shoulders, through a thin veil of trees, is the long, green reach of Antelope Flats. At the far edge, a twist of cottonwoods can be seen cradling the Snake River as it tumbles southward to meet the Gros Ventre and the Hoback. But rising abruptly past the Snake, almost shouting through the blue Wyoming sky, is the one truly unforgettable part of this high-country scene—the Tetons themselves. The views along this walk, mostly across a lovely patchwork of forest and meadow, are sparkling, even mesmerizing. In some ways, it is as if you've suddenly entered the beating heart of the Rocky Mountains.

As you've undoubtedly noticed, Shadow Mountain supports a healthy collection of aspen, the beautiful white-barked deciduous tree with leaves that flutter in the slightest puff of air, hence its common name "quaking aspen." One famous myth says the leaves of all aspen began to tremble when the wood was chosen to fashion the cross of Christ. The more observable explanation, useful but rather colorless, is that the leaves twist because they have a flat stem at the point where they attach to the leaf.

At 0.2 mile into the walk the trail passes a meadow filled with yarrow, larkspur, balsamroot, showy goldeneye and the tall spikes of green-leaved gentian. A thick, green curtain of Douglas fir and subalpine fir rises to the left. The bark of the subalpine fir, incidentally (the tree with a spire-shaped crown and needles curving upward in tight bunches), is often eaten by deer and elk. Look for nibbled patches along the trunks of this grove. From here the trail slopes gently downward through a young forest of fir, spruce, lodgepole and limber pine, soon coming out on a bench that affords spectacular views of 26,000-acre Jackson Lake, far to the northwest. This long, sweeping valley was scoured into its present shape by a river of ice nearly 2,000 feet thick that crept out of the Absaroka and Wind River ranges.

Continue for a short distance, reaching our turnaround point in 0.6 mile, at a stretch of trail that descends through a delightful meadow. Grand Teton, with an elevation of 13,770 feet, looms straight ahead. This is a particularly fine place to assume the prone position in a thick mat of lupine and showy goldeneye. It's good for the soul to on occasion lie back and grab a mouse-eye view of worlds peppered with wildflowers, capped by puffs of summer cloud.

WALK #20—GROS VENTRE SLIDE

DISTANCE: 0.8 mile
ENVIRONMENT: Mountain
LOCATION: Bridger-Teton National Forest. Head north out of Jackson, Wyoming, on U.S. Highway 89/191 for approximately 7 miles to the Gros Ventre Road, and turn right. At 1.2 miles north of Kelly, the Gros Ventre Road turns right, toward Slide Lake. Our walk begins 4.8 miles from this last turn, at the Gros Ventre Slide Overlook.

A wet June morning, 1925. The early songs of the wrens and tanagers have come and gone; only the raucous calls of magpies and Steller's jays can be heard with any regularity. The Gros Ventre River tumbles eastward out of the Red Hills toward its rendezvous with the Snake, as it has done countless mornings before. And then, without warning, an event of catastrophic proportions occurs. From a point 9,000 feet up on a high ridge south of the river, an enormous slab of earth, a mile long and over a third of a mile wide, tears loose from its mountain moorings and comes rolling toward the river—a frightening tidal wave of rock and timber. So much momentum is packed into these 15 million cubic tons of shale and sandstone rubble that it completely buries the river, screams up and over the road where you now stand and continues to roll a short distance up the north side of the red-rock valley wall. In less than three minutes, the calamity is over.

As a result of the river blockage, the lake to your left (Lower Slide Lake) begins to form, rising quickly against the earthen dam. But less than two years later, in May 1927, this dam gives out. A great wall of water races down the channel toward the town of Kelly, 6 river miles downstream. A forest ranger sees what is happening, and makes a frantic call to warn the people below. Some refuse to listen; six people drown.

And so went the tale of the Gros Ventre Slide, one of the largest observed earth movements in the world. That this slice of mountain country was unstable was hardly news to the people who lived in the region. A smaller, slower slide blocked the Gros Ventre river channel several miles upstream years before, creating Upper Slide Lake. Land and mud slides in several of the nearby drainages were also common, which made the proposition of building a road up the Gros Ventre River a chancy project at best.

There are several theories as to what actually caused the Gros Ventre Slide. One attributes the soil instability of this region to a slow

Yellow-bellied Marmot

but steady melt of glacial ice still buried deep in the ground. The meltwater saturates the earth, slowly loosening the unstable rock foundations until the ground gives way. Another theory says that these mountains are simply still settling, and as sheets of soft rock, such as gypsum, dissolve in the presence of ground moisture, the landscape collapses. Unlike the Gros Ventre Slide, most of the time these collapses are slow, quiet events. Whatever the reason, viewing the aftereffect of events like the Gros Ventre Slide, with its great rubble piles and tilted timber, or Quake Lake on the northwest corner of Yellowstone, should dispel any notions you may have about the Rockies being composed of unchanging, static environments.

In its present state, the Gros Ventre Slide Nature Trail is not so much a loop as a single path with two spikes taking off of it, but this should change by late 1992. Begin to the left of the overlook, making your way through a sparse forest of limber and lodgepole pine surrounded by thick mats of fireweed and buffaloberry. Buffaloberry, which is somewhat bitter when eaten right off the bush, was nevertheless an important food source to many Native American cultures. The fruit was collected by women in late summer, who would usually beat the bushes soundly with a stick. Most of the berries were then dried in the sun to be used over the winter. A foamy treat known in Montana as "Indian ice cream" was made by placing a few berries in a little water and then beating them with a stirring device until they reached a pink froth. About 0.2 mile into the walk the trail will fork; continue right and proceed up a huge jumble of rubble, much of which hardly looks 60 days let alone 60 years old. The giant slabs of sedimentary rock on this rise give a good clue to the formation of the Gros Ventre Range. For millions of years this area was an ancient sea bed, where ocean debris filtered down through dark waters to form layers of sediment that would eventually harden into rock. Much later, pressures inside the earth thrust these beds of rock upward to form mountains, which were then sculpted into their present shape by glaciers, as well as the incessant rush of wind and weather.

Continue along these slabs past black elderberry and common juniper onto a bench lush with purple fireweed blooms and the tattered, yellow heads of groundsel. From here the trail descends over a maze of sedimentary rock down to the shore of Slide Lake, a quiet, peaceful stretch of water framed to the east by the beautiful russet flanks of the Red Hills.

If the new section of trail has been finished when you take this walk, you'll simply retrace your steps for approximately 200 to 300 feet, and then take a right turn, following the path to another overlook at a bench above the lake. If this new trail isn't done yet, you'll need to go all the way back to that first fork in the trail near the parking area, and then follow the more northerly path out to the second overlook. This path winds through a sparse forest sprinkled with buffaloberry and dwarf juniper. Notice the tilted trees, still growing after having slid here 60 years ago from their original home high on the mountain to the south.

WALK #21—SNOW KING NATURE TRAIL

DISTANCE:	0.75 mile
ENVIRONMENT:	Mountain
LOCATION:	Bridger-Teton National Forest. The chairlift to this trailhead is located on the south end of Jackson, Wyoming, at the Snow King Ski Resort. Park near the corner of Snow King and Cache streets. Summer hours for this chairlift are typically 11 A.M. to 6 P.M. June through September.

Although a few hearty walkers may feel that riding a chairlift up Snow King will rob them of that special sense of accomplishment that comes from plodding up 1,500 vertical feet under their own power, others will consider it a welcome way to reach the high country. The cruise up the face of Snow King is over meadows bursting with lupine, yarrow, buckwheat, an occasional sticky geranium and, in late July and August, bright lavender fireweed blooms flying from clusters of tall green stalks. There are, incidentally, two stories as to how fireweed got its name. One says that the blooms resemble flames, and the other, more commonly accepted notion is that the name comes from the plant's ability to colonize areas that have been burned or otherwise disturbed. (The plant spreads quickly from a network of underground stems.) Bear, deer and elk find fireweed to be quite tasty, as do some people, who boil and eat the young leaves and shoots.

American Elk

When you reach the top, take a few minutes to visit one of the two observation platforms on either side of the chairlift. The one on the right, near the snack shop, has an interpretive sign that will help you identify distant peaks, but the one on the left, being slightly quieter, may be more appropriate for mental drifters.

And this is definitely a view to drift with. To the north the Tetons seem to literally explode from the earth, gray horns of granite ripping through the sky like mythical ramparts guarding the brink of the world. To the Snake Indian people they were known as the "hoary headed Fathers." To the northeast, just outside of Jackson, Flat Creek meanders through the National Elk Refuge, seasonal home for thousands of elk who pour down from the surrounding drainages each year, prodded by the cold sting of winter.

Because so much of the elk's traditional wintering range has been lost to development, the animals that concentrate here must be given supplemental feed during a portion of their stay. Part of the cost for this food (perhaps $250,000 a year) is actually earned by the elk themselves. Males shed their antlers each year while in the refuge area. Boy Scouts then collect these under a special-use permit and sell them at a rather famous auction held each May at the Jackson town square. People come from around the world to purchase these antlers, both to make crafts as well as to grind them into various health mixtures. By the time the last ring of the auctioneer's gavel is heard, $40,000 or more may have been collected. The Boy Scouts use most of these earnings to buy feed

Balsamroot

in the form of alfalfa pellets, which is then donated to the elk refuge.

Looking along the base of the Tetons (in Grand Teton National Park) you can see a ribbon of cottonwoods marking the course of the Snake River. From here the Snake continues south for about 30 miles through thick glacial deposits, then turns east to a do a fast dance through the magnificent Snake River Canyon before entering Idaho at Palisades Reservoir. At one time or another the Snake River Valley (often referred to as the "Mad River") was used as a highway, hunting ground or meeting place by nearly every trapper worth his beaver pelts. Over your right shoulder is the western fringe of the Gros Ventre Wilderness.

The Snow King Nature Trail begins directly across from the chairlift unloading ramp; be sure to pick up a trail guide near the start of the walk. The path begins in an open area sprinkled with yarrow, scarlet gilia, lupine, buckwheat and big sagebrush. By the way, sagebrush (or wormwood) is not the same "sage" used for seasoning meats, as anyone who has tried it could certainly attest to. In the Rockies, the type of sage used for seasoning is a small annual plant, actually a member of the mint family. Nevertheless, sagebrush has been ingested by man for centuries, often in the form of a hot tea taken for an upset stomach or to induce sweating during fever. This tea, which tastes incredibly bad, has also been shown to be of some help in relieving painful menstruation.

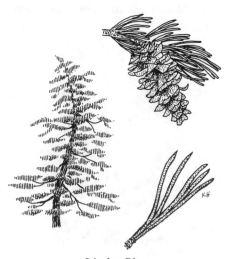

Limber Pine

The trail meanders along a meadow sprinkled with balsamroot and showy golden eye, fringed to the north by fir and pine. At the outer-most point in the loop, another trail leaves the nature path heading west. Follow this path out past wind-clipped limber pines to a promontory affording fine views to the south. About 1,500 feet below is the Snake River, writhing toward its rendezvous with the Hoback River, named for mountain man John Hoback.

WALK #22—DOG CREEK

DISTANCE: 2.4 miles

ENVIRONMENT: Forest

LOCATION: Targhee National Forest. This walk is located southwest of Hoback Junction, Wyoming, on U.S. Highway 89/26. The walk begins on a dirt road that takes off from the west side of the highway, approximately 0.5 mile south of mile marker 137. There is a small turnoff where you can park, directly across the highway from our walking road.

While it's possible to drive 300 or 400 yards down this dirt road to where the actual trail part of our walk begins, you'd be missing one of the finest slices of habitat to be found for miles around. After paralleling U.S. Highway 89/26 for a short distance, our walking road heads west across a small bridge. On your right will be a wetland absolutely overflowing with a lush weave of bird and plant life. Red-winged blackbirds chatter from the stalks of cattails, while an osprey traces circles in the sky. Mallards and cinnamon teals float quietly in fringes of reeds. A pair of great blue herons, surprised by your approach, explode from the water into a glorious dance of sweeping wings, soon to take refuge among the tall spruce on the other side of the pond. (These herons, incidentally, make routine feeding trips of 25 miles or more, very often to fishing sites located along the Snake River Plains to the north.)

Don't leave this marsh without paying your respects to the common cattail, which can be found in relative abundance just to the east of the bridge. This is perhaps the most widely used wild plant in America. Even today people eat the tender insides of the young shoots (they're rather like cucumbers), boil the spikes and eat the flowers off as one might do with an ear of sweet corn and bake the starch-laden rootstalks. Besides being a good source of tinder, Native Americans commonly placed cattail "fuzz" in baby wrappings to prevent chafing, and also wove the leaves of the plant into mats that would serve as flooring in the family tipi. Geese and even elk will eat young cattail shoots in the spring, while pheasants, marsh wrens and red-winged blackbirds hide their nests in the tall stalks.

Continue west on this dirt road for about 200 yards, to a point just past a corral on the right. Here the actual trail begins, meandering above a pleasant, open creek bottom peppered with asters, sticky geraniums, harebells, timothy grass and yarrow. This latter plant, 1 to 2 feet high with clusters of small, white flowers and fern-like leaves, is often passed off as "just another weed." In fact, yarrow is one of the most widespread healing herbs in the world, having been used by everyone from Native Americans to old-world herbalists.

Perhaps the most common use of this overlooked little plant was to crush the leaves and apply them to bad cuts and lacerations in order to control bleeding. Laboratory experiments have identified the presence of a chemical called achellein, which reduces the clotting time of blood. (The name of this substance, as well as the genus name of yarrow, *Achillea*, comes from the belief that the ancient

Osprey

Greek Achilles used yarrow, or a related plant, to help control bleeding in his soldiers during the battle of Troy.) Several North American Indian tribes used a tea made from the leaves to break fevers, and at least one Rocky Mountain tribe boiled the plant in water to create a solution that helped aching muscles and joints.

As you walk along the north side of Dog Creek, you'll be afforded a glimpse to the west of the forested flanks of the Snake River Range, a rugged collection of limestone and shale peaks, fresh, tumbling streams and yawning meadows bursting with wildflowers. These rugged mountain folds were trapped extensively during the 1830s, in the heyday of such legendary frontiersmen as David Jackson, Jedediah Strong Smith and William Sublette, heroes whose free trapper lives ended abruptly when silk hats suddenly replaced beaver as the "nouveau" look on the streets of Boston and Paris. The majority of those notoriously uninhibited rendezvous you may have read about, where trappers drank, lied, drank, purchased wives, drank and, in their spare time, traded beaver pelts for food and staples for the coming year, took place south of here, along the wide sage flats lining the Green River Valley.

A short distance into the walk, about 50 yards past the point where the trail becomes a single footpath, is a tiny spring guarded by a remarkably big, grandfather Engelmann spruce. This grand, old patriarch is perhaps 300 to 400 years old. Imagine what adventures have occurred beneath its branches, the people who may have taken rest against its strong trunk. About 40 yards past this old tree, to the left of the trail, are the remains of a beaver dam, courtesy of the furry fellow who brought to America the entire romantic, boisterous era of the free trapper. Once an area is sufficiently flooded, beavers build fine lodges complete with protected underwater entrances. Nearby, below the level of freezing ice, a cache of aspen or willow branches is kept on hand to feed mom, dad and the kids through the long, cold Wyoming winter.

Our turnaround is located 1.2 miles into the walk, at a point where Beaver Dam Canyon and Creek spill into Dog Creek from the southwest. Those so inclined may want to explore this side canyon for the chance of seeing its namesake, the beaver. But whether you set eyes on this little engineer or not, it would be hard not to enjoy a slow, aimless drift through the canyon's quiet nooks and crannies.

WALK #23—GRANITE CREEK

DISTANCE: 2.5 miles

ENVIRONMENT: Forest

LOCATION: Bridger-Teton National Forest. Follow U.S. Highway 189/191 south out of Hoback Junction for approximately 12 miles to Granite Creek Road, and head east. You'll reach a parking lot for Granite Creek Hot Springs in 10 miles. Park here and cross Granite Creek to the hot springs facility; our north-bound trail takes off from between the plunge pool and the creek. *Note:* An excellent alternative to this starting point can be found 1.5 miles south of the hot springs at the Granite Creek/ Swift Creek trailhead. Though this route adds 3 miles to the walk, it has two added benefits: first, the vehicular bridge here allows use of the trail in off hours, when the footbridge at the hot springs is gated and locked; secondly, starting at the Granite Creek/Swift Creek trailhead will take you past beautiful Granite Creek Falls, located approximately 0.5 mile south of the hot springs.

Not being particularly adept at sign language, when the Plains Indians tried to tell French trappers that the people of these mountains were known as "always hungry," the French misread the sign—both hands passing over the stomach—as "big bellies," or Gros Ventres. And so the people and the mountains have been known this way ever since. While these 25 square miles of high country may lack the abrupt drama of the Tetons, they nonetheless form a fantastic tapestry of grassy summits and wind-scoured badlands, soft-shouldered hills and peaks and deep gorges of red, gray and purple rock. The Gros Ventre Wilderness supports an excellent population of wildlife, including bighorn sheep, bear and moose, and was once the main migration corridor for thousands of elk bound for Jackson Hole each year at the first slap of winter.

These mountains are much older than the Tetons. Much of the Gros Ventre is composed of layers of colored sedimentary rock formed over countless millennia at the bottom of ancient seas. These sea floors were later uplifted by violent forces deep within the earth, their outer flanks eventually colliding with an overthrust block that was slipping slowly to the northwest. Many of the well-defined shapes you see today are the result of more recent geologic activity—creeping rivers of glacial ice, and the incessant pounding of wind and weather.

If all this isn't enough to entice you, surely the hot mineral waters of Granite Hot Springs will. Although a commercial facility, this pool, built in 1933 by the Civilian Conservation Corps, remains wonderfully close to its humble beginnings. The last time I visited, people were still walking down a dirt road, paying their money to a couple of kids and changing their clothes inside a plain cabin with wooden pegs driven into log walls. They would then make a quick dash across the grass to slip into clear, hot mineral water, bubbling into the pool beneath a backdrop of towering rock walls and pockets of cool, green forest. Hot springs rely on the fact that fresh water continually percolates through the earth to a layer of searing hot rocks. These rocks, which often overlie a magma chamber, heat the water to high temperatures, a process which increases the pressure enough to allow it to again rise to the surface of the earth.

The views of the sheer granite walls of Granite Creek Canyon are especially fine along the first 0.25 mile past the hot springs. These walls plunge to ground level in a series of short steps, each fall broken by a steep ridge peppered with hardy trees, many sinking their roots into rock cracks on the edge of oblivion. (Trees, by the way, are another, sometimes overlooked agent of erosion. Their powerful root systems split the rock along tiny fault lines, causing it to eventually fall and crumble on the ground below, piles of rubble that are then one step closer to becoming soil.)

If you're walking this path in midsummer, at 0.3 mile you'll come to a beautiful meadow of asters, cinquefoil, thistle, scarlet gilia and balsamroot. This latter plant, easily identified by its large, olive green, arrow-shaped leaves, produces tasty seeds not unlike those of the sunflower. Many Native Americans also ate the tender inner section of the immature flower stems. Wind your way in and out of wildflower meadows and pockets of fir, spruce and an occasional aspen for another 0.35 mile, finally reaching a small pond on the fringe of a grassy meadow. This is a good example of pond succession, a neat trick of nature where water is turned into wildflowers. As the plants that surround the pond's perimeter die and drift to the bottom, they are broken down and accumulate as layers of soil. This slow, but steady, process decreases the depth of the pond until it finally reaches a point where plants can successfully live across the entire surface of what was once open water. From this point the remaining water fills in fairly rapidly. What was once liquid becomes an extension of the surrounding meadow.

If you're here in late July or August, about 50 yards past the pond on the right you'll see what appear to be a collection of sunflowers from which someone has plucked all the yellow petals, as if a desperate, love-struck romantic came through here playing "she loves me, she loves me not," each time getting the wrong answer. In fact, these are western coneflowers, and they bear their flowers not in long rays like most composites, but as a collection of tiny blooms on a dull-colored cone.

Our turnaround point is at a long, jumbled line of granite talus, approximately 1.25 miles into the walk. Here you'll likely hear the strained, high-pitched "eeek, eeek" of the pika, sometimes referred to as "rock rabbit." In most places it takes a sharp eye to actually see one of these dancing bundles of fur, both because of their coloring, and because they tend to travel through hidden passages in the jumbles of broken rock. A farmer of sorts, the pika actually harvests various types of vegetation—often 15 or 20 different species at a time—and then lays it out on flat rocks to dry. Once it is properly cured, he gathers it up and stores it away for winter, when he will still be active under a deep blanket of snow.

Great Basin

WALK #24—KILLPECKER DUNES

DISTANCE:	3.2 miles
ENVIRONMENT:	Desert
LOCATION:	Southwest Wyoming, Bureau of Land Management. Head north out of Rock Springs on U.S. 191. In 0.3 mile past mile marker 10, turn east onto Sweetwater County Road 17. Continue for 15.4 miles and make a left turn. Follow this road for 6.3 miles, to a small two-track road taking off to the right. Drive to the end of this road and park beside an old railroad bed, approximately 0.65 mile from your last turn. Begin the walk by heading north (left) on the railroad bed.

This walk through a long, lonely reach of Wyoming desert follows the bed of an old railroad built 30 years ago to haul iron ore from the Atlantic City Mine. Although much of the area you'll be traversing is currently under study for wilderness designation, very few people ever come to this windswept quilt of sage and sand. The dunes you'll see here, the majority of which lie to the east and north, are just a small slice of a sandy field that stretches from the state of Idaho all the way into the Sand Hills of Nebraska, making them second in size only to the dune fields of the Sahara.

The further you immerse yourself in this environment, the more enticing it becomes. There are secret draws running into great hummocks of bare, blond sand, where one can easily imagine being adrift in the wilds of Arabia. During the winter, large fields of ice and snow accumulate along the lee side of the dunes. The blowing wind eventually covers these fields with an insulating blanket of sand, forming what is known as an eolian ice cell. These cells, located throughout the Killpecker Dunes, release their cool cargo through the summer into small ponds that dot the area. Because of this unique phenomenon, you'll find a surprising variety of waterfowl here, as well as mule deer, and the only desert elk herd in the state of Wyoming.

Bobcats, mountain lions, coyotes, red foxes and kangaroo rats also live in this wild maze of stone and sand, and patient explorers will find many of their tracks in the moist soils that surround the ponds. (On a hot day look for small burrow entrances that have been plugged with earth; kangaroo rats use such coverings to regulate temperature and humidity inside their burrows.) A particularly thrilling experience in this area is to glimpse wild horses running through the sage, their manes flying in the desert wind. There are approximately 1,500 wild horses in this region, which represent roughly 60 percent of Wyoming's total herd.

As you climb from the parking area up to the old railroad bed, notice the towering, pointed butte off to the east. This is a volcanic plug known as the Boar's Tusk. It was uncovered countless millennia ago as the relentless forces of wind and water peeled the softer rock from around it, leaving broad, sage-covered valleys at its rocky feet.

Turning to the north, the path traverses a broken carpet of big sagebrush, greasewood and rabbitbrush. The sagebrush and grease-

Mountain Lion

Pronghorn

wood are special favorites of the pronghorn, which you may well see grazing in scattered bands across the flatlands. These beautiful animals, with their brilliant white rump hairs that can be raised to alert other members of the herd to danger, are the best runners on the continent. They are remarkably fast, able to achieve speeds of nearly 70 miles per hour for very short periods. Perhaps even more important to their survival, however, is endurance. Most prong-horn are able to lope along at 20 miles per hour for more than 15 miles, a pace that will leave even the most determined predator with his tongue hanging in the dust. Add a pair of eyes that can spot movement miles away, the fact that they need very little sleep and the ability to eat almost anything that grows (including cactus), and you've got one of the truly great survivors of the American West.

Several ponds can be found along this walk, but one of the first of any size is located on your right about 0.5 mile into the walk. Notice the carpets of salt grass lining the fringes of these water pockets, which for part of the year are a beautiful shade of gold. In another 0.5 mile is another fine water pocket on the left, this one lined with reed grasses and Baltic rush. Those who approach quietly may well see a small flock of mallards here. The ponds that pepper the Killpecker dune field vary greatly in size, and range in depth from several inches to 8 feet. Some are quite sterile, while others support a wide range of life, including tiger salamanders, tadpoles and, in the deeper pools, freshwater shrimp. The best time to see tiger salamanders, which are the largest land-dwelling salamanders in the world, is late in the evening after a good rain.

After 1 mile you'll enter the wilderness study area, marked on both sides of the road by small, brown signposts. Along 0.3 mile farther is an excellent covey of pools on the right side of the railroad bed, framed to the east by a soft collage of sand dunes and grassy bluffs. This is an excellent place to leave the railroad bed and do some serious rambling in this amazing environment. Work your way back a quarter mile or so to the fringes of the dune fields. Walk up the quiet draws. Notice how the drooping heads of the bunch grasses trace lazy circles in the warm sand. Keep your eyes open for the tracks of harvest mice and short-horned lizards, and for shore birds, who often come here to feed along the edges of these cool, clear pools of water. When you're ready, slowly make your way cross-country toward the south, rejoining the railroad bed near where you parked your car.

WALK #25—EMIGRANT TRAIL, SOUTH PASS

DISTANCE:	1.5 miles
ENVIRONMENT:	Desert
LOCATION:	Southwest Wyoming, between Lander and Rock Springs. Head east on Wyoming Highway 28 out of Farson to the Continental Divide, which is clearly marked by a sign along the road. Shortly after this sign, and 0.25 mile east of mile marker 33, turn right (south) onto Sweetwater County 74. In 2.9 miles you'll cross a small two-track road. Park here, and begin your walk along this road to the west.

If there is one walk in all the American West that feeds a fantastic array of historical fantasies, it would have to be the Oregon Trail. For decades families, farmers and gold seekers, politicians, preachers and prostitutes rolled across these 2,000 miles of trail on their way to new lives in the wild West. They came by horse, by mule, by trail wagon and by foot. Some would recount it as the greatest adventure of their lives. Others, however, were destined to return east again by the same route, convinced that the tales of milk and honey that first pulled them west had been the grandest of lies. Still others would never make it west at all, ending up in crude, shallow graves along the trail, victims of disease, exhaustion or the wrath of Indians.

In the long, arduous journey from Independence, Missouri, to Oregon City, in Oregon's Willamette River Valley, South Pass was a breath of fresh air. No route offered an easier crossing of the Continental Divide. In fact, many emigrants didn't realize they had crossed the divide at all until someone gave a joyous shout at setting eyes on Pacific Creek several miles west of here, realizing that its waters were flowing west, instead of east.

The actual discovery of this important pass came long before the first of 350,000 west-bound emigrants began cutting wagon ruts through these fields of sage. In the early 1800s, the great financier John Jacob Astor had attempted to dip his fingers into the money pots of the fur trade by buying the Canadian North West Company, which the owners flatly refused to sell. Undaunted, Astor launched an all-out effort to capture the entire fur trade of the western sector of the continent. One of Astor's employees, a man named Robert Stuart, inadvertently stumbled across South Pass while he was returning from the West Coast with important dispatches. But it would be 14 years before the first wheeled vehicle rolled across this route, and three decades until wagons full of emigrants began crossing in earnest.

So exceptional was this route that it soon became the common corridor for several other west-bound trails. In 1847, Mormons fleeing persecution in the East began streaming across South Pass bound for Utah. A year later, when gold was discovered at Sutter's Mill, thousands of eager miners rushed over South Pass to seek their fortunes in California. Still a dozen years further down the road, the Pony Express mail-route riders began using South Pass on their courageous, galloping horseback rides to carry the mail between California and Missouri. In fact, a station for the Pony Express lies just a few miles west of here, at Pacific Springs.

As you begin your walk west along this short stretch of the Emigrant Trail, over your left shoulder will be the Oregon Buttes, a set of rugged swales rising from a sweep of high, flat tableland. This area is a favorite nesting site for raptors, so keep your eyes to the sky for soaring golden eagles and red-tailed hawks. Also common along this road are several large, round dens, a few of which are serving as homes for coyotes. Like the raptors, they too are here to dine on the plethora of mice and ground squirrels that frequent these lonely reaches of high desert.

About 0.25 mile into the walk you can look off to your right (north) and see the ramparts of the Wind River Range, one of the most beautiful of all the western mountains. In the middle 1800s, the famed explorer John Charles Frémont climbed one of the higher peaks in the Winds, which now bears his name. Like most of the mountains of the Rockies, the Winds saw no small number of miners pouring into their granite folds during the latter half of the 19th century. It was in part this stampede by miners, along with a huge influx of workers who came to build the Union Pacific Railroad, that led the residents of this region to press for a territory called Wyoming—a request that was finally granted in 1869. Unfortunately, neither the hopes for gold nor the railroad-construction jobs lasted for very long. A year after the territory was created most of the newcomers had moved on, leaving the entire region with a scant 9,000 people.

At 0.75 mile you'll enter a fenced area, in the center of which are two markers—one for the Oregon Trail, and the other commemorating the first pioneer women to cross the pass in 1836. You can actually continue walking this stretch for several miles, but we'll make this our turnaround point. It's the perfect place to grab a seat next to a clump of sagebrush and cast your thoughts out onto the Wyoming winds. How amazing all this must have looked from the seat of a wagon 140 years ago. What a strange mixture of feelings would have been brewing in those families—feelings of fear, of hope, of sheer exhilaration for the new lands that lay ahead, ever to the west.

WALK #26—HONEYCOMB BUTTES

DISTANCE: 4.8 miles

ENVIRONMENT: Desert

LOCATION: Southwest Wyoming, Bureau of Land Management. Exit on Interstate 80 at Bar X Road, located approximately 46 miles east of Rock Springs, Wyoming. Proceed north on Sweetwater County Road 21 for 41.9 miles, where you'll turn right (north) onto Sweetwater County Road 74, following the sign toward Oregon Buttes. At 4.3 miles from this intersection take a faint road heading off to the right (northeast). Drive 2.5 miles (stay left at the fork 0.6 mile in) to a large wash at Bear Creek. Park here, and continue walking to the northeast on the same road. Do not attempt this drive after a rain! *Note:* Continue north along County Road 74 past Oregon Buttes to reach the Oregon Trail walk described on page 80.

If you're up for a trek through country so wide and lonely that it can leave you feeling like the only person on earth, then Honeycomb Buttes is definitely the place. Here wild horses still thunder across the bunchgrass plains, and large herds of pronghorn huddle in the sagebrush. Golden eagles and red-tailed hawks hang on the desert winds, attentions fiercely tuned to the ground below for the tiny flash of a grasshopper mouse or kangaroo rat. The buttes themselves, visible to your left as you begin the walk, are a complex maze of sharply eroded shale canyons, where, at least in modern times, very few human feet have ever trod.

This little-known tract of land is a part of the Red Desert, which in turn is cradled by the windswept arms of the Great Divide Basin. This basin is the unique product of a split in the Continental Divide that occurs to the southeast, one branch of its rocky spine running past Rawlins, and the other heading toward Pacific Springs, to the west. Although most of us were taught in some long-ago geography class that raindrops falling on the slopes of the Continental Divide either go to the Gulf of Mexico or the Pacific Ocean, such is not the case here. No raindrop, no snowflake, no stream leaves this basin. Were the climate to change even slightly toward the wet side, this would once again be an inland sea.

Along the first section of this trail are fine views of Continental Peak to the north, and hard back over your left shoulder, Oregon Buttes, which once formed a prominent landmark to pioneers on the Oregon Trail. The plant life along the first 0.5 mile of this road is a loosely woven mat of rabbitbrush, sage and greasewood, as well as a mix of wheat grasses and prairie cordgrass. It was this latter plant, tall and stout, that fueled many of the over-optimistic mid-19th-century reports that this region was a paradise, with grass growing "high as a horse's belly."

At 0.6 mile the road begins to deteriorate into a layer of cracked bentonite, a no-nonsense sign that this is the last place on earth you should be with a car after a good thunder shower. Around this area you'll pass through a small depression where water routinely accumulates, partly due to a clay lining beneath the topsoil that keeps it from percolating into the earth. These playas, as they're called, are easy to spot because of the conspicuous lack of sagebrush, which is quite intolerant of saturated soil. When they

Burrowing Owl

occur as large tracts lined with carpets of bunch and wheat grasses, dry playas can look remarkably like slices of the Serengeti, shimmering in the summer sun.

Continue along this road until you reach the North Fork drainage, approximately 1.4 miles into the hike. From here we'll leave the road, working our way along the streambed for about a mile, to a quiet, windswept amphitheater of red and gray shale. There are countless nooks and crannies in this soft-shouldered maze, each one serving up solitude in portions that few of us are used to. There is growing support for making portions of the Red Desert into wilderness, a proposition that seems more likely to happen now than a few years ago, when energy prospectors combed these flats and draws.

There are those who continue to think of this area as a veritable wasteland; one government official, in fact, suggested that it was "the perfect place for a nuclear waste dump." But as we continue to fill the long reaches of the West with the filigree of progress, we will need more and more of these spare, lonely places, these subtle flows of rock and sky. In some ways it is here, as much as at the shores of blue alpine lakes, that the real essence of wildness can best be found.

Northeastern Wyoming

WALK #27—ROCHELLE HILLS

DISTANCE: 1.4 miles

ENVIRONMENT: Prairie

LOCATION: Thunder Basin National Grassland. Take Wyoming Highway 59 out of Douglas for approximately 35 miles, and, at a place where the highway veers to the northwest, leave it to head north on the Steinle Road. In just over 5.5 miles, the Steinle Road turns east, and continues for another 6 miles to the Dull Center Road. Turn left (north). In a little under 10 miles, you'll turn left onto the Rochelle Hills Road. Continue north and then west on this road for 11.4 miles to a small dirt road taking off to the north. Park here and begin your walk northward along this route. *Note:* These roads can become slick after a good rain.

The Rochelle Hills are a complete surprise in a land that, at least from Wyoming Highway 59, appears to be a place of only subtle cuts and swells, a slightly crumpled blanket of wheatgrass, cheatgrass and sage. This small road will lead you into a very different place, one cool and thick with ponderosa, with high, sheer escarpments that make dizzying plunges toward the prairie below. There is no shortage of quiet, wooded pockets for sitting and daydreaming, or of high perches from which to watch prairie falcons, golden eagles and Swainson's, ferruginous and red-tailed hawks hanging high on the winds above Thunder Basin.

Our walk begins in a large meadow of cheat, bluebunch wheat, blue grama, June and little bluestem grasses, surrounded by a thick wall of ponderosa pine. Blue grama, incidentally, the plant with curled, flag-shaped heads and a low, matted base, is the most common shortgrass on this prairie, as well as the most nutritious for grazing animals. Blue grama tends to form thick mats of tough sod that are very resistant to erosion. It's interesting to consider how the grasses of the prairie allow wild and domestic animals alike to store up the maximum amount of energy possible. In spring or early summer blue grama is the main entree. As this becomes more limited later on, the animals move over to buffalo grass, or to the tops of needle and thread grass. It was through such cyclical grazing that, at one time, millions of bison were able to sustain themselves on the Great Plains.

And then there are the ponderosa, lending stature and beauty to this high, windswept escarpment. This is among the most widely distributed pines on the continent, and is an extremely important source of commercial wood products. The nuts of the ponderosa were collected and eaten by various Native Americans, and still provide a good food source for chipmunks, jays and squirrels. Another animal that seems fond of this pine is the porcupine; look for sections on these trees where this lumbering pincushion has peeled away the tasty bark. Porcupines are rather solitary animals, but will huddle (carefully!) together during extremely cold weather. As you might guess, porcupines have few enemies. Some clever, hungry coyotes, however, have developed the ability to roll the porcupine over and attack its soft belly. But woe to those who miss their mark! A mouth full of these tough, barbed quills has caused many a predator to starve to death because it became too painful for them to ingest food.

Even with these ponderosa breaks, more than likely you'll notice a rush of wind here. While such constant blowing is not relished by most humans, for the pronghorn who live here it is a vital link to life. Unlike deer and elk, pronghorn have almost no body fat. As a result, there is no option to wait out a bad winter storm; they must eat virtually every day of their lives. Were it not for the winds blowing the big sagebrush you see here free of snow, the pronghorn would most certainly not be able to survive.

In 0.7 mile you'll reach our turnaround point, at a high perch offering tremendous views of the prairie lands to the west, north and east. According to geologists, much of the region lying before you was once the same height as these pine breaks. The escarpment is simply capped with a protective layer of scoria, or "clinker," which kept wind and water from eroding it away. Basically, scoria is a layer of shale that the heat from a burning underground coal seam hardened into rock; pieces of the brick-colored stone can be found all along the top of the pine breaks.

On a clear day, you can look to the northeast and easily see all the way into the Black Hills of South Dakota. It was to a large degree events in this region that led to some of the last, and bloodiest, encounters in the western Indian wars. Despite the fact that the Black Hills had been made a part of the Great Sioux Reservation by the Treaty of 1868, in 1874 General George Armstrong Custer led a wagon train of soldiers into the region and found gold. Predictably, in no time at all miners were pouring into the area, totally indifferent to the fact that they were storming Indian lands. This invasion, combined with strong efforts the following year to prohibit native peoples from roaming unsettled territory, sent an unprecedented number of reservation Indians packing. They joined spring hunting parties to the west in great numbers along the streams south of the Yellowstone River. It was one such congregation of perhaps 10,000 Blackfoot, Oglala, Sioux and Cheyenne along the Greasy Grass (Little Bighorn River) that Custer found that fateful June day in 1876, when he and more than 200 of his men met their deaths on a windswept Montana prairie.

WALK #28—SCHOOL CREEK

DISTANCE:	1.75 miles
ENVIRONMENT:	Prairie
LOCATION:	Thunder Basin National Grassland. From Wyoming Highway 59 turn east onto Wyoming Highway 450, toward Newcastle. Proceed for about 15 miles, and turn right (south) onto School Creek Road. In approximately 0.5 mile, turn left (east) onto a two-track road. Park in 0.2 mile, just this side of a small stream channel.

A stream winding across the prairie can be a ribbon of magic, bringing an explosion of willow, cottonwood, rush and cordgrass to these long, yawning fields of grass and sage. Here in the thickets great congregations of birds may be seen, and, hiding beneath a cloak of darkness, raccoons, badgers, long-tailed weasels, muskrats, coyotes and, on occasion, mountain lions. After spending some time investigating the who and what of this riparian corridor, climb up past it toward the east to a roadway running beside a small reservoir, and turn right. If you creep up on this reservoir slowly, you may well spot a sizable group of mallards. These birds, with their green heads and beautiful chestnut breasts, are the most plentiful of all the North American ducks, and the ancestors of our domestic ducks. As you continue along this roadway you'll pass through thick mats of cheatgrass, as well as occasional clumps of plains prickly pear. To your left you'll see an escarpment covered with ponderosa pine. This long, broken ridge line runs north all the way into Montana, where it forms a portion of the famed Missouri Breaks. It marks one of the largest coal seams in the West. The Black Thunder coal operation, which you passed coming east from Wyoming Highway 450, is just one of several mines operating on the 500,000 acres of Thunder Basin National Grassland. On the other side of the pine breaks is the town of Newcastle, a former hotbed for poker players, founded on coal in the late 1800s.

At 0.25 mile you'll reach a large flat covered with greasewood. The salty leaves of greasewood are quite edible in limited quantities, and were a source of greens for many Native Americans. In the animal world, jackrabbits are particularly fond of the plant. The greasewood has definitely expanded its territory in Thunder Basin, and in other areas of the northern plains as well. Some researchers believe that over the years, through a complex altering of the environment due to overgrazing, the alkalinity of bottom-

Locoweed

Badger

land soils has increased, making the land more appropriate to the growth of greasewood than to more traditional native plants.

In a short distance you'll come to our turnaround point at a "T" intersection. Rather than return by the same route, however, head cross-country to the School Creek drainage, visible a hundred yards or so over your left shoulder (north), framed by a light peppering of cottonwoods. You can follow this back toward the reservoir you passed earlier in the walk. As you make your way across the landscape, keep your eyes out for badger holes, recognizable by their distinctive half-moon entrances, as well as the more rounded openings of fox and coyote dens. There are also prairie rattlesnakes here, which, while they have no more interest in you than you may have in them, should nevertheless be watched for.

The trees of this meandering drainage serve as perches for the bald eagles that can be seen here from November through March. During periods of intense cold the eagles congregate in the tree-lined hummocks immediately to the north, in a section of the pine breaks known as the Rochelle Hills. Also in these hills is a herd of about 90 elk, a surprising occurrence, since these regal animals are usually found in more extensive reaches of the high country.

Making your way up through this braid of old stream channels, look for the tracks of raccoons in the jigsaw blocks of wet clay. These remarkable animals, which may weigh up to 25 pounds and live for a dozen years, are extremely agile and clever—two traits that allow them to escape death at the jaws of much larger and

Raccoon

Red Fox

faster predators. Raccoons will eat almost anything, but in this area their diet consists mostly of small animals, fruits, bird eggs and carrion. True to the tales we all grew up with, raccoons do wash much of their food before eating it, a fact reflected in their Latin species name, "lotor," or "washer."

Earlier I suggested that changes in the environment due to overgrazing have increased the alkalinity of certain bottomland soils. But over the past 75 years, overgrazing has brought about an even more devastating change to these riparian corridors. Because the lushest grass cover of the prairie is found along its streams and rivers, it is no surprise that cattle have always made their way to these areas first. By staying along the banks for long periods of time, completely devouring some plants and trampling others, the protective cover of vegetation is eventually destroyed. This allows the stream to cut deeper and deeper into its banks.

This means that over decades, rather than drifting across the floodplain in the usual series of oxbows and meanders, the stream begins to channelize itself, cutting down instead of across. Unfortunately, the beautiful wide bands of cottonwoods that line the bottomlands of the western prairies, important both for their

Blue Grama

control of erosion and as wildlife habitat, are completely dependent on the normal drifts of stream channels for their propagation. The flooded silts along a drifting stream channel are what allow cottonwood seeds, only viable for a few weeks, to take hold and grow. A patch of trees located far from the stream got their start as a group at a time when the stream channel was closer to that location; this is why you'll see cottonwoods growing in clusters that are essentially the same age.

All this means that the wide prairie belts of cottonwoods, such as those near Little Thunder Creek along Wyoming Highway 450, are on the way out. As these trees die off, and most here are nearing the end of their life cycle, they will not be replaced by others. Eventually there will only be a narrow ribbon of cottonwoods along the immediate stream channel. Although this situation is to an extent correctable with proper land management, for years few people in either the government or the private sector have been willing to pursue the matter. Cattle continue to graze the stream bottoms unchecked, and the land continues to suffer.

On the way back, take a closer look at the escarpment off to the east, composed of sedimentary rocks topped with a layer of brick-colored scoria. Scoria is created when the heat from burning underground coal seams bakes the layers of shale above them, much as a clay pot is fired inside of a kiln. Coal seams, by the way, can ignite by a number of methods, including spontaneous combustion. You are walking near an extremely large underground coal seam, 70 to 100 feet thick.

WALK #29—THUNDER BASIN FLATS

DISTANCE: 1.5 miles
ENVIRONMENT: Prairie
LOCATION: Thunder Basin National Grassland. From Wyoming Highway 59 3 miles south of Wright, head east on Wyoming Highway 450, toward Newcastle. Just over 3 miles from this junction, turn onto a small dirt road taking off to the south. This road forks just south of the highway; park at the fork and begin your walk on the right branch.

Although Thunder Basin National Grassland is rarely even noticed by travelers hurrying past on Wyoming Highway 59, it is in fact a rich tapestry of varying environments—broad, grassy plains; quiet, shimmering creeks and unexpected pockets of forest and badlands. The paths we'll be walking in this area (see pages 87 and 89) will explore three of these ecosystems, starting with a yawning expanse of grass and sagebrush, capped by a wide, blue arc of Wyoming sky.

There are several plants along the beginning of this trek that you'll see again and again as you walk or drive across this slice of high prairie. Let's begin by taking a look at big sagebrush, the plant sporting a woody stem and blunt, gray-green leaves, which exude a pungent odor when crushed. This plant covers literally millions of acres in the American West, and is the most common type of artemisia, or "wormwood," found in the deserts of the Great Basin. Big sagebrush is no relation to the sage used as a cooking spice, which is a member of the mint family.

The presence of sage and another common plant here, western wheatgrass, is a typical mix in those sections of the American prairie marked by colder temperatures and fairly dry conditions (12 to 14 inches of moisture per year). Head west from here and, very generally speaking, you'll encounter more sage and less grass; head east and the opposite will be true. Sagebrush does yield to grasses for several years after a fire goes through, but in some areas of Wyoming there is hardly enough grass to sustain a major fire.

About 100 yards down the road you'll also see needle and thread grass and a serious non-native invader of the prairie, cheatgrass. The former plant bears its pointed seeds on the end of long hanging "threads." These coiled threads actually twist every time there's a change in humidity—a trait which helps ensure germination by actually screwing the seed into the ground. The latter plant, cheatgrass, is a relatively short grass with very blond, flag-shaped heads. It has taken over much of the Wyoming prairie, and is of very little value to either domestic livestock or wild grazers. To a great degree this is the result of poor management practices, in particular allowing cattle to graze in one place for too long. An alternative management method, a lesson derived from the millions of bison that once roamed here, is simply to keep the cattle moving as they graze, a pattern which allows, and to some degree actually stimulates, the growth of more desirable native plants.

While you may sense a sameness to this land the first time you find yourself out in the middle of it, there is really no shortage of diversions. The beautiful pronghorn, which is able to subsist on a remarkable variety of plants from prickly pear to sagebrush, is very much at home here. In the winter pronghorn may be seen huddling in scattered groups across the landscape, dining on the leaves of big sagebrush plants that have been blown free of snow by the restless winds. Cottontails are here as well, as is the beautiful sage grouse. Sage grouse, not nearly as numerous today as a hundred years ago, are known for their fascinating courtship rituals. Each spring the males return to established display grounds and begin complex courtship dances. Feathers of the neck, tail and wing are spread, and special air sacs in the breast are inflated, showing off the downy mat of creamy-white plumage that surrounds them. Loud popping noises rise from the chest, audible across remarkably long distances. After some time females will begin walking through the display area, eventually coming to rest in front of the mate of their choice.

At 0.5 mile into the walk you'll come to a *playa*, which is a depression in the terrain, sometimes lined with an underground cap of clay, that fills with water each spring. These shallow pockets remain wet well into summer, providing both cattle and wildlife with drinking water. Notice that the plant life here is quite different from that of the surrounding landscape. Most obvious is the absence of sagebrush, a gap you'll see wherever there are saturated soils.

Continue to walk south for another 0.25 mile or so, far enough away from the highway that you can sense the deep quiet on the prairie, the one pervading sound being a whisper, a rush or, on occasion, a roar of prairie wind.

WALK #30—JOYNER RIDGE

DISTANCE: 1.5 miles
ENVIRONMENT: Prairie
LOCATION: Devil's Tower National Monument. There
is one main road in this monument. Approximately 1 mile before reaching the visitor center, a smaller, paved route takes off to the left (north). Follow this a short distance to a signed parking area for the Joyner Ridge Trail. This is a loop trail; begin by taking the left fork.

It is with good reason that Wyoming is occasionally referred to as the "state of firsts," especially when it comes to natural resources. Yellowstone became America's first national park in 1872. The Shoshone National Forest, immediately to the east of Yellowstone, was the first national forest. And, thanks to Theodore Roosevelt, in 1906 this preserve became the nation's first national monument. (Perhaps the most surprising of all of Wyoming's string of "firsts," though, has nothing to do with the natural world. In 1869, the Wyoming territorial legislature became the first known governing body in the world to grant women full rights to vote and hold public office.)

From a distance, the great spire that is Devil's Tower is an intriguing curiosity. But when you get close enough to stand at its base—a full thousand feet across—and look up at its beautifully fluted sides soaring 867 feet into the Wyoming sky, it becomes a thing of real stature. At the beginning of this walk you'll have a fine view of the tower off to your right, across a beautiful quilt of mixed-grass prairie peppered with ponderosa pine. (If you're a science-fiction movie fan, you may recognize Devil's Tower from a scene in *Close Encounters of the Third Kind.)*

Devil's Tower is really a column of igneous rock. Sixty million years ago, about the time that the Rocky Mountains were on the way up and dinosaurs were on the way out, this tower was a giant, molten volcanic neck lying more than a thousand feet below the surface of the earth. As it cooled underground, the volcanic rock fractured into the beautifully fluted four-, five- and six-sided columns that you see today. While the igneous rock that makes up Devil's Tower is quite hard, that which surrounds it— sandstone, shales, limestone and gypsum—is quite soft. Thus, over millions of years the patient forces of wind and water wore away the surrounding landscape, leaving this enormous citadel to stand watch over the plains.

As you might have guessed, Devil's Tower represents an irresistible temptation to climbers. In fact, today more than a thousand people make their way to the top each year. The first ascent of the tower was made by a local rancher named William Rogers on the Fourth of July, 1893, to the cheers of a thousand onlookers; two years later, Roger's wife duplicated the feat. Perhaps the most memorable trip to the top was made by George Hopkins in 1941. George didn't climb a single foot, but rather dropped to the 1.5-acre rock platform by parachute. Unfortunately, a rope the plane dropped to enable him to make his descent missed its mark and fell over the side, leaving George stranded for six days until a young mountaineer from Dartmouth was brought in to rescue him. The event received an extraordinary amount of public attention.

As you make your way along the Joyner Ridge Trail (named after a former custodian of the monument), notice what seems to be a very distinct line between the ponderosa forest and the grasslands. Actually, the line isn't nearly as firm as it first appears. Prairie and forest are in a constant dance, advancing and retreating according to the climate of preceding years. In the forest to the left keep your eyes open for white-breasted nuthatches, wood pewees, mountain bluebirds and hairy woodpeckers; on the mixed-grass prairie to the right watch for nighthawks, meadowlarks, kingbirds and song and chipping sparrows, as well as red-tailed hawks and turkey vultures.

In 0.75 mile you'll come to a bench running on the edge of a large ravine. Far below in the distance is an open prairie parkland of bluestem, blue grama and needle and thread grasses, narrowing into a bottleneck fringed by deciduous woods. In 0.1 mile from where you first join this ridgetop, the trail will descend in a series of switchbacks into the ravine. From here you can get fine views back up toward the tops of the sculpted sandstone cliffs, each curve of rock throwing back pale, parched colors in the morning sun.

At the upper end of this bottleneck you'll enter a fine woodland, a soft collage of bur oak, green ash, ponderosa pine, chokecherry and wild plum. Rouse yourself early enough to walk here just after sunrise and you'll be treated to a marvelous chorus of bird song—chickadees, northern orioles, house wrens, yellow warblers, northern flickers, warbling and solitary vireos, red-breasted nuthatches and rufous-sided towhees, to name but a few. As you make your way up this ravine the forest becomes less dense, and occasional cuts in the canopy let in enough light to allow grasses to rise from the path. (Keep your eyes peeled for white-tailed deer!) Lining the roadway will be tall clumps of a grass known as big bluestem. This species typically grows several feet high; extensive fields of big bluestem growing farther to the east made many an early settler think that he had arrived in the land of milk and honey.

At the end of the ravine is a large open parkland of mixed prairie—in fact, the very one that you were following along the first section of the walk. A short distance past an interpretive sign at the beginning of the park, take the path leading off to the right, which will take you back to the parking area. Before you get in your car and drive away, take one last look at Devil's Tower. Speculation about the origin of those deeply fluted sides by various Indian tribes gave rise to a number of colorful interpretations. Most of the stories say that a giant bear was attempting to get at a small band of people who had the good fortune, magic or physical agility to end up high above the earth on the platform of Devil's Tower, just out of reach of the great bruin. The deep furrows you see in the side of the pillar were made by the bear's claws, scratched into the rock as he tried in vain to reach the frightened humans. A beautiful painting depicting this legend hangs in the visitor center.

■ COLORADO ■

COLORADO
...

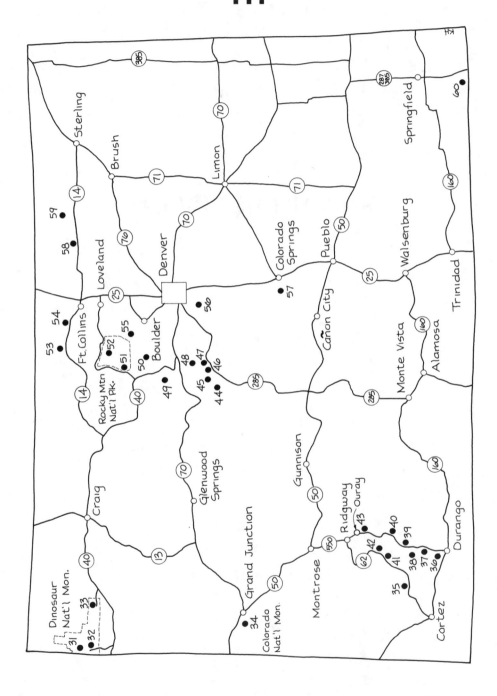

Colorado Plateau

WALK #31—WHIRLPOOL CANYON OVERLOOK

DISTANCE: 3.2 miles

ENVIRONMENT: Desert

LOCATION: Dinosaur National Monument. Head north from monument headquarters on the Harper's Corner Road. Just north of mile marker 22, on the right side of the road, is the Echo Park Overlook. Park here and walk back south along the Harper's Corner Road for 0.1 mile until you come to a dirt road taking off to the west. This is our walking path.

If you've ever had a desire to amble across the middle of nowhere, this is the walk for you. You'll be following a small, dirt ranch road that seems almost to float through a vast blanket of pungent sage, the distant line of eroded cliffs and mountains shimmering like mirages in the summer sun. Turkey vultures with enormous 6-foot wing spans hang on the desert thermals, carving circles in a parched blue sky. If you stand completely still for a moment, you'll notice a remarkable lack of sound here. To look across this tremendous yawn of open space, unable to cock an ear to even the slightest whisper or lilt of bird song, is a strange, almost overpowering experience. It can be a real relief to again strike up the comfortable rhythm of feet tapping time against the dirt.

If you haven't noticed them already as you drove on the roadway to the trailhead, this walk may introduce you to the large reddish brown to black insects known as Mormon crickets. These 2-inch-long creatures are actually a form of wingless grasshopper, their nickname deriving from the extensive damage they did to the crops of Mormon pioneers in 1848, until they were finally gobbled up by California gulls. In some years their populations absolutely explode, and millions of them—both dead and alive—can be found lining the pavement of the Harper's Corner Road. Strangely, when such large numbers occur, the insects will often begin a mysterious migration in an apparently random direction, never stopping or detouring around any obstacle in their path, be it a river, fence or even a sheer cliff.

You can tell the female of this species by the long pointed structure (ovipositor) that extends from the abdomen. Eggs are laid in the soil during the summer, and will hatch the following spring. While these insects may hardly seem like a palatable pâté to us, for some Native Americans they were a very important source of food.

In 0.8 mile you'll pass through a fine collection of junipers, and then begin descending gently, soon reaching a place where the land drops away into a magnificent canyon. In these layers of rock is a story stretching back to some of the earliest pulses of life on earth. The upper gray shales and limestones before you rest atop 500-million-year-old reddish brown rocks that once formed head-lands on a vast, silent sea known as the Lodore Ocean. Beneath even this is the billion-year-old red sandstone that forms the roots of the Uinta Mountains. The narrator of this incredible tale is the Green River, 2,500 feet below you and just out of sight, cutting ever deeper into the foundations of the earth.

It was in 1869 that the intrepid, one-armed explorer John Wesley Powell became the first man to descend the mighty Green and Colorado rivers by boat. Having already lost one of his crafts at Disaster Falls and very nearly losing another one at Hell's Half Mile (both in Lodore Canyon), Powell was hardly a stranger to the incredible force the Green could muster. Thus it was probably not with complete calm that he and his men approached the mouth of the canyon that lies before you.

"All this volume of water," he writes, "confined, as it is, in a narrow channel and rushing with great velocity, is set eddying and spinning in whirlpools by projecting rocks and short curves, and the waters waltz their way through the canyon, making their own rippling, rushing, roaring music." Through difficult lining and portaging maneuvers, Powell's party made it past the point where you now stand, to find a wider, but even faster river farther down. "What a headlong ride it is!" he later wrote, "shooting past rocks and islands. I am soon filled with exhilaration only experienced before in riding a fleet horse over the outstretched prairie." Later, floating in the calm waters of Island Park just to the west, Powell decided to christen this Whirlpool Canyon, the narrowest of all the gorges they had seen thus far.

The road continues along this edge, becoming fainter and fainter, finally fading out completely a couple hundred yards from where it first joined the edge of the canyon. Continue along the ridge past the end of the road for another 200 yards through a piñon-juniper forest to a narrow open area strewn with rocks. This is our turnaround. From here you can look north into a deep canyon that lies along the Island Park geologic fault. This beautiful gorge, its floor carpeted with tall grass and cottonwoods, was carved by Jones Hole Creek, which runs clear as crystal into the murky waters of the Green. The word *hole*, incidentally, was a term used by early trappers and explorers to designate valleys throughout the West.

WALK #32—CANYON OVERLOOK

DISTANCE:	0.3 mile
ENVIRONMENT:	Desert
LOCATION:	Dinosaur National Monument. Head north from the monument headquarters on the Harper's Corner Road. Turn at the signed road to the Canyon Overlook and Picnic Area, just north of mile marker 15. A short distance after making this turn the road will fork; the left branch goes to the picnic area, while the right goes to the overlook. Park at the overlook.

The view from Canyon Overlook is certainly one to remember, with mile after mile of folded stone, licked by wind and sculpted by patient fingers of water into a fantastic tapestry of domes, cliffs and twisted canyons. Standing on this high perch looking into the rugged landscape below, it's easy to agree with the Dinosaur National Monument brochure: this place is, and seems likely to remain, "a secret of the present, known to few travelers."

This walk is much shorter than most of our treks. I've included it because it offers a wonderful opportunity to see how what may seem like subtle differences in the landscape can completely alter the vegetative complexion. Leaving your car parked at the Canyon Overlook, begin the walk by descending the paved road to the picnic area lying just to the north. While this stretch can, of course, be driven, the warm smell of sage and sand on the wind, the clean summer skies overhead and the rush of rabbits and squawk of jays make a slow saunter on foot the only truly appropriate way to travel.

Depending on the time of your visit, you'll likely find the roadway fringe leading to the picnic area dappled with color—the deep blues of lupines, the fiery reds of scarlet gilia and the soft white petals of the primroses. As is common in other parts of the monument, junipers and piñon pines add a smattering of blunt green to the scene. These trees seem especially beautiful when viewed from a distance, as you can see in the great sweep of forests visible far below in Pearl Park, tossed like a tattered quilt at the bare feet of a sandstone gulf.

While you may have noticed a couple of changes in the look of the plant life as you made your way down, things really begin to get interesting about the time you reach the turnaround circle adjacent to the picnic area. Here in this small island surrounded by concrete is, of all things, a small huddle of aspen, a tree usually no more at home in a high slice of desert than would be the beavers that so relish its sweet white bark. From here things become even

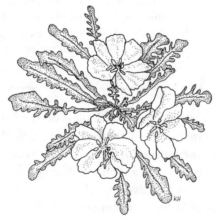

Evening Primrose

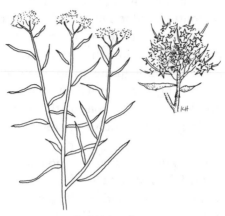

Rabbitbrush

more interesting. Walk out along the small finger of land extending
beyond the picnic area in a clockwise direction. Joining the occasional piñon pine and juniper is a beautiful assemblage of curl-leaf
mountain mahogany, as well as several fine old Douglas firs.
Almost nowhere else along this drive, most of which is through a
land washed with sage, rabbitbrush and greasewood, will you see
this kind of plant community. So why here?

The first thing that may come to mind is elevation. Remember that the higher you go, the cooler the air becomes. Since cool
air cannot hold as much moisture as warm air, moisture-laden
clouds rising over an uplifted landscape tend to drop their water at
high elevations. In many places near here you can be standing in
shorts in a warm, dry desert, looking at 3 feet of snow on the high
line of the surrounding mountains.

The next thing to consider is exposure—how the land is
oriented to the sun. As it turns out, this is a great part of the secret
to this arboreal oasis. The face of this land slopes gently downward
almost due north, the one direction that offers the least amount of
exposure to the sun. Rain that falls here stays a little longer,
because the warm, dry fingers of the sun can't pull it from the earth.
The snow that comes also lasts a little longer, melting drop by drop
into the soil instead of quickly evaporating back into the atmosphere. These extra drips of water, each one bringing the promise
of life, are what enable the trees you see here to survive when all
around there is the strong song of the desert.

Looking north and just slightly east from the overlook at the end of this promontory, hidden in the folds of Weber Sandstone, lie the grassy glades of Echo Park. Here the Green River exits beautiful Lodore Canyon to join the Yampa, which has been on its own stunning journey through the grand twists of rocks known as the "Goosenecks." Together they will twist like a great snake, past the rugged roil of Whirlpool Canyon and the silence of Island Park, through the sunlit gorge of Split Mountain and out into the sage-covered flats beyond.

More than a hundred years ago, Echo Park was the home of a quasi-hermit named Pat Lynch. The life of this feisty Irishman was never dull. He was once stranded and held prisoner on the coast of Africa, and was also a naval veteran of the Civil War, reportedly with the crew that sunk the Merrimac. He came to settle in this rugged land in the vicinity of Echo park, laying "claim on this bottom for my home and support." Often living in caves once used by Indians, Pat grew to love this place as few Europeans had before him, or have since. It is wonderful that in this modern day one can still lose oneself in Pat's footsteps, meandering along the Green, up Moonshine Draw and down Iron Springs Wash, finding the land still filled with that piercing, silent beauty, that clear ring of enchantment that haunted Pat Lynch until the day he died.

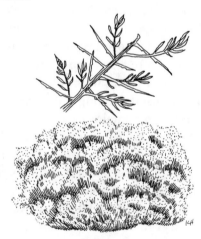

Greasewood

WALK #33—YAMPA RIVER

DISTANCE: 2 miles
ENVIRONMENT: Desert
LOCATION: Dinosaur National Monument. From U.S. Highway 40, approximately 40 miles west of Craig, Colorado, turn north on a signed highway toward Deerlodge Park Campground. The walk begins from this camping area, approximately 11 miles from U.S. Highway 40.

By the time the Yampa River reaches this beautiful parkland, it has already traversed an amazing variety of environments. Rising 100 air miles to the east, in the high spruce-fir forests that flank the Continental Divide, the Yampa tumbles through meadows splashed with wildflowers and across floodplains heavy with sage, eventually punching its way westward through the hard heart of the Juniper Mountains. Here at Deerlodge Park it makes a slow, lazy amble through a grove of grandfather cottonwoods before disappearing into a silent, mysterious world of 300-million-year-old limestones and ancient quartz sand dunes, now hardened into a maze of shimmering white canyons.

This walk begins beneath the magnificent Deerlodge Park cottonwoods, along a path which follows the south bank of the Yampa through a blanket of tall grass. Besides forming an extremely beautiful environment in which to walk, the vegetation growing along the Yampa was once part of a garden of useful plants that Native Americans relied on heavily. Various parts of the cottonwood, for example, contain populin and salicin, both of which are related to the active ingredient in common aspirin; Native Americans were using cottonwood (and, to a lesser extent, aspen) to break fevers and reduce inflammation long before the first Excedrin headache. Some Indians ate the sweet sap of the cottonwood, while the buds and fruits were commonly used to produce colorful dyes.

As you continue along the river, look for the stiff, segmented, hollow stems of horsetails, also known as scouring rush. This latter name hints at the fact that early peoples used the abrasive stems of the plant to polish stone pipes and arrowheads, while pioneer women would routinely dry and bundle the stems to clean pots, pans and even wooden floors. Before such things as sandpaper or fine grades of steel wool, British woodworkers used horsetails as their primary means to finish cabinets and fine pieces of furniture.

The braid of trails running through the grassy areas that fringe the Yampa sand bars can become faint in places. You may wish to do a little walking in the upper reaches of the sand bars themselves, noting the surprising amount of life that can spring from these sandy soils, including an abundance of cottonwood seedlings and tamarisk. Once out of the cottonwoods, in about 0.25 mile, you'll enter a much more open area covered with sagebrush, cacti, rabbitbrush and saltbush. By the way, the leaves and seeds of the rabbitbrush—the tall bush with slender leaves and great clusters of tiny golden flowers—are a favorite of the cottontails you may see dashing across your path.

If you're walking through this area during mid- to late summer, you'll undoubtedly spot the black and white plumage and long tails of magpies or, at the very least, hear their harsh cries rising from the river corridor. Magpies typically do not congregate during the nesting season, but suddenly become much more sociable after the rigors of parenthood are completed. Their harsh yak! yak! can be rather startling when you're used to the gentle croak of the ash-throated flycatchers, or the somber coo of mourning doves.

Just under 0.5 mile into the walk you'll reach a parking lot. This marks the western terminus of the road system into Deerlodge Park. (If you happen to be walking out along the sand bars at the time, this parking area will be on your left at the point where a large block of sandstone protrudes to the edge of the river.) We'll follow a footpath leaving from the southwest corner of the parking area, climbing up through the rocks onto a small bench above the river.

From the parking area to our turnaround point, the look of the land is quite different from what came before. Across the river are large blocks of severely tilted sedimentary rock, evidence of the fact that these lopsided peaks were squeezed on either side by enormous pressures inside the earth. Later erosion by wind and water, a process that occurs rather quickly in soft sandstones, gave these rocks the dramatic face they wear today. Grain by grain, the relentless forces of erosion are delivering these mountains to the Yampa, which then speeds them away to the Green.

At 0.65 mile the trail heads away from the river to cross a rocky sandstone wash. Notice how different the vegetation is beneath these narrow walls. Here water is regularly channeled from the face of the surrounding plateaus, allowing a fine garden of wildflowers, cottonwoods and squawbush to exist where they otherwise could not. At 0.9 mile our path will turn south, bound for the rocky corridors of Disappointment Draw and Indian Water Canyon. You may wish to exit the trail here and walk along the sand bar to the point where the river disappears into a massive buttress of rock. From here it will continue west as it has done for countless millennia, cutting through first the soft, Tertiary sediments, and finally the harder limestone and sandstone blocks laid down by a series of ancient oceans.

WALK #34—JOHN OTTO TRAIL

DISTANCE: 0.5 mile
ENVIRONMENT: Desert
LOCATION: Colorado National Monument. Leave Interstate 70 at Fruita (exit 19), and drive south on Highway 340 for 2.5 miles to the monument's west entrance. From the entrance, it's a scenic 4.5-mile ascent on the Rim Rock Drive to the monument headquarters and visitor center. The John Otto Trail begins about 1 mile past the visitor center on the left (northeast) side of Rim Rock Drive.

Any road-weary traveler on Interstate 70 would do well to make a leisurely detour into Colorado National Monument. In this tapestry of quiet sandstone chambers is a world far different from that of on-ramps and off-ramps, where the monotonous whine of tires gives way to the whisper of cottontail feet and the coo of rock doves.

This 20,000-acre pocket of solitude owes its existence to the fervent efforts of one man, John Otto, for which this trail has been named. Otto came to the region in 1906, and wasted no time in assuming the role of chief promoter of the region. Of the Grand

Valley below he would claim that rich soil and abundant sunshine grew "peaches as big as the moon," and pumpkins "big as railroad oil tanks." But he held an even greater admiration for this soaring canyon country, expending an enormous amount of effort writing letters and raising money in order to have it declared a federal park. His perseverance paid off in 1911 when President Taft signed legislation making the area a national monument, with Otto himself as the first custodian. For this position Otto was paid a whopping $1 per month.

Otto's antics were, more often than not, the talk of the local grapevine: the way he would disappear into these canyons for weeks on end with only his beloved burros for company; his suggestion to name the preserve "Smith National Monument Park," thinking that such a name would cause the millions of Americans named "Smith" to visit the area; the time he suddenly married Beatrice Farnham from New England (her wedding present being a burro), only to have his bride discover to her dismay that a tent and pack stove were about as much of a domicile as John was able to handle.

This walk begins in an open forest of piñon and juniper, two trees that occur together throughout much of the American Southwest. On the ground here you'll also see the stiff, multi-jointed green stems of Mormon tea. Its nickname refers to Mormon pioneers who commonly used the plant to make a tasty tea, although Native Americans and Mexicans were using the plant for medicinal purposes long before Brigham Young set foot in Utah.

Mormon Tea

This particular species of Mormon tea has trace amounts of ephe-drine, which is recognized around the world for its value as a decongestant. (Asian varieties have much higher concentrations of this chemical.) Many people of the Southwest still drink tea made from this plant to relieve allergy and cold-related congestion.

While this canyon country may look frightfully devoid of any plants that could sustain human life, those who know it well might consider it a garden of plenty. Besides Mormon tea, the leaves and "berries" of the juniper provide a treatment for urinary tract disorders, while the piñon (a good example is 50 yards down the trail on the right) offers delicious, high-energy nuts containing nearly 60 percent fat. In addition, the piñon produces a quick, hot fire. Early settlers discovered that the wood of the singleleaf ash, also found here, made extremely durable tool handles. And finally, the buds, flowers and fruits of the yuccas along this trail are fine sources of food, while the leaves of the plant once provided material for making rope, sandals and mats.

The trail descends gently, offering fine views of the Grand Valley, 2,000 feet below, framed in the distance by the beautifully layered Book Cliffs. In just over 0.2 mile the path ends at a wonderful sandstone perch. Here you can stand wrapped in warm sun, with a dry desert wind tumbling up the canyon walls. Listen for the raucous call of the pinyon jay, and the fast rush of wings as swifts dance along the precipices looking for insects. To your right is beautiful Monument Canyon and the 550-foot-high spire of Wingate Sandstone known as Independence Monument. This monolith, as well as the Pipe Organ formation directly in front of you, are remnants of much larger ridge systems, long since beaten back into grains of sand by eons of ice, wind and water. The one thing that has kept these spires from suffering the same fate is a protective layer of light-colored cap stone (Kayenta formation), which consists of rock sediments that have been glued together by silica and calcite. True to his love for this land, John Otto scaled Independence Monument on the Fourth of July in 1910, planting an American flag on the summit.

Southwestern Colorado

WALK #35—PRIEST GULCH

DISTANCE: 2.5 miles
ENVIRONMENT: Forest
LOCATION: San Juan National Forest. The trail takes off from Priest Gulch Trailhead, located on the north side of Highway 145, approximately 25 miles northeast of Dolores, Colorado. Pick up the path by leaving the parking area and following an old roadbed now closed to motor vehicles; the trail lies past the end of this road, on the other side of a fence. Alternatively, you can cross Priest Creek on a bridge that lies adjacent to the trailhead, and then turn left. (A right turn would put you on the Calico Trail.) Taking this latter route, however, means that you'll have to ford the creek in about 0.25 mile.

Priest Gulch traverses the very best of the Colorado forests. Aspen blanket the hills and hummocks as far as the eye can see, their soft canopies streaked here and there with the dark olives and frosty blues of Engelmann and Colorado blue spruce. Though beautiful any time of year, the shrinking days of autumn trigger a particularly splendid change in the aspen, as the airy green color of chlorophyll drains from the tree, leaving a sea of blazing-gold leaves shimmering in the October sun.

Many a mountain man used to scan the high pockets of the Rockies in search of the aspen's fluttering leaves and striking white trunks. For to find them often meant finding the beaver, who has a particular penchant for the sweet bark of the tree, and a wily way of using the twigs and branches to construct dams and lodges that the best of engineers would envy. (The beaver also likes to keep a stash of aspen branches beneath the freezing level of his pond, thereby ensuring a good supply of food throughout the winter.) Beaver continue to munch aspen bark in wet pockets of this forest, while deer and elk browse the leaves and twigs. Alas, aspen is a transition forest, and, lacking fire or any other disturbance, it will eventually be replaced by the conifers you see growing nearby.

The same shift in hat fashions that ultimately saved the aspen-loving beaver from being trapped to extinction sent the mountain man the way of the passenger pigeon. "We are done with this life in the mountains," wrote mountain man Robert Newell, who 150 years ago saw the writing on the wall. "Done with wading in beaver dams, and freezing or starving alternately, done with Indian trading and Indian fighting. The fur trade is dead in the Rocky Mountains, and it is no place for us now, if it ever was."

Our short trek along Priest Gulch is a fairly gentle one. After two very short climbs in the first 0.2 mile, the path levels off to become an easy streamside meander. At 0.5 mile you'll come to a small meadow 50 yards long, speckled with the white umbels of yarrow blooms, and the lemon-colored heads of yellow salsify. Salsify, by the way, was introduced into this country from Europe, where it has been cultivated for 2,000 years for its tasty, fleshy root. Depending on whom you ask, a cooked salsify root tastes like a parsnip, an artichoke or even an oyster (hence one of the plant's nicknames, "oyster plant"). Salsify has done very well at establishing itself in the new world, in part due to its ability in late summer to launch thousands of seeds into the wind on tiny white parachutes.

Just before leaving this small meadow, note the two large, dead trees on your left. While many people might look at these according to the number of cords of firewood they would produce, such trees are actually very important to resident wildlife. Three-toed woodpeckers, for example, would relish either of these snags as a place to rear their young, as might the beautiful, weasel-like marten.

Throughout this section of trail, particularly along the stream just after leaving this first meadow, you'll notice the long, slender leaf bunches and, in June and July, the beautiful lavender flowers of the Rocky Mountain iris. This is one of the most beautiful of all the mountain wildflowers, and only grows in areas where water lies close to the surface of the ground. The fresh roots are reported to contain strong poisons, although when dried they have been used for decades as a treatment for syphilis, as well as in the making of a strong diuretic.

Sixty yards past the first meadow the trail wanders through a forest of conifers draped with lace lichen. After reaching a second open area in 1 mile, make a stream crossing and begin a gradual climb up a narrow ridge. Just after topping this ridge at 1.25 miles, you'll enter one of the most beautiful aspen meadows you could ever hope to find. These lovely trees, some 80 to 100 years old, form a stunning fringe around a grassy parkland peppered with iris, yarrow and salsify. To the west is a high wall wrapped in spruce and aspen that separates this drainage from Little Taylor Creek, while in the distant north stands the high, lush ridge line of Stoner Mesa. If you make a short descent down a 35-foot hill on your right, you'll come to a very secluded section of Priest Creek—a perfect pocket in which to sit and soak up a Rocky Mountain afternoon. For those who aren't ready to turn around, this trail continues on for 6 more miles, first crossing Forest Road 542, and then eventually joining the Calico Trail.

WALK #36—JUNCTION CREEK

DISTANCE:	2.6 miles
ENVIRONMENT:	Forest
LOCATION:	San Juan National Forest. From Durango town center, head north on Main until you reach 25th Street, and turn left. This street first becomes Junction Creek Road, and then, at the point where it enters the San Juan National Forest, it turns into Forest Road 543. Our walk begins at the forest boundary, on the left side of the road.

This walk will take you through a mixed conifer forest that blankets the bottom and sides of a lovely, meandering mountain valley. The artist responsible for much of this scenery is Junction Creek, the fine little stream on your left that for thousands of years has sliced its way through these thick slabs of sedimentary rock on a headlong dash from the high reaches of the La Plata Mountains. A century ago this waterway ran dark with sediments from mining operations near its headwaters; today only spring snowmelt and summer showers cloud its otherwise crystal complexion.

The early portion of the trail winds through a narrow open area, complete with a mat of tall grass cradling the cinnamon trunks of ponderosa. This tree, also known as yellow pine or, when young, as blackjack pine, tends to grow in relatively open parklands like this one. Held against a distant range of mountains or a flush of Colorado sky, it seems to absolutely sing the essence of the American West. Many Native Americans of the area collected the seeds of the ponderosa, which they ate raw or made into bread.

Also common along this section of the trail is Gambel oak, a member of the beech family whose thickets of lobed leaves can be found woven into much of the ponderosa understory. While the nuts of nearly all of the oaks served as major sources of food for Native Americans, Gambel oak was especially prized since its acorns tended to be less bitter than those of other varieties. Preparing acorns meant first grinding them into a fine meal, often in a stone mortar or metate. The ground nuts were then placed in a basket lined with leaves, and water was poured through them to

Downy Woodpecker

remove the tannic acid. Acorn meal could be stored for long periods in pottery containers, and its flavor (as well as that of acorn mush) could be altered by adding other nuts or berries, or even meat. So important a food source was Gambel oak that it, like the nuts of the piñon, actually influenced the ebb and flow of large bands of people. Today a common consumer of Gambel oak is mule deer, which have a fondness not for the nuts, but for the plant's thick leaves.

The trail continues above the creek through collections of purple asters, scarlet gilia and yarrow. Besides depending on adequate moisture from summer showers, the particular blossoms that you see splashed onto this landscape depend a great deal on what time of year you happen to be here. Were you to drift very, very slowly through this forest you'd see a soft, carefully orchestrated explosion of yellows, scarlets and creams, each bloom marking the steady drift of summer. Beyond blooms, a beautiful fusion of greens can be seen here, created by the outstretched arms of blue spruce, alder, ponderosa and cottonwood.

One mile down the path, keep your eyes and ears open for the raucous call and deep blue flash of Steller's jays, the soft toot of nuthatches and the sporadic drum of sapsuckers.

While most people realize the influence of fire and disease on this landscape, few of us stop to consider that the dry, loamy soil underlying this forest also adds a great deal to the pace of change. At 1 mile into the walk you can look high across the creek and see evidence of a large slide of land, now patiently being stabilized once again by the long root fingers of young conifers. Just to your right at this point, on the bank alongside the trail, is a sizable collection of exposed root systems—more evidence of how much of this land is routinely carted off by wind and water. The hold these trees and plants have on these mountainsides forms a tenacious net—one which a careless fire or misplaced clearcut can easily destroy.

At roughly 1.2 miles, the pathway enters one of those hidden pockets that add no end of appeal to walks in the southwestern uplands. Protected from overexposure to the sun and fed by fine lines of water, the land here shifts dramatically from a coniferous forest fairly bereft of understory life, to a place exploding with aspen, coneflowers, box elders, chokecherries, mountain maples and thimbleberries. Something very different is happening here.

The dry, fine-edged odor that laced the ponderosa pines has melted into air that runs thick with the smells of damp earth and herbs. The lilt of bird song is heavier; a cool moisture rubs your face and arms. It is a profound lesson in the power that both water and exposure have to alter the face of the land.

In 0.1 more mile is our turnaround, at a point where the trail joins another pathway coming in from the left. This is the south-ernmost portion of the newly constructed Colorado Trail, a re-markable 470-mile dance across the high country from Durango to Denver.

WALK #37—LOWER HERMOSA CREEK

DISTANCE: 3 miles
ENVIRONMENT: Forest
LOCATION: San Juan National Forest. From U.S. Highway 550, 0.25 mile north of mile marker 32, turn west onto Hermosa Creek Road. Immediately after making this turn, take a right onto La Plata County Road 201. Follow this for roughly 4 miles, where it will dead-end at the trailhead.

For much of its 30-mile tumble from the high, rugged peaks of the central San Juans to the northwest, Hermosa Creek is paralleled by a wonderful footpath, the two of them meandering through a vast, endless quilt of rich forest communities. As you'll see on this walk, simple turns of the trail can have surprising consequences. For instance, a small drainage nook hidden from the warm, drying fingers of the sun will support a flush of life far different from that which surrounds it. You'll find an entirely different array of flowers peppering the ground, and the dull, blunt complexion of ponderosa and fir may yield to the summer-bright greens of aspen and alder. With such changes, of course, comes a different array of animal life—the buzz of honey bees where there were none before, glimpses of deer looking for leaves to browse and the light chirp of bushtits instead of the raucous calls of Steller's jays.

Our trail begins in a semi-open coniferous forest, with fine, broad views of Hermosa Valley stretching to the northwest. It was on just such forested mountain trails that the proud Ute Indians once roamed summer through fall. In addition to gathering herbs and berries, they also hunted elk, deer and rabbit; after the hides of the animals were tanned, they often became items to offer in trade with tribes living in the uplands of northern New Mexico. Every component of this forest had a name and, more often than not, a use to these people. Roots and bulbs, pine nuts, seeds from various grasses, acorns from the Gambel oak that grows so profusely here—even the Abert's squirrels that dance and chatter in these ponderosas—were considered important food sources. Branches from willows and alders were used to make water baskets, which were then sealed with the pitch from the conifers that surround you. Sweet sap was collected from aspen in the spring. In short, here was firewood, housing material, clothing, trade items, dinner and dessert.

According to a Ute legend, long before any people roamed the earth, the creator Sunawavi began to collect and cut sticks, which he then placed in a large bag. Day after day this went on, much to the curiosity of Coyote, who had stood nearby watching the entire process. One day, while Sunawavi was away, Coyote could no longer contain himself and opened the bag. When he did, thousands of people ran out and scattered in every direction, each speaking different languages. When Sunawavi returned he was extremely angry. He had planned to distribute the people evenly

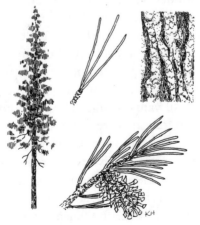

Ponderosa Pine

across the land so that they could live in peace, but now there would be much war, each tribe trying to get better and better land. Considering the small collection of people who remained in the bag, Sunawavi decided to name that one group the Ute. They would remain few in number, but be endowed with great courage, able to stand against all others.

And so the story seemed to unfold, at least until the arrival of hungry miners to the San Juans in the latter half of the 19th century. The Utes were not aggressive fighters; they sold a major portion of the high country to the north to the U.S. government simply to avoid a war. Yet still the newcomers wanted more, until Sunawavi's special people were removed from all but a minuscule section of Colorado Territory. Today in this part of the state, only words hint at this nearly forgotten people—Ouray, Ignacio, Uncompahgre, Weminuche; words, and the sprawl of the vast green forests that nurtured them for countless centuries.

Notice how, in about 0.3 mile, as you walk along an exposed, south-facing bench, the vegetation changes dramatically. Instead of ponderosa and white fir there is a profusion of Gambel oak interspersed with juniper. This latter tree, readily identifiable by its beautiful blue "berries" (they're actually the tree's cones), is sometimes mistakenly referred to as cedar. Once consumed by the Utes, today they are an important food source for many birds. Later, roughly a mile into the walk, the trail cuts across the sheltered drainage of Swampy Creek, an environment rich with wildflowers, shrubs and smatterings of deciduous trees.

Although ponderosa pines have been present throughout much of this walk, adding a stately, truly western feel to the landscape, nowhere are they more beautiful than at our turnaround point, approximately 1.5 miles from the trailhead, growing in a beautiful, open parkland perched on a rim high above Hermosa Creek to the southwest. In fact, if you leave the trail and walk to your left for 30 or 40 yards, you'll find an abundance of perches beneath these great trees that are just perfect for mentally drifting away with the breezes that roll out of the La Plata Mountains to the west. Though the ponderosa is often cited as one of the most "common" pines on the North American continent, here it seems anything but. In this slice of mountainscape these cinnamon-colored giants are real magic, particularly "uncommon" in the amount of beauty they offer to anyone who lingers beneath their branches.

WALK #38—UPPER HERMOSA CREEK

DISTANCE: 2.8 miles
ENVIRONMENT: Forest
LOCATION: San Juan National Forest. From U.S. Highway 550, just north of the main entrance to Purgatory Ski Area, turn west onto Forest Road 578, following the signs for Sig Creek Campground and Hermosa Park. Continue past the campground for several miles to a road taking off to the left across a meadow to the East Fork of Hermosa Creek. Park here, and cross the stream on foot. The walk continues on this road for a hundred yards, becoming a trail after crossing through a gate. *Note:* This trail has several gates; please be sure to close each one as you pass through.

This is a splendid walk through a combination of high, open meadows and quiet spruce-fir forest, ending at a small streamside park. A hundred years ago the road you drove in on was a toll route connecting the mining region near Rico with transportation facilities at Rockwood, 15 miles north of Durango. Because any investor worth his bank rolls was hesitant to back a mining region unless there was an adequate, reliable means of transporting the ore, road building in the 1870s was pursued at a fever pitch, often over some of the most incredible topography imaginable. Yet the actual building of these roads, which often meant blasting through solid rock, was only the beginning. Gatekeepers were employed to collect fees, and the constant beat of weather meant work crews armed with picks and shovels had to be on hand to fill in ruts, as well as clear the endless flows of mud, rock and snow. Toll-road fever began to wane in the 1880s with the arrival of the railroads. At that point, every mining-camp promoter quickly shifted his energies to trying to woo the iron horse into his particular pocket of the San Juan high country.

In 0.3 mile is a fine view off to the right of the mountains that give rise to Hermosa Creek. From here the watercourse tumbles southward for more than 20 miles through stately forests of Engelmann spruce, Douglas fir, ponderosa, juniper and white fir, finally unleashing its precious cargo into the Animas River, 10 miles north of Durango. This gentle trail follows the course for nearly the entire distance, and would be a wonderful one-way walk for those with the time, energy and an extra car.

As the path turns south Hermosa Creek enters a shallow ravine, flanked on the west by fine collections of aspen mixed with spruce and fir. Aspen are especially adept at colonizing disturbed ground, although if no further disturbances occur, they will ultimately be replaced by more shade-tolerant species. It is these shade-tolerant trees—in this case spruce and fir—that ultimately form what is known as the climax forest.

The open ravine continues to drop southward, becoming narrower and narrower until the grassy creek banks are eventually replaced by forest. In 1.5 miles you'll reach the East Fork of Cross Creek, just after passing through a wooden gate. Cross this stream and continue on for about 50 more yards, where you'll find a small grassy area beside Hermosa Creek, directly opposite a sheer rock wall. This is our turnaround point.

Along this latter stretch of trail you'll stand a good chance of meeting some of the more common feathered residents of the forest—the black-crested head and bright blue body of the Steller's jay, the blunt gray body and piercing scream of the goshawk and that ever-busy, fluffy gray insect eater, the mountain chickadee. This latter bird sports nearly the same familiar tune (chick-a-dee-dee-dee) as does its lower-altitude cousin, the black-capped chicka-

Pine Grosbeak

dee, though, all in all, it seems to have a coarser, more throaty sound. Always found near coniferous forests, in severe winters these hardy little birds may work their way down to the lower stretches of Hermosa Creek, where the sting of winter is a bit less severe. Also keep an eye out here for red crossbills (the name refers to the specially evolved crossed bill, perfect for opening pine cones), as well as pine siskins and golden-crowned kinglets.

Steller's Jay

WALK #39—SPUD LAKE

DISTANCE: 2.2 miles
ENVIRONMENT: Mountain
LOCATION: San Juan National Forest. From U.S. Highway 550, approximately 15 miles south of Silverton, head east on the signed Lime Creek Road. Continue for 3.5 miles until you see a large lily pond on the right. The parking area and trailhead for Spud Lake are just past this pond on the left.

There is something special about Potato Lake, known by its close friends simply as Spud Lake. It's an inviting kind of place, a soft, sparkling destination set in an ancient braid of rock and fringed by a pleasant medley of aspen, spruce and willow. Even before you set foot on this trail you may feel a tug from the large, beautiful lily pond located along the southern edge of the entrance road. Water lilies produce long, sinewy rootstalks that twist through the depths of their host pond or lake like so much spaghetti. Lemon-colored flowers are visible through much of the summer, perched on the tops of hearty green leaves that grow thick enough to actually insulate a body of water from the heating effects of the sun. Seeds of the yellow pond lily can be collected and roasted (as was commonly done by Native Americans), producing a food that tastes remarkably like popcorn.

The first stretch of the Spud Lake walk is through a fine grove of aspen, the occasional brief climbs made easier when done to the accompaniment of black-capped chickadees, yellow warblers and red-shafted flickers. Besides providing homes for many types of birds, the buds, bark and leaves of the aspen provide food for a variety of local animal life, including deer, elk, beaver, grouse and even snowshoe hares. Each autumn they also provide mankind with stunning beauty, the green of summer seeping away into a wash of brilliant gold, flashing like Caesar's coins in the early October sun. Incidentally, the delightful ceaseless quiver of these leaves (the common name of the tree is actually "quaking" aspen) is due to flat, supple leaf stalks that yield to the slightest breeze.

When you are 0.3 mile into the walk, you'll catch fine glimpses to the northwest of a strikingly handsome peak known as Engineer Mountain. This great uplift, an easily recognizable landmark from various points around the region, is a massive block of sedimentary and hardened volcanic rock sitting on a layered bed of sandstone, limestone and shale. These lower layers were laid down during repeated intrusions of ocean water. In fact, fossils of the shellfish that lived in these ancient seas can be found in abundance in the limestone layers of this and other nearby mountains. How strange they seem here, stranded high and dry in a cold world of soaring, wind-scored rock—far, far away from the warm seawater soup that nurtured them 300 million years ago.

At 0.75 mile the path skirts a fine pocket of willow—always a sign that water is not far away—and then proceeds past a tumble of granite talus (large, loose rocks), providing a fine home for a couple of indomitable pikas, or, as they are sometimes referred to, rock rabbits. These tailless bundles of energy, which look rather like guinea pigs, are most famous for their practice of harvesting grasses and laying them to dry on a rock in the sun; once dried, the pika gathers them into neat little bundles and stores them for use during winter. While the pika's small size and gray coloring make them hard to spot, chances are you'll hear their shrill "eeek eeek" ringing out from beneath the cover of a nearby rock pile. Despite their efforts to keep a low profile, these tiny farmers occasionally end up as dinner for hungry coyotes and hawks.

At just over a mile the trail passes a couple of old beaver ponds, the fringes of the second one sporting a small crop of scouring rush, or horsetail. This primitive plant consists of dark green, segmented stems, and derives one of its common names from the silica in its stem that, when dried, is an excellent substance for polishing wood, metal and even certain types of stone. Pioneer women often used scouring rush to clean metal pots and pans.

Just past these small ponds is Spud Lake itself, flanked on the north by Potato Hill, and on the east by the rugged West Needle Mountains, a glittering, ancient massif of feldspar, quartz and other metamorphic ingredients squeezed into being through the heat and pressures of a restless earth. There's something about this lake that welcomes you, makes you feel like a local as soon as you arrive. Though a fairly popular spot with Durango residents for fishing and picnicking, I recommend nothing more than a long, lazy soak in the Colorado sunshine, listening to tongues of waves softly licking the shoreline.

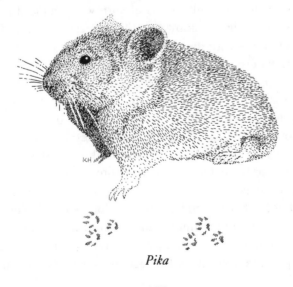

Pika

WALK #40—MOLAS TRAIL

DISTANCE: 3 miles

ENVIRONMENT: Mountain

LOCATION: San Juan National Forest. The parking area is located along the east side of Highway 550, approximately 1.5 miles north of Molas Pass, and 6 miles south of the town of Silverton. There is a sign at the highway turnoff for both Molas Lake and Molas Trail. The main dirt road continues past the parking area, descending northeast to Molas Lake. Our walk, however, begins adjacent to the highway along a small, rutted dirt road heading south from the west end of the parking lot.

This area is truly a high-country delight. For much of the walk the trail flows gently downward through a rolling, open parkland thick with grass, willow and wildflowers, occasionally brushing elbows with dark green pockets of spruce and fir, and soft, milk-white stands of aspen. Lending grandeur to the scene are the mighty Grenadier Range to the northeast, and the aptly named Needle Mountains to the southeast, soaring into the sky in a magnificent chain of parapets and sheer, granite ridge lines.

Besides the fine collections of yarrow, asters and harebells growing in these high meadows, you'll see an abundance of willow along this route—testimony to the fact that you are indeed in the high West, where deep, lingering snows mean an abundance of moisture to support such plant life. You can often use the vegetation patterns of the highest alpine meadows to determine particulars about the climate. Thick, shiny, dark mats of sedge and rush grasses, for instance, usually grow in sheltered depressions where the snow lingers for much of the year. Willow, on the other hand, can flourish only in habitats with more prolonged periods of exposure to the sun.

Willow has been used for centuries for the relief of headaches and the treatment of inflamed joints; in addition, boiling the bark in water results in an excellent antiseptic which can be applied externally to infected cuts or lacerations. Native Americans of the area once used the supple twigs of the plant to make collecting baskets. Willows are still important to the wildlife that make their homes in the San Juan high country. Leaves are considered tasty browse by mule deer, while beavers have an outright passion for the bark. Hidden beneath thick mats of willow leaves can be found the nests of white-crowned sparrows, who each year wing their way to the San Juans from as far away as Mexico. Besides offering superb hiding places for nests, temperatures beneath a willow mat are typically several degrees warmer than that of the air above—a fact that helps make the hatching of sparrows' small, spotted blue eggs a surer bet in this chilly environment.

A short distance down the road the Molas Trail takes off to the right, curves in a wide horseshoe turn to the left with views of privately owned Molas Lake, finally heading southeast again toward the Needle Mountains. This entire open area resembles a crumpled blanket peppered with small depressions, one of the most obvious of which contains Molas Lake. This type of land form is known as a *karst*, which is an ancient limestone bed that has been slowly dissolved into a tapestry of sinks and basins. The smooth, gentle roll of many of the surrounding hills is the result of careful sculpting by an immense blanket of ice, which during the Pleistocene Ice Age covered all but the highest peaks.

In 0.5 mile the trail reaches a small, rocky perch above a shallow valley. At the bottom is a cold, clear stream, dancing quietly toward the Animas River. Stealing the scene in the background is mighty Mt. Garfield, just over 13,000 feet high. From this point the trail descends fairly sharply for a couple hundred feet, and then follows a fine open area fringed with timber for nearly 0.75 mile. This stretch offers superb walking, nothing to distract you but puffs of scarlet, lemon and lavender blooms scattered across the meadows, huddles of conifer spires poking at the sky and the outstretched wings of red-tailed hawks hanging on the summer breeze.

At 1.3 miles the path suddenly enters a fine spruce-fir forest—a good place to watch for nuthatches and northern three-toed woodpeckers. Before long you'll pass a small sign on the left advising against cutting trail switchbacks. In 40 or 50 yards past this sign, keep an eye out to the right, near a small cluster of aspen, for a spur trail taking off up a short incline. It is the perch at the top of this spur that forms our turnaround point.

The vantage point from this spur is pure mountain fantasy— a quilt of soaring, rugged mountains that form the western flanks of the rugged Weminuche Wilderness. From these summits the high country takes a long, dizzying plunge to the banks of the Animas River, visible a thousand feet below where you now stand.

Along the Animas you'll be able to barely make out the line of tracks belonging to the Durango and Silverton Narrow Gauge Railroad, the longest continuously operated steam line in America, now a meticulously restored passenger line. Originally established by the Denver and Rio Grande to serve the mines of Silverton, the spur was completed in July 1882 after a Herculean effort (much of it during midwinter!) to punch the line through the tortuous twist of canyons and rugged mountain folds that mark so much of the route. Given the fact that the fate of most mining camps was firmly tied to the reins of the iron horse, Silverton could not have been happier that the effort to link it to Durango was successful. As a result, to a large degree, by the middle of the decade this oldest of the San Juan mining camps was producing a cool million dollars a year in precious minerals.

WALK #41—EAST FORK TRAIL

DISTANCE:	2.2 miles
ENVIRONMENT:	Mountain
LOCATION:	San Juan National Forest. This trail takes off on Forest Service Road 204, which leaves from the south side of Colorado Highway 145, 2 miles west of Lizard Head Pass, and 0.6 mile west of mile marker 58. (An east-facing sign giving the elevation of Lizard Head Peak is located across the road from where the walk begins.)

In all of southwest Colorado there are few walks offering such easy access to such incredible mountain beauty as the East Fork Trail. You'll be traversing a plateau of rolling, open meadowlands fringed with spruce and fir—a vast, park-like setting rimmed with precipitous, rocky peaks.

After taking a right at a fork just 40 to 50 yards from the highway, the road continues to climb moderately through a meadow peppered with alpine wildflowers. In 0.3 mile you'll reach an old sheep cabin perched on a grassy bench. (Please respect the privacy of the owners by not touching or damaging this property in any way.) From this point the path forks again, the right branch being the most obvious. You'll want to take the fainter route to the left, through a large, moist, grassy meadow filled with cinquefoil, bistort, buttercup and tall huddles of false hellebore. If you have any doubts, note that the proper route heads 180 degrees away from Lizard Head Peak, which is the spire-shaped mountain directly to the north. Watch your step, as the meadow may be wet.

About halfway through this meadow you'll spot the remains of a small pond on the right side of the trail. Now little more than a high-country puddle, this body of water was once much larger; as happens with most ponds, it is in the final throes of succession. The additional moisture around the edge of a pond provides opportunities for a plethora of green plants to set up shop that could never survive otherwise. Each season these shoreline plants, as well as those able to live in open water, die off and sink to the bottom. Thus the edges of this pond have been slowly but surely filled in, shrinking the size of the open water. One day there will be no pond at all—just a slight depression filled with the same kinds of grasses and wildflowers that grow in the surrounding park.

From this meadow the trail climbs in small tiers for 0.5 mile to a signed intersection with the East Fork Trail. Almost from the moment you set foot on this trail fantastic views open up to the west and south, as if a grand curtain was being slowly drawn open to reveal an alpine paradise. The first rush of scenery will be off to your right past a small grove of aspen. Far below this high perch toward the southwest is the Dolores River, tracing a graceful, shimmering arc at the feet of immense, broad-shouldered mountains. Just out of sight around the far reaches of the river is the tiny hamlet of Rico.

In the 1870s, Rico was one of four major mining towns, along with Ouray, Silverton and Lake City, that would end up riding a long, wild rollercoaster of boom, bust and boom again. Inexpensive mining with rockers or gold pans, like those that provided such easy, rewarding pickings in the California gold fields, didn't produce nearly such satisfying results in the San Juans. By the late

1870s men working in this area had come to realize that the real riches of these mountains—gold and, especially, silver—could only be retrieved by "hard rock" mining, which involved sinking shafts into the earth along quartz veins. But making money the hard-rock way meant having money in the first place, because drills, rails, mining cars and timbers all had to be purchased before operations could begin in earnest. In the San Juans, then, a miner was most often tied to a company. Here few poor men ever trailed their burros down to a creek, returning a few days later carrying saddlebags filled with gold.

When the Rico Argentine Mining Company closed its doors 25 years ago, many people thought it was the bust that would finally break Rico's back. By the mid-1980s, only about 50 residents were left. Today, however, there are new, fledgling signs of life here—hopeful shop owners trying to eke out a living from passersby who are more interested in looking for rushes of scenery than for rushes of silver and gold.

As you continue along this steep bench, the sound of the Dolores River laughing far below, views begin to open up to the south, toward a great, forested basin capped by granite peaks. Still farther on, as the steep bench begins to flatten and the ridge line to your left melts away, even more mountains become visible to the east. Standing in this great alpine park thick with grass and the royal blue of harebells, it would be hard to imagine a more magnificent mountain setting. To the north is 14,246-foot Mt. Wilson and the fat, gray finger of Lizard Head. To the east lies Grizzly Peak, to the south Hermosa Peak and Bolam Pass and to the west the Dolores River, flying down the high country on its way to meet the mighty Colorado.

Our turnaround occurs 0.25 mile after getting onto the East Fork Trail, at a point where the path crosses a small lip of land and begins a gentle descent into a shallow ravine. You can, however, continue southward on this trail for 4 more miles, a good portion of it equally gentle, and equally spectacular.

WALK #42—LAKE HOPE TRAIL

DISTANCE: 2 miles. (The round trip distance to Lake Hope itself, which involves a long, steep climb, is about 5 miles.)

ENVIRONMENT: Mountain

LOCATION: Uncompahgre National Forest. From Colorado Highway 145, about 12 miles south of Telluride, turn southeast on the entrance road to Trout Lake. Follow along and then past the east side of Trout Lake for just under 2 miles to a fork, where you'll turn left up a hill. Continue to climb on this road for a couple of miles to the signed trailhead, which takes off from the right side of a sharp horseshoe turn to the left.

While the trail up to Lake Hope itself—a cobalt-colored jewel set in a field of precipitous rock—is beyond the easy walking nature of this book, the first mile of the pathway offers spectacular mountain vistas, as well as vast gardens of alpine wildflowers. The entrance road to the trailhead does have enough potholes to keep you honest; in most years, however, the route isn't anything that a passenger car can't negotiate. Early morning is an especially fine time to walk here, as summer sunlight pours like warm honey across the face of this tumbling mountainscape.

The first section of our path traverses a fine, subalpine fir forest, offering occasional glimpses through the trees of sheer, white waterfalls running off the high ridges near Sheep and San Miguel mountains. At 0.25 mile you'll cross a shallow stream basin where you'll see a swath of conifers either uprooted or broken several feet above the ground, like so many matchsticks snapped between a giant's fingers. This is testimony to the enormous power of the avalanche, a frequent occurrence in the high country of southwest Colorado.

A short distance into the walk look for a large, rust-colored mountain lying to the east. This is Vermillion Peak, and it gets its strange coloration from the igneous gasses that once poured up through the earth along cracks in the mountain, oxidizing the iron in the rock. This peak, like its neighbors, is slowly being eroded by wind, water and ice; assuming that there are no further uplifts here, one day, very far into the future, Vermillion Peak will crumble into a featureless plain.

At just over 0.3 mile the forest on the right opens up, offering great views of Lizard Head and massive 14,017-foot Wilson Peak off to the northwest. Many of the smooth, U-shaped valleys in this region were sculpted by the slow grind of glacial ice. Glaciers did not, however, cover the jagged upper tips and ridge lines of the peaks you now see, which poked above the frigid landscape like islands in a frozen sea. (Those mountaintops which remained above the ice are known as nanataks.) The land here is a tortured blend of rocks—feldspars, huge slabs of sedimentary material and multi-colored, highly eroded volcanics like San Juan tuff, which is made up of tightly compressed cinders and ash. It was tuff, incidentally, that came sliding down on a sheet of slippery shale to block the Lake Fork of the San Miguel River, creating magnificent Trout Lake in the process.

As you reach a point about 0.5 mile down the path, keep an eye out for what many have called the most beautiful alpine wildflower in the world, and the state flower of Colorado—the blue columbine. These flowers were once picked in enormous quantities to adorn the households and restaurants of early mining towns—so much so that in many regions the flowers soon became scarce. Eventually, laws were passed prohibiting their harvest.

Make your way slowly along this relatively flat section of path, through gardens overflowing with bluebells, twinberries, paintbrush,

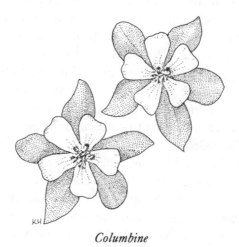

Columbine

clover and cow parsnip. On your left will be enormous scree slopes, which are steep flanks of mountain covered with small rocks that have been broken down by constant freezing and thawing. Our turnaround is in 1 mile, at a point where the trail makes crossings of several small snowmelt streams. Just to the left are two waterfalls, dripping like lacy white veils over the gray lips of volcanic rock. Still more wildflowers can be found here, their feet planted in moist alpine soil, their heads basking in a wash of mountain sunshine. Besides those species mentioned earlier, look for scattered bouquets of delphinium, marsh marigold and sticky geranium.

WALK #43—AMPHITHEATER

DISTANCE: 0.7 mile
ENVIRONMENT: Mountain
LOCATION: Uncompahgre National Forest. Head south out of Ouray on U.S. Highway 550 for 1.1 miles, where you'll see a road taking off to the left toward Amphitheater Campground. Continue through the campground to the end of the road; our trail takes off from here toward the south.

This is a short, relatively quick walk offering double scoops of the same magnificent mountain scenery that cradles the roadway for so much of its run into Ouray. Ouray, by the way, was named after the great Chief Ouray of the Ute Indians. Hardly had the ink dried on the treaty that guaranteed the Utes nearly the entire western quarter of Colorado, when prospectors began to flood into the area in a mad search for silver and gold. To head off the growing risk of a clash, in 1873 the peaceful Utes were persuaded to sell about four million acres of the most mountainous part of this region to the government, which would then open it to mineral exploration. The surrounding valleys, however, were to be left alone.

Alas, only a few years later a wave of protest by settlers against the Native Americans, much of it beginning here in Ouray, started gathering tremendous force. By the end of the decade, the roar of "The Utes Must Go!" had reached across the entire state. A writer for the *Denver Times* brashly declared, "He who gets in the way of [the Western Empire] will be crushed." And so Ouray and his people were crushed, if not physically, then in spirit, sent off to live out their days on a Utah reservation.

After running through a beautiful open forest for approximately 200 yards, the trail comes out on an open bench sporting clumps of Gambel oak, with views of both Ouray and the great swell of mountains that rise from its western flanks. Like their neighbors in Telluride and Silverton, early residents of Ouray felt certain that their mining camp could grow into the greatest of settlements. But in these parts, becoming anything more than a tumble of shacks and shanties required capital investment, and lots of it. Such moneys were used to build a transportation system (second in importance only to the minerals themselves), as well as to buy equipment for getting at the valuable ore, which, in the San Juans, was most often buried deep within the earth.

To this end, mining camps did everything in their power to attract money. Pamphlets and newspapers, locally the *Ouray Times* and the *Solid Muldoon*, painted incredibly rosy pictures of the wealth that could be had for the taking. Local accomplishments and attractions, be it a new brass band or a toll road, were lavished with praise, while it was left to rival papers in nearby towns to point out things like murders and horse thefts, which they did with absolute relish. Ouray distributed thousands of maps showing roads to the wealthiest mines, and rich ore samples were sent on cross-country displays in hopes of catching the attention of potential investors. In Ouray's case, at least, all of this was hardly without merit; thus far the district has produced over $125 million in silver, gold, copper, lead and zinc.

After walking a short distance along the bench, you'll intersect another path running east-west. Turn left here, and proceed for about 0.1 mile up a steep incline. To your right is a magnificent view of the amphitheater, which is composed of ancient, gray volcanic deposits known as San Juan tuff.

The path turns slowly to the north, and then heads back east again. Shortly after turning east you'll see a small spur trail taking off to your left, leading to a fine overlook of the valley below, as well as Sister or Twin Peaks. This is our turnaround. The massive collection of summits and ridge lines visible from this point are a complex collection of "redbeds," made of sand and muds deposited 200 million years ago by streams running off the high Uncompahgre Plateau, as well as by volcanic intrusions and layers of limestone laid down in ancient seas. Wind, ice and water continue to split these highlands into bits and pieces, which are then carried off by a network of fast, icy streams. It is a grand stretch of the imagination to think of this mountainscape being torn down grain by grain, year after year, turning it once again into a flat, featureless plain.

North–Central Colorado

WALK #44—HOOSIER PASS

DISTANCE: 0.8 mile
ENVIRONMENT: Mountain
LOCATION: Pike National Forest. Located approximately 11 miles north of Fairplay, on Colorado Route 9. Park at the pass parking area, located on the west side of the road. Our walk begins across the highway near a series of cross-country ski trails, on a road climbing to the east.

Notched into the high, rocky folds of the Continental Divide, 11,542-foot Hoosier Pass derives its name from a group of Indiana men (Hoosiers) who worked a placer-gold operation nearby. Indeed, armed with a history book and a map, it doesn't take long to realize that you are absolutely surrounded by towns, creeks, gulches, mountains and lakes that bear the fanciful names bestowed on them by a group of hardy, hopeful mining men the likes of which the West had never seen. The town of Fairplay, 11 miles to the south, was so named by a group of miners who discovered gold there after having been snubbed in their attempts to work other diggings nearby. Tarryall Creek, a half dozen miles to the east, supposedly got its title from a posse who "tarried" long enough in its pursuit of Ute Indians to dig for, and find, gold. Lost Lake, Mosquito Pass, Gold Basin, Georgia Pass—all were named out of the troubles, dreams or fondest memories of the men who came here looking for the magic "color" that would make those long, back-breaking days and cold mountain nights all worthwhile.

Begin this walk by crossing over to the east side of the highway and climbing up to a road which takes off uphill from the base of a cross-country ski-trail complex. (The large rock and concrete flume visible on your left, incidentally, once carried water for Colorado Springs.) The walk up is a steady climb, and the high altitude will require that you take your time and breathe in as much of this spruce- and fir-spiked air as you possibly can. In 0.25 mile the path begins to level off, arriving 0.1 mile farther at a small, flat plateau dotted with both needle and mutton grasses, false buckwheat and spike trisetum. Also here in summer are several beautiful alpine wildflowers, including harebell, shrubby cinquefoil, globe gilia, bistort, false dandelion and death camus.

Hoosier Pass is rapidly becoming one of the most famous botanical sites in the state of Colorado. The unusual east-west alignment of this mountain, as well as its particular elevation and soil composition, have allowed some extremely rare plants to flourish here. One 2-inch-tall species with white blossoms, known as braya, is found nowhere else in the world; another, armeria, has been found only at this site, on the Arctic tundra and in Siberia. (Speaking in general terms, the plants growing across the northern hemisphere's 3.5 million acres of alpine tundra are fairly consistent. In other words, the majority of species found on Hoosier Pass would also be found in other tundra locations, from the European Alps to highlands of central Asia. A few of these form links with vegetation that existed over 70 million years ago.)

Just before reaching our turnaround point at this open, grassy area, you'll see one or two examples of tree *flagging* adjacent to the road. This is the phenomenon in which conifers sport branches only on the lee side of their trunks, the others having been pruned away by the cold, scouring fingers of the wind.

The view to the south from this knoll is a spectacular one. Far below you can see the South Platte River complex running to the south, a band of silvery braids framed on all sides by thick stands of willow. Rising abruptly to the southwest is the line of weather-beaten mountains comprising the Mosquito Range. On the lower slopes of nearby Mount Brass is the Windy Ridge Bristlecone Pine Scenic Area, a 150-acre tract of high country devoted to the species with the singular distinction of being the oldest living tree on earth. (The oldest living plant, however, is thought to be the creosote bush of the desert Southwest.) And finally, the town lying 11 miles to the south is Fairplay, once rather notorious for the wild, unruly behavior of its residents.

One of the more interesting tales about Fairplay concerns a miner named Rupe Sherwood and his trusty burro companion,

Prunes. Though dogs may be considered man's best friend today, for 19th-century miners there was no beating a good burro, or, as they were frequently dubbed, "mountain canaries"—a title which refers to their tendency to let out in a chorus of high-pitched braying whenever the mood strikes. In Prunes, Rupe Sherwood had much more than he actually expected when he laid down his $10 for the stout little animal in 1879. Not only did Prunes routinely carry his share of ore—heck, most burros could do that—but Rupe was also able to routinely send Prunes down the mountain all by himself to the general store. The storekeeper would remove the shopping list that he carried, fill the order and off Prunes would go back up the mountain to his master, his packs full of supplies. Over the years, Prunes and Rupe became something of a legend through-out this part of Colorado.

The mountain mining life was a hard one, but these two buddies didn't seem any worse for the wear. Prunes died in 1930, at the ripe old age of 63. He's buried on Front Street in downtown Fairplay, with an elaborate tombstone and bronze plaque marking the spot. Rupe passed on at 81; true to his last wish, the townspeople buried his ashes next to the monument of his ever-faithful companion.

WALK #45—GEORGIA PASS

DISTANCE: 2 miles

ENVIRONMENT: Mountain

LOCATION: Pike National Forest. From U.S. Highway 285 in the town of Jefferson, head north, following signs for Michigan Creek Campground. Continue past the campground, climbing until you reach the top of Georgia Pass. Park here. From the pass you'll see two roads; one descends to Breckenridge, while the other (Forest Road 268) limbs toward Glacier Ridge. Our walk begins along this latter route. *Note:* While Georgia Pass is also accessible from the Breckenridge side, this road is appropriate for four-wheel drive vehicles only.

If you've come to the Colorado Rockies for the views, here is one walk that most certainly will not disappoint you. This line of high peaks and ridges—just one wave in a sea of such dramatic mountainscapes—happens to form that great spine of the American West, the Continental Divide. (In fact, the first 0.6 mile of this walk will more than likely become part of the great Continental Divide Scenic Trail, a 3,000-mile pathway from Canada to Mexico.) Drops of rain or snowmelt falling to your left (north) are destined to return to the Pacific Ocean, while those on your right (south) are bound for the Gulf of Mexico. Standing here at Georgia Pass, it seems hard to dispute Colorado's claim of having the highest mean elevation of any state in the country. More than a thousand of its peaks scrape these powder-blue skies at over 10,000 feet above sea level; 54 of them come in at over 14,000 feet.

As you make the steady climb up Forest Road 268, you'll see a slow but steady transition in the forest that fills these high-country nooks and crannies. Engelmann spruce, for instance, grows 25 to 30 feet tall near the beginning of the walk, but as you make your way up onto the higher, more northerly exposed ridges, some rather curious changes take place. Besides becoming smaller, you'll notice a peculiar phenomenon known as "flagging," which refers to trees that sport branches only on one side of their trunks.

White-tailed Ptarmigan

The bitter blasts of wind that roar across this high ridge, often nearing 100 miles per hour, actually prune away branches on the windward side, leaving only the lee growth intact. On even more exposed sites, the spruce may grow in such dwarfed versions that they more resemble shrubs than trees. These wind-scoured mats of vegetation, which in this area consist mostly of Engelmann spruce and subalpine fir, are known as *krummholz*, a German word that translates roughly into "elfin timber." The Colorado Rockies krummholz belt typically occurs on exposed ridges in areas where monthly average temperatures rarely exceed 50 degrees. Since the growing season may be as short as seven weeks, trees grow at an incredibly slow rate. Though they appear small, these spruce mats may actually be well over a hundred years old. (That more famous champion of high-altitude living, the bristlecone pine, can be a thousand years old but measure no more than a few inches in diameter.)

Just over 0.6 mile into the walk you'll come to an intersection on a flat, high plateau covered with cushion plants and, for a few weeks each summer, the brilliantly colored forbs that mark the alpine tundra. Here we'll turn right onto a small road heading south. Because the alpine tundra is incredibly fragile, it's very important that you stay on established roads and trails. A tin can lying over a patch of tundra plants can kill them in less than a month; their return can take a quarter of a century. Recent studies conducted in Rocky Mountain National Park have reconfirmed the delicate nature of these ecosystems, having identified several types of tundra plant communities that, if disturbed, may take as long as a thousand years to recover.

As you proceed southward, notice on your left the remains of a hanging glacial snowfield—a cold, white remnant of the last ice age, when all but the highest peaks were covered with thick slabs of grinding ice. Ahead of you, becoming more expansive the farther you go, are fantastic views of South Park, an expansive intermontane valley resting on beds of 200- to 400-million-year-old sedimentary rock. South Park has figured prominently in the exciting comings and goings of Colorado. Through these fields of high grass tramped many a hopeful miner, some bound for Blue River, some for Breckenridge, and, by 1860, a great many for the infamous California Gulch located to the west, along the upper reaches of the Arkansas River. This valley reportedly got its name when a veteran of the California gold rush named Abraham Lee dipped a gold pan into a small stream here and declared, "Boys, all California is in this here pan!" Well, maybe not all of California, but the discovery did earn this small group of Georgia boys over $50,000 in the first three weeks of digging. The summer of 1860 was barely half over before 8,000 people had crammed their way into California Gulch.

Just four years later, South Park was the scene of an intense manhunt for a gang of Confederate bandits led by brothers Jim and John Reynolds. Each time this gang would pick off a stage passing through South Park, they presented their victims with the grand lie that they were breaking ground for a force of Texas Rangers on their way to destroy Denver. With a good share of the populace already fearful that southerners were banding together with disgruntled Indians to overthrow the region (such alliances were attempted), this particular story spread like wildfire, causing near-panic in towns up and down the Front Range. The locals were not amused in the least by such shenanigans. Each of the captured gang members eventually ended up with a bullet in him; one was even decapitated, and his head preserved and put on display in the nearby town of Fairplay.

The road curves around toward the west again, making a short climb at 1.2 miles onto another high plateau. At 1.4 miles it turns south onto a spur of land that overlooks the drainage that you drove up on your way to Georgia Pass. Along this stretch of ground is a part of the Colorado Trail—470 miles of scenic trail linking Durango to the city of Denver. From this point you should be able to see a small pathway following along a series of posts to the north. If you spot it, you can follow it northward until it rejoins Forest Road 268, a short distance east of where you parked. If you can't spot it from the road, however, don't aimlessly comb the tundra looking for it; just turn around and return the way you came. This is too fragile of an environment to engage in cross-country rambling.

WALK #46—LOWER BURNING BEAR CREEK

DISTANCE: 1.3 miles
ENVIRONMENT: Forest
LOCATION: Pike National Forest. From U.S. Highway 285, 0.6 mile east of mile marker 207, turn north onto Forest Road 120. The trailhead, as well as a small parking area, is on the right, approximately 2.8 miles north of U.S. Highway 285.

Whereas the upper reaches of the Burning Bear Creek Trail meander along the forested feet of a soaring mountainscape (see page 147), the stroll along this lower end of the pathway is a bit more subdued—a short, sweet amble along a small mountain stream singing through a huddle of aspen. In autumn this trail is particularly appealing, the aspen leaves glimmering like gold dust in the late September sun, the smell of dry grasses wafting through the cool Colorado air. Although the path climbs throughout its 0.65 mile, all but a very short stretch about 0.2 mile into the walk is fairly gentle. Do keep in mind that signed private property is nearby; please respect the privacy of these landowners.

Just a hundred yards into the walk you'll join the aforementioned stream. This delightful little watercourse, known as Lamping Creek, gathers its waters to the northwest of here, just a few miles this side of the Continental Divide. True to the definition of the Continental Divide, its waters are bound for the Gulf of Mexico, first via the South Platte River across the windswept prairies of northeastern Colorado, then along the Platte, drifting through the long reaches of Nebraska grain fields until it reaches the Missouri River south of Omaha. It finally reaches the mighty Mississippi at St. Louis, which will carry it 700 miles farther southward, melting into Gulf waters through a sprawl of marshy fingers just outside of Venice, Louisiana.

At this point, however, the stream is little more than a friendly trickle through the forest, the source of life for a beautiful array of wildflowers and stout mountain alders. The bark of this latter tree, which you can see near the beginning of the trail, was often boiled by Native Americans of the region to produce a beautiful reddish orange dye. This was used to color moccasins and feathers, both of which held the dye quite well without any additional preparation. The women of tribes to the north reportedly made a tea from alder bark that helped them regulate their menstrual periods.

At 0.2 mile into the walk you'll come to a faint road taking off to the left; this is a private driveway, so continue straight, up a short, but relatively steep section of trail. At the top you will have left many of the aspen behind for a mixed conifer forest of lodgepole, juniper and an occasional bristlecone pine. Bristlecones, incidentally, are among the oldest living things on earth; core samples taken from trees in the White Mountains of California revealed several bristlecones to be more than 5,000 years old! It's incredible to think that such trees were beginning to grow before construction of the Great Sphinx, before Egyptian astronomy, before alphabets—a full thousand years before Stonehenge was erected on what is now British soil.

Bristlecones are the hardiest of trees, achieving their greatest splendor under conditions of poor soil and frightful cold that other species find intolerable. Growing ever so slowly in such places, their wood becomes extremely dense, a collection of small, tightly clustered cells that are impervious to either insects or decay. They are unflinching survivors, the oldest trees often carrying nutrients to a single living branch via a thin line of bark, the rest having been scoured away by a thousand seasons of wind and ice.

The trail continues to climb steadily along a bench perched above Lamping Creek, lined with fine collections of yarrow, cow parsnip and sticky geraniums, as well as an occasional columbine and monkeyflower. This is a perfect stretch to leave the roadway and spend some time streamside, listening to the lilt of chickadees and the buzz of nutcrackers. Also in here you'll notice a sizable collection of aspen stumps whose trees were long ago chewed down by beaver. (Look at these closely; you can still see the rodent's narrow teeth marks in the weathered wood.) It has been suggested that beaver, with their incredible efficiency at cutting trees and flooding large areas of ground, have more impact on the land than any other mammal besides man. What's more, the size of these tree stumps should convince you that their timber-harvesting operations are hardly limited to saplings.

A beaver's pond provides a protective area around his lodge, while the deep water allows for food storage beneath the winter ice.

This environment also favors the growth of alder, willow and cottonwood, which, not by accident, happen to be among this furry engineer's favorite foods. The fate of the beaver in this area is not known. Quite possibly, though, their "pond, sweet pond" slowly filled with sediment until it could no longer support their preferred lifestyle.

At just over 1.6 miles is our turnaround point, where the stream crosses the road. More ambitious walkers can continue up the trail for a quite a distance before encountering any substantial climbs.

WALK #47—UPPER BURNING BEAR CREEK

DISTANCE: 3.5 miles
ENVIRONMENT: Forest
LOCATION: Pike National Forest, south of Georgetown. This walk is located along Forest Road 118 (Guanella Pass Road), just south of Burning Bear Campground. You'll find a large parking area on the east side of the road for access into the Mount Evans Wilderness. Park here and walk south along the highway for 0.15 mile. Our trail takes off to the right, heading northwest, adjacent to a horse corral.

This walk along upper Burning Bear Creek—a corruption of a 19th-century fire known as "Burned Bare"—is a stroll through an absolutely delightful high-country collage of clear, tumbling waters, open meadows and thick, green forests. The trail begins in a quilt of shrubby cinquefoil, with excellent views to the north of the soaring spine of the Continental Divide, just west of Guanella Pass. In about 50 yards the path makes a sharp left turn onto a footbridge crossing Burning Bear Creek. Suddenly the hushed veil of forest drops around you. Here is the pungent smell of conifers, and the springy feel that comes with walking a path thick with years of fallen needles. Burning Bear Creek now flows in a whisper off to your right, a twisted course of oxbows and meanders, visible only occasionally between tall clumps of willow.

While nearly everyone is drawn to the carpet of growth that sprouts from the banks of a mountain stream, few of us, save the ardent fishermen, stop to ponder the myriad of life that exists in the water itself. Living in a stream like this one is not an easy proposition. The strength of these currents can be a force to deal with, especially in early to midsummer when they are fed by snowmelt. Most stream insects set up housekeeping in locations well away, or at least protected from, the main pull of the currents—most often in the nooks, crannies and crevices provided by the jumble of streambed rocks. Furthermore, some insect larvae have developed disc-shaped suction cups at the rear of their bodies which they use to anchor themselves to the surface of rocks. Since going out for food is so dangerous, most of these creatures have their meals delivered. Some have funnel-shaped appendages that are used to collect passing plankton; the caddis fly, on the other hand, actually weaves a small net which it floats into the stream to trap bits of food.

This assemblage of tenacious stream creatures makes up much of the trout's daily diet. Trout, of course, also have to contend with the relentless force of currents. Over millions of years they have developed a long, lean shape that offers little resistance to flowing water. They also spend the majority of their time in quiet pools formed by large rocks or sharp bends in the stream.

Just over 0.25 mile into the walk you'll reach a section of trail marked by signs reading "Snowpack Studies—Please Stay on Trail." This is a joint project between the Forest Service and the

Evening Grosbeak

Soil Conservation Service, and is used to predict the amount of spring runoff likely to occur from these mountains.

Watch here for mountain chickadees, Steller's jays, Clark's nutcrackers, and the beautiful yellow body and heavy beak of the evening grosbeak. These latter birds tend to congregate when food is hard to come by, and in late autumn or early spring walkers may see dense bands around a good supply of seeds or buds. Also in these woods are red crossbills, the male of which is a rust-colored bird about 6 inches long, with a bill that is actually crossed at the ends. It's no accident that this peculiar design happens to be perfect for inserting into pine cones and splitting the scales open, making it easy for the crossbill to remove the nuts with its tongue.

The path bends slowly around toward the left, offering in 0.75 mile fine views of the red, iron-rich peaks to the west that form the lower ramparts of the Continental Divide. A fine meadow will accompany you westward for nearly half a mile, coming to an end as you enter a thick cloak of lodgepole pine. This tree, one of the most widespread in North America, got its common name from the fact that thin lodgepole were once commonly used by Native American peoples to construct their tipis, or lodges. Lodgepole is one of a group of trees sometimes referred to as "fire pines," because many of the tree's cones will not open until licked by the flames of a forest fire. This quality ensures that the tree, which does best in open sunlight, will be among the first to get things growing again after a fire has destroyed the existing forest.

Speaking of fire, notice here the fairly large amount of dead timber lying on the forest floor. The dry conditions in the West mean far less bacterial activity occurs on the forest floor than, say, in the woods of the East. It requires a long, long time for these dead trees to be broken down into soil again. Before the arrival of modern man, periodic fires, usually the result of summer lightning strikes, would race through the forest clearing the ground of such debris, while at the same time killing off harmful parasites and returning nutrients to the soil. By adopting a policy of stopping all forest fires, we inadvertently caused a buildup of combustible materials on the forest floor. When a big fire does strike in such a forest, it can be much more devastating than it would have ordinarily been, since the increased amount of fuel allows it to rage hotter and higher than it ever would have normally. Such lessons have not gone unheeded; today in the national forests you'll see controlled burning projects specifically designed to reduce the fire load on the forest floor.

In 1.7 miles the trail makes a gentle descent from a low bench, dropping to the same level as a small stream that has been gurgling off to your right for the last 0.25 mile. This is our turnaround point. Before heading back, though, leave the path and walk north a short distance to this watercourse. Here you'll find several quiet pockets of willow and aspen, washed in the cool whisper of water dancing down the bedrock. This is a particularly delightful place to bird watch, picnic or take a long afternoon snooze in the mountain sunshine.

WALK #48—GUANELLA PASS

DISTANCE: 3.5 miles
ENVIRONMENT: Mountain
LOCATION: Pike National Forest. About 12 miles south of Georgetown, on the Guanella Pass Road (Forest Road 118). The pass can also be reached from the south by taking the Guanella Pass Road north from U.S. Highway 285, northeast of Kenosha Pass.

The high path to Square Top Lakes lies a half dozen miles or so east of the Continental Divide, and offers a fine opportunity to taste the brilliant, yet extremely delicate fringes of the alpine tundra. Like the Arctic tundra with which it shares many traits, this is a place of extremes. Due to the thinner atmosphere, the sun beats down with three times the intensity that it does in low elevations; reflected off a snowfield, over time it can be enough to blind you. In winter bitter winds howl across these smooth slopes at speeds close to 100 miles per hour, whipping snow into strange patterns, dumping it into protected pockets until it forms blankets 20 feet thick, while in more exposed places the rock surfaces are scoured completely clean.

Such conditions, however, have hardly left this high valley devoid of life. Besides the beautiful mosaic of willow growing here, there is no shortage of bunchgrass, Rocky Mountain sedge, tufted hairgrass, alpine avens, haircap moss, buttercup, marsh marigold and Parry's clover. To really get a feel for just how packed with life these high gardens can be, you almost need to be lying on your stomach with your nose in the mat. Alpine plants grow small and close to the ground, first so that they can escape the drying and damaging effects of the wind, and secondly, because when you're facing a growing season of only 12 to 16 weeks, it makes little sense to waste your time producing stems.

The view to the southwest along this stretch of Continental Divide is a fine one, the forested western flanks of Geneva and Arrowhead peaks tumbling southward into the Platte River Mountains. It was along another fork of the Platte River, south of this high perch where you now stand, that 27-year-old Zebulon Pike headed west in late November 1807 in his search for the headwaters of the Red River. Pike had already been beaten back by snow during an attempt to climb the high peak that would one day bear his name, but still he pressed on at this frightfully late date, horses so weary that many had to be abandoned, food running so low that it was only the most amazing strokes of hunting fortune that kept him and his men from total starvation. Yet Pike, driven on by an intense desire to have his own place in the explorers' hall of fame, pressed on through the increasingly bitter days of early winter, eventually clambering back out onto the plains via the Royal Gorge of the Arkansas River, more confused about the real source of the Red River than ever. (It was on some unknown high peak west of

White-crowned Sparrow

here that Pike claimed to have seen the headwaters of the Yellowstone, which in fact rises several hundred miles to the north. This mistake undoubtedly caused more than a little confusion for some trappers, who then would have expected to find New Mexico just a short trek from the Tetons.)

In 0.4 mile you'll reach a fork; stay to the left. The thick huddle of willows growing on the hillsides in this area has done much to prevent soil erosion, particularly during those times when cattle manage to escape into the area from an adjoining allotment. These willow thickets are also the home for white-crowned sparrows, who migrate to this high landscape each year from as far south as Mexico. This delightful little bird can sometimes be heard singing even at night. Willow thickets not only protect the birds from predators, but actually tend to hold in heat so that their eggs will stand a better chance of hatching in this cold environment.

There are a few steep sections at about 1 mile in, and, at this high elevation where there is less oxygen, plan to stop once in a while to avoid getting overly tired or developing a headache. Heaven knows there's plenty of scenery to ponder, from Duck Lake a mile to the south, glimmering like a sapphire in the midday sun, to the long tumble of high ridges fading into a fine blue haze 70 to 80 miles distant.

After topping a small crest at 1.5 miles, you have only to make a gentle descent and then an easy, arcing climb to arrive at the lower of the two Square Top lakes, named after the large block-shaped peak immediately to the west. The stream you followed on the last

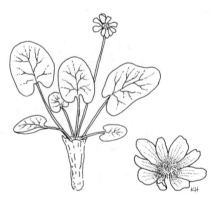

Marsh Marigold

stretch of the walk begins in this rugged lake basin; it tumbles through a wonderful wildflower-strewn corridor into Duck Lake, ultimately bound for the North Fork of the South Platte River. For the adventurous among you, there is another lake just above this one, similar in size, at the base of the sheer scree slope visible to the northwest. Such lakes often are frozen into July, with water temperatures rarely going above 50 degrees at any time of the year. The barren, rocky parameters mean that very little organic food is available to the lake. Consequently, few life forms can be found here; only deep, clear, steel-blue waters—a tranquil, rock-rimmed jewel of the high divide.

WALK #49—SAINT LOUIS LAKE TRAIL

DISTANCE:	2.4 miles
ENVIRONMENT:	Forest
LOCATION:	Arapaho National Forest. Head south out of Granby on Colorado Highway 40 for approximately 15 miles. At 0.9 mile south of mile marker 226, in the center of the town of Frasier, turn right (west) onto Eisenhower Drive. In a few blocks, take a left on Norgren Street and then, a few blocks later, a right on Mill. Mill will lead you to our trailhead, which is 12.6 miles from where you first turned off the highway.

While this walk requires steady climbing, it offers a fine soak in a classic, central–Rocky Mountain spruce-fir forest—a place with layer after layer of dark, wild beauty. After crossing a wooden footbridge over cold, frothing Saint Louis Creek, the path meanders along a route lined with sticky geranium, gentian, columbine, pipsissewa, monkeyflower and, in the more open areas, the beautiful, purple shooting star. Pipsissewa and monkeyflower, incidentally, were often utilized by Indian peoples of the region, the former to break down kidney stones (its common name is derived from a Cree Indian phrase for "breaking into pieces"), and the young leaves of the latter as a source of raw greens. Pioneers in the West who picked up on this use of monkeyflower often referred to the plant as wild lettuce.

There is a wonderful, cool moistness to the high-country spruce-fir forests. The great blankets of snow that fall here—sometimes several feet in a single day—linger long into the summer, huddles of tight, green aprons shielding it from the warm fingers of the sun. In 0.25 mile you'll break out of the forest briefly to skirt a meadow brimming with grass and willow. Then, after climbing a short rise away from the stream, it's back into the thick of the woods; this time, however, into a more mature slice. Dark cathedrals of old, stately Engelmann spruce tower above the footpath, some of which were standing here well before the exploration and settlement of the Rocky Mountain West.

Spruce and fir represent what is known as a *climax forest*, meaning that they form the last in several stages of plant succession; this succession commonly begins with grasses, then proceeds to shrubs and aspen and finally to spruce and fir. Like several other species of trees, both spruce and fir are able to sprout new growth off of low branches that come into contact with the ground, a phenomenon that increases as the growing environment becomes more severe. Although mammals and birds are not as abundant in the spruce-fir forest as in other kinds of forest, this walk seems to have a peculiar abundance. Deer and elk are joined by martens and snowshoe hares, while three-toed woodpeckers, pine grosbeaks, nuthatches, pine siskins and creepers add to the feathered population. Especially common along the upper reaches of the trail are Clark's nutcrackers. At first glance it may appear that this bird consumes pine nuts without bothering to even swallow them. Actually, it has a special storage pouch under the tongue that allows it to collect several seeds and then pack them away to other dining areas.

In 0.8 mile is a creek crossing, and, 0.2 mile later, you'll have the rather unusual treat of stereo streams—one on the right and another on the left—as you make your way up the back of a narrow finger of land. Look off to your right in this area for young Engelmann spruce. The year I was here several were showing the effect of black snowmold—a dark, molasses-like glob that hangs off of lower branches. Snowpack often holds these branches against the ground through the spring, which, as mentioned earlier, is actually a necessary step for the branch to sprout as a new tree. If the snow lingers too long, however, snowmold fungus is able to establish a firm hold.

At just over 1.1 miles the trail tops a small plateau, overlooking a beautiful stream. Our turnaround point is the bank of this stream, which is reached by making a short, sharp descent to the right. Besides being a great place for wildflowers, take a look at some of the delicate groundcovers lying at the cool, moist feet of the spruce and fir. Twinflower is here, along with wood nymph and wintergreen. If, on your way back to the trailhead, you look closely, you may also see the delicate, lavender fairy slipper. Fairy slipper is also known as Calypso orchid, a name taken from the character of a beautiful sea nymph in Homer's *Odyssey*.

WALK #50—ARAPAHO PASS

DISTANCE: 6.2 miles

ENVIRONMENT: Mountain

LOCATION: Roosevelt National Forest. From the town of Nederland, turn west off of Colorado Highway 72 onto a paved road leading to Eldora. In 4.8 miles this road will fork; stay right, and continue for 5 more miles to Buckingham Campground. Our trail takes off from the north side of this campground. *Note:* The last 5 miles of this drive are on a narrow, rutted road, not suitable for large recreational vehicles.

The walk to Arapaho Pass is a gentle, open climb through a soaring slice of high country—a ragged geological wonderland of granite, gneiss and schist. Thin ribbons of ice water pour off the mountain walls, and elk and deer can be seen moving quietly through the shadows of fir, spruce and limber pine. Being at 10,000 feet the snow here lingers on well into June, though the fact that the trail traverses a south-facing slope makes much of the route accessible earlier than it would be were it on the other side of the valley. Mid-September can be an especially fine time to visit, as the

Colorado sky turns a brilliant cobalt blue, the aspen leaves ripen to gold and the trail becomes lined with the bright red bangles of buffaloberry and twisted stalk.

The mountains that surround you here, many of them a part of the Indian Peaks Wilderness, have overlooked a great deal of Colorado's frontier history—the rush to mine silver and gold (and during World War I, tungsten), the long and often vicious struggle to quell the Arapaho nation and in general, the rise and fall of hopes and dreams in an atmosphere of astonishing furor and frenzy. Walk almost any direction, and some incredible piece of history will be there to greet you. Follow this divide south about 6 miles, for instance, and you'll come to Rollins Pass, the place where railroad magnate David Moffat, desperate to further his dreams of a transcontinental railroad line, would find himself locked in the folly of trying to run a railroad through the unbridled fury of winter at 11,600 feet. Continue a little farther and you'll come to Silver Plume, where in 1887 a wealthy, broken-hearted miner of 40 would play a mournful song on the violin, turn and shoot himself in the heart and fall into a grave he had dug with his own hands.

Our path begins with a gentle climb through an open weave of fir and limber pine, underlain by currant, whortleberry, harebell, buffaloberry, twisted stalk and fireweed. Just 0.2 mile from the trailhead the path breaks out into the open, beginning a fine, long run through a world dominated by mountainous terrain. As you make your way toward the summit, notice the spire-like shape of the subalpine fir and Englemann spruce trees dotting the sides of the valley. Perhaps inspiring people in the high country to often build chalets with steep roofs, the steeple shape of spruce and subalpine fir allows these trees to toss off even the heaviest snowfalls. Besides their shape, another good clue to spotting a spruce-fir forest even from a great distance is its dark foliage. There is perhaps nothing more beautiful in all the West than golden aspen leaves held against the dark green branches of Engelmann spruce and subalpine fir.

Besides the currant and buffaloberry already mentioned, one of the more common shrubs you'll be seeing along your walk is shrubby cinquefoil. From the end of June through early August this member of the rose family blooms with bright yellow, five-petaled flowers, adding wonderful splashes of color to the surrounding terrain. Shrubby cinquefoil, which is not a first choice in food for either domestic or wild animals, is known as a *habitat indicator species*. This means that in the places where shrubby cinquefoil grows, biologists can tell whether an area is being overgrazed (and, therefore, has too many animals on it) by how severely the cinquefoil has been browsed. Decisions about how many cattle can be on a specific range, or how many hunting permits to issue in any given year, are to some extent made by studying the condition of indicator species like this one.

As you continue the easy climb toward Arapaho ridge, keep your eyes and ears open for the Clark's nutcracker, a bold, noisy bird that, in addition to the raucous, crow-like call that most easily identifies it, has a rather pleasant repertoire of soft croaks and chortles. True to its name, the nutcracker does enjoy feasting on conifer seeds, sometimes loading extras into a small pouch located just under its tongue. But the nutcracker is hardly a purist, and will readily dine on berries, insects and even carrion. The range of this bird is extensive, stretching through conifer forests from Alberta all the way to Baja, California.

On the rocky outcrops that line much of the trail you'll find paintbrush, stonecrop and yarrow, while in the moist meadows are bluebells, gentians and monkshood. Monkshood sports beautiful purple blossoms somewhat akin to larkspur, and takes its name from the fact that the upper sepal forms a hood similar to those worn by monks during the Middle Ages. All parts of the monkshood plant are poisonous, especially the seeds and roots.

At just over 2 miles you'll come to an intersection with the Arapaho Glacier Trail; stay left, following the sign to Arapaho Pass. Notice the old steam boiler and hoist wheel sitting off to your right. These are relics from the Fourth of July Mine, which, true to its name, was founded on the Fourth of July in 1872. (The trail you're walking is actually a remnant of an old wagon road built to serve this operation.) Like so many Colorado mines, the Fourth of July was to be the lode to end all lodes—first touted as a rich source of silver, and later, as a source of copper that would rival the great deposits of Anaconda, Montana. Two months after its initial discovery, the *Rocky Mountain News* made the rather bold prediction that this mine contained ore sufficient "for a hundred thousand men to mine for generations to come."

The area where you're now standing was the location of the mine's shafthouse. A large log structure stood here, inside of which was a horse-powered winching system used to raise and lower the ore buckets, as well as a blacksmith shop that tended to the sharpening of tools. If it was like other mines of the day, the shaft probably reached a depth of about 200 feet before the winching became arduous enough to require that the horse-driven system be replaced with a steam-driven hoist. The boiler you see here, brought in for just that purpose, was the same kind used in locomotives. A fire was built in a tightly constructed firebox located at one end, and the heat from it passed through the long tubes in the bottom of the cylinder, which were surrounded by water. As the water expanded and finally became steam, it pushed a piston that, in turn, powered the hoist used to raise ore and rock from the mine. It's not altogether clear whether the miners actually had a chance to use this system, or if so, to what degree. (An early photo of this location shows no evidence of any wood or coal.) Such boilers required tremendous amounts of fuel; four cords of wood a day was not unusual. Obviously, in high-mountain locations like this one such consumption would add terrifically to the amount of labor needed to run the operation.

Most of the activity on the Fourth of July Mine occurred at the bottom of the canyon, about 500 feet directly below this trail junction. Near this location was a steam-driven power plant, an air compressor to drive the drills and provide ventilation, quarters for the mine manager, a two-story boardinghouse, storage sheds, bunkhouses and stables. Alas, despite herculean efforts and grandiose predictions, significant amounts of ore—either silver or copper—never materialized.

A little over a mile from this junction is Arapaho Pass, where you'll find yourself smack-dab in the middle of a striking panorama. Behind you to the east stretches the dull, yellow skin of the plains, while in every other direction is a grand, seemingly endless tumble of mountains. The trail you see directly below, running past the edge of a small lake, continues northwest for another 7 or 8 miles to Monarch Lake; the path to your left, on the other hand, leads to Middle Park (a few miles south of Granby) via Strawberry and Ranch creeks. If you can arrange transportation, the trip from Fourth of July Trailhead to Monarch Lake, about 12 miles in length, makes for a wonderful summer or early-autumn dayhike.

WALK #51—EAST SHORE TRAIL

DISTANCE: 2.5 miles
ENVIRONMENT: Forest
LOCATION: Rocky Mountain National Park. Head north out of Granby on U.S. Highway 40, and turn right onto U.S. Highway 34. Proceed for approximately 11 miles, and make a right turn 0.9 mile past mile marker 11, at a sign reading "Arapaho National Recreation Area." Then immediately make another right turn, following signs toward Shadow Mountain Dam. Park at the dam and walk across it to the east side. Our walk begins here, taking off to the south (downstream) along the Colorado River.

This stroll along the western fringe of Rocky Mountain National Park is a true delight. For the most part the landscape is a quiet, mellow quilt of high country, an easy mix of lodgepole forest and riparian meadows. But there's also a wonderful sense of wildness here—a thick, exciting feeling that pervades so much of Rocky Mountain National Park, arguably the most beautiful of all the high-mountain preserves. Besides sporting a stunning collage of rocky peaks, more than a hundred of which soar to over 12,000 feet, Rocky Mountain National Park has an almost overwhelming collection of hanging glacial valleys, plunging waterfalls and cold, crystal streams. One of those watercourses, visible on your right flowing through a gentle glacial valley, forms the quiet, clear beginnings of the greatest river in the West—the mighty Colorado.

A short distance from the Shadow Mountain Dam you'll find yourself in a beautiful meadow stitched with sedge, marsh marigolds, elephantella, shooting stars and Calypso orchids. Here you may spot red-tailed hawks running surveillance along the upper fringes of the grass, ever watchful for a tasty deer mouse or ground squirrel. Hawks and eagles, in general, play an extremely important role in this ecosystem by controlling the population of such small mammals; if left totally unchecked, these prolific little rodents over-populate, quickly eating themselves out of house and home.

Also eyeing the rodent population here with anxious stomachs are coyotes, which you may hear in the evening engaged in a rousing chorus of yips and yowls. There are few animals that have as tenacious a survival instinct as the coyote, especially in the face of man's often vigorous attempts to exterminate him. (The name *coyote*, incidentally, comes from the Aztec word "coyotl.") Indeed, this beautiful little canine seems more abundant than ever, conducting his business from Costa Rica to Alaska, from the thick of wilderness to the backyards of the suburban areas that have so encroached upon his territory.

One of the reasons the coyote has been so successful in hanging on to a shrinking environment is because when it comes to dinner, he's wide open to suggestions. True, the ground squirrels, voles, rabbits, mice and pocket gophers living in this area provide a significant portion of his diet. But he will also eat birds, snakes, weasels and occasionally even skunks! What's more, he's hardly above consuming either carrion or garbage.

Coyotes may spend several years with the same mate; the male becomes extremely busy in the spring as he scours the countryside looking for enough food to feed both himself and the nursing female. Five to seven pups are born without hair, unable to open their eyes for nearly two weeks. The home den is left behind when the youngsters are about 10 weeks old, at which time they join the family in wide-ranging hunting forays. The kids will strike out on their own in the fall, just about the time aspen leaves begin raining down on the forest floor.

At 0.25 mile you'll cross a marshy grassland environment on a wooden walkway. At the far end is a fork; stay to the right. A short distance later you'll enter private land, so be sure to stay on the trail as you make your way through this stretch of classic lodgepole-pine forest. (The lodgepole is an easy tree to identify in this area, since it is the only one with its needles growing in bundles of two.) Lodgepole can form dense blankets of timber in the Rockies, and is found in scattered stands from Mexico to Alaska, making it one of the most widely distributed pines in North America.

While most of this long, quiet stretch of forest is a homogeneous blanket of lodgepole, there are a few mats of common juniper and kinnikinnick lending splashes of green against the dull brown carpet of lodgepole needles. One of the reasons these needles take so long to decompose is that, like most conifer needles, they are covered with a waxy coating that's especially impervious to bacteria. This coating, combined with the fact that the essentially arid nature of this climate doesn't go very far in promoting decay, has helped create the deep layers of needles you see here today.

About 0.75 mile into the walk a trail from Grand Lake comes in from the left. Grand Lake is a beautiful, deep, natural lake lying to the north, formed by the lateral and terminal moraines of two distinct glaciers that ground their way across this landscape during the last glacial epoch, which ended roughly 25,000 years ago. Continue straight, past an area of timber that has been shredded by a ferocious windstorm, finally joining the Colorado River again in another 0.5 mile. This lovely fringe of river shore is a perfect place to soak up the very best of the Rocky Mountain wilderness. It's an unforgettable experience to sit here and ponder the fact that this tranquil, whispering ribbon of water is embarking on a remarkable 1,400-mile journey to its ultimate destination at the Gulf of California. The Colorado is a splendid river, the mighty architect of Colorado's Glenwood, Utah's Glen and Arizona's Grand canyons, patiently peeling away grain after grain of rock to create some of the most outstanding rock labyrinths the world has ever known.

Golden-mantled Ground Squirrel

WALK #52—MILL CREEK BASIN

DISTANCE: 5.2 miles
ENVIRONMENT: Forest
LOCATION: Rocky Mountain National Park. From the
town of Estes Park, head east on U.S. Highway 36 to the Beaver Meadows Entrance Station. At 0.1 mile past the entrance station, turn left, following the signs for Moraine Park. Follow this route for 3.7 miles, at which point you'll turn right onto a road that leads in 0.2 mile to the trailhead. (This turn is marked with a sign that says "Hollowell Park.")

Those fortunate enough to have rubbed elbows with the entire length and breadth of the continental Rockies are almost always amazed at the sheer variety of mountainscapes to be found here. There are high volcanic plateaus studded with lodgepole pine, and sheer, yawning reaches of lichen-covered talus and scree; there are fan-shaped limestone palisades rising from the foothills like the backs of petrified dinosaurs, and great ramparts of granite towering above thick, somber forests of subalpine fir. But in all this region, were you forced to pick one area that most embodies the glory of the Rockies, an area that gives the fullest expression to our grandest fantasies of the high country, it would be hard to do better than Rocky Mountain National Park.

These peaks are in fact only the last of several ranges that have been pushed into the sky by mighty forces deep within the earth. This process began many millions of years ago, when North America started to drift westward across beds of fluid, molten rock. Eventually the continent began grinding across vast stretches of the Pacific Ocean floor, submerging parts of that floor into the depths of a fiery cauldron of molten rock, while at the same time causing great internal pressures on this region, crumpling and pleating it into long chains of folded rock.

No sooner does any mountain range rise, however, than it begins to yield to the forces of erosion. The mountains you see today, which began to surge from the sea roughly 75 million years ago, aren't even close to what they looked like fresh out of their initial uplift; wind, water and ice have been sculpting them for centuries, creating enormous, glacier-scoured valleys, as well as a dramatic collage of cliffs, canyons and palisades. All other things being constant, one day this high country, like all the high country that stood here before, will dissolve into a great, flat plain.

While the walk up Mill Creek isn't nearly as dramatic as many other trails in the park, it is generally much quieter, a fact that may allow you to feel more fully submerged in the roll of this ancient landscape. The path begins in a fine, open stretch of montane, peppered with big sagebrush and antelope bitterbrush, as well as with smatterings of yarrow, sulfur flower, lupine, paintbrush and gumweed. As you make your way westward toward the mouth of a small canyon, notice the sharp differences in vegetation there. The drier, south-facing slope is dominated by sagebrush and loosely scattered groves of ponderosa pine. But as that slope drops to the bottom of the ravine, where more moisture is available, the ponderosa and sage yield to small groves of aspen, and along the banks of Mill Creek itself, thick mats of willow. And finally, on the north slope of the canyon, which for the most part is spared the drying effects of the sun, the forest grows thick and dark. While elevation, soil type, annual precipitation and even incidence of fire have a lot to do with what grows in any given place, the simple orientation of a slope—south versus north—also has an enormous impact. (With this fact in mind, anyone interested in hitting mountain trails during early summer would be well advised to look on a topo map for those paths that traverse south-facing slopes.)

At about 0.6 mile the path leaves the montane and enters a lovely forest. At first you'll find primarily ponderosa, aspen and bushy mats of common juniper growing along the trail; as the path continues, however, look for Engelmann spruce, mountain maple, false Solomonseal, twisted stalk, fireweed, harebell, sticky geranium and along Mill Creek, willow and mountain alder.

While Mill Creek is not an imposing stream, what it lacks in stature it more than makes up for in grace. It contains a delightful series of small plunges and cascades, many framed by rocks covered in soft green blankets of moss. At just over 0.75 mile the aspen are particularly beautiful, their ivory trunks spreading out in hushed groves from the banks of the creek. This is also a good place to look for the shiny green, sharply toothed leaves of chokecherry.

While most of us would only appreciate the fruits of chokecherry after it had been sweetened into a syrup or preserve, many Indian peoples relished them just the way they are. Some Plains Indian tribes set up camps in chokecherry groves for the specific purpose of harvesting the fruits and pounding them—pits and all—into small cakes, which they would then dry in the sun; they did this in a lunar cycle known to them as the "black cherry moon," a reference to the dark color of chokecherry fruits at full maturity. Eastern Indians have long used a tea made from the bark of chokecherry to treat coughs and various respiratory ailments—a practice that the American colonists soon incorporated into their own culture.

At about 1.3 miles the trail splits, the right fork going to Cub Lake, and the left to Bear and Bierstadt lakes. Take a left here, following the path across Mill Creek, up a hill through a small grove of aspen, and finally into a sizable forest of lodgepole pine. Notice how much more homogeneous the vegetation is in the lodgepole forest, the understory bare but for patches of whortleberry and a few clusters of kinnikinnick. At a little over 2 miles is another fork in the trail; take a right here, following the signs for Cub Lake. Cross Mill Creek once again, wind through an open meadow for about 0.3 mile, and then turn right again. (This is the same trail you would have been on had you taken a right at that first trail junction.)

The scenery on the back side of this small loop is really quite beautiful. There are long, open benches dotted with sagebrush, ponderosa, common juniper and Douglas fir, as well as a particularly striking grove of aspen, much of it rising from bright patches of columbine, bedstraw, fireweed and sticky geranium. This forest is a fine spot to cast a few daydreams on a warm summer day, to lie back in the flora and let the magic of this park wash the worry and woe from the nooks and crannies of your heart.

WALK #53—MOLLY LAKE TRAIL

DISTANCE: 2 miles
ENVIRONMENT: Forest
LOCATION: Roosevelt National Forest. Head north on U.S. Highway 287, which is located north-west of Fort Collins, and turn left on Red Feather Lakes Road. Proceed west for 24.6 miles, and turn left (south) onto County Road 162. Continue for 2 miles. Our walk-ing road is Forest Road 267, located on the east side of County Road 162. Park at the junction of these two roads, and begin your walk through a gate to the east.

The walk to Molly Lake is along an ever-so-gentle roadway, currently closed to motorized vehicles. A series of numbered posts have been placed along the route which correspond to information on a sheet available at the trailhead, making the walk a perfect one for learning a few of the more common plants that pepper this rolling, "way-out-West"–looking landscape.

Occasionally on this walk you may see piles of woody debris, commonly known as slash. These are the result of Forest Service efforts to control infestations of the mountain pine beetle, which commonly attacks both lodgepole and ponderosa pine trees. The eggs of these insects are laid beneath the bark during August and September, allowing the larve to obtain nutrients from the trees throughout the winter months. By the following summer the surviving larvae have turned into flying beetles, which then take off to set up shop in other conifers nearby. Curiously, it's not so much the insects themselves that do the most damage to these trees, but rather a fungus they carry that attacks the cells used to transport nutrients up the trunks and out to the branches. Unlike the slow death caused to both ponderosa and lodgepole by the parasite dwarf mistletoe (visible at stop 3), conifers hit by mountain pine beetles are typically dead within 18 months following the initial infestation. Trees weakened by other forces are particularly susceptible to pine beetles. Healthy stands are more or less safe, especially with a little help from hungry resident woodpeckers, who find the beetles quite tasty.

There is a very pleasant mix to this forest—shiny greens of ponderosa and lodgepole, dark mats and spires of common juniper and Douglas fir and shimmering stands of aspen, the latter particularly beautiful when their leaves melt to gold in the crisp air of autumn. Also growing in dark, shiny mats (complete with light pink bell flowers in the spring or red berries in the fall), is the beautiful creeper known as kinnikinnick. The name *kinnikinnick*, incidentally, is an Algonkian Indian word which applies to any of several plants that are used in traditional Native American smoking mixtures. Kinnikinnick was just one part of homemade tobacco, frequently being added to red willow or red-osier dogwood leaves. This mixture became a favorite of the trappers who roamed this high country during the first half of the 19th century.

Because the name kinnikinnick is occasionally given to other plants, it's sometimes safer to refer to this lovely little creeper by its other common name, bearberry, a title that refers to the fact that most bears find the fall fruits much to their liking. (Appropriately, the Latin species name of this plant means "bear's grape.") Most humans, on the other hand, find these fruits more palatable if they are boiled first. Kinnikinnick leaves are a source of the tannins used to cure fur pelts, and are still used for this purpose in many parts of Russia. In addition, some Native American people made tonics and diuretics from the plants; the Cheyenne, for instance, used the berries for treating colds and flu.

Stop 10 will allow you a close inspection of a tree killed by a porcupine's insatiable appetite for tender tree top bark. Porcupines are the largest land rodents in this area (beavers are larger), and, when spotted lumbering across the floor of an open forest, can look remarkably cumbersome. In trees, however, these slow-moving pincushions are really quite graceful. Their love for the inner bark of conifers can wreak havoc in a forest, often either by completely girdling the trunk of the tree, thereby stopping its nutrient flow, or by destroying the entire upper section of the tree by removing its bark. Porcupines are also famous for chewing on sweat-soaked tool handles and canoe paddles. Despite popular belief, porcupines cannot "shoot" the quills that line their back sides.

Just before you reach the turnoff to Molly Lake you'll see a rough path leading to an overlook of the Lone Pine Valley. Standing above this long, lonely roll of timber and grass, "Lone Pine Valley" seems like a particularly appropriate name, the kind some cowboy—and there have been plenty here—might dream up on a moonlit autumn night while out checking the doggies. In fact, if ever there was a place where the sunsets should be accompanied by harmonica music, this is it.

Just under 1 mile is a small road taking off to the left. This is the route to Molly Lake, a pretty little watering place for deer and cattle, framed on the north by rolling hummocks of grass, and to the south by fine clumps of aspen, their leaves fluttering with every sigh of summer breeze.

WALK #54—GREYROCK MEADOW LOOP

DISTANCE:	6.5 miles
ENVIRONMENT:	Mountain
LOCATION:	Roosevelt National Forest. This trail is located on Colorado Highway 14, approximately 17 miles west of Fort Collins. Although the trail begins by crossing a footbridge over the Cache La Poudre River, the parking area for the walk is located on top of a hill on the south side of the highway. The turnoff for this parking area is 0.5 mile west of mile marker 114.

When writing about the footpaths of Colorado, it seems almost irreverent to not include one solid, hearty plod up a mountain. While this 6.5-mile trek does gain 2,000 feet in elevation, it is by no means as rugged as many in this region. Give these wooded, bird-filled ravines, these warm, brown hills of grass and the rugged, soaring vistas the slow, deliberate attention they deserve, and you should be able to handle this walk just fine. You may want to make note of the fact that this is an especially good path to take in early spring or late autumn, when most other mountain trails are locked in winter white.

The walk begins with a crossing of the beautiful Cache La Poudre River. This rather ponderous name is French for "Hide the Powder," a title bestowed on it by a group of rendezvous-bound trappers who, caught by an autumn snowstorm, had to bury their gunpowder, as well as several other items, and return for them the following spring. Rising in the cold high country along Trail Ridge Road in Rocky Mountain National Park, the Cache La Poudre flows through increasingly arid country on its way to the South Platte River.

Once over the river, continue west through fine clumps of dry-land vegetation, including narrowleaf yucca and an occasional plains prickly pear cactus. Like nearly every other plant you see here, from ponderosa to rice grass to snakeweed to juniper, these plants were utilized by the Native Americans who once made their homes in these lovely hills. Both the young shoots of the yucca and the fruit, or "tuna," of the prickly pear were sources of food. In addition, the white, curling fibers of yucca leaves served as sewing thread, while whatever needles were necessary could be fashioned from the sharp tips.

The Native Americans of Colorado were as overwhelmed as any native people in the nation when European-style progress rolled westward. By the 1860s, sweeping the Indian onto reservations and then gaining title to his lands was a territorial obsession; in fact, newspapers throughout the state routinely lambasted any military leader who seemed reluctant to make war against the natives. (After the gruesome 1864 Sand Creek Massacre, in which soldiers under the command of a former minister launched a surprise attack that killed 200 Cheyennes, mostly women and children huddled under a white surrender flag, one paper reported that the state's soldiers had "again covered themselves with glory.") With precious careers on the line, it became more and more common for high-ranking officials to resort to outright deadly assault to convince constituents that they were serious. Scalps of Indians were often put on public display, often as intermission entertainment at local theaters, to reinforce the notion that Colorado Territory was under strong, heroic leadership.

Continue climbing gently along the trail (this section was constructed by the Civilian Conservation Corps) to a junction in 0.6 mile. Here we'll stay to the left, although those interested only in getting to Greyrock Mountain can cut their distance (though not their effort!) by taking a right. The next 1.5 miles of pathway will require the most effort, so plan to take frequent stops among the open stands of ponderosa or in the shade of junipers, the latter huddled like fat old men in the dusty washes. At the 2-mile mark you will cross a high ridge that offers sweeping views up Cache La

Poudre River, as well as to the south, toward the peaks of Rocky Mountain National Park. The mountains you see before you are actually quite young, having been fully uplifted for only the past five to seven million years. Instead of the dense cloak of spruce-fir forest that blankets higher slopes, here the land is covered by thin layers of grass and ragged groves of ponderosa. Buff-colored sedimentary rocks line the ridge lines and canyon headwalls, some forming strange, fierce shapes, looking haggard and parched when held against a cloudless sky.

The path continues to climb more gently toward the east, finally reaching a small perch that offers long, long views across the western fringes of the Great Plains. From here you'll descend into Greyrock Meadow, a beautiful blend of rock and grass, with Greyrock Mountain itself rising on its granite pedestal to the east. Your last climb will be up the west flank of Greyrock Mountain to a crossing point south of the actual summit. Just past this you'll meet up with the Greyrock Mountain Trail. Turn right and start the long, steep descent back toward your starting point along the Cache La Poudre.

The trip down is through a wonderful, wooded canyon, which most of the time is thoroughly washed in the fluty echoes of bird song. Keep eyes and ears open for Say's phoebes, warbling vireos, western bluebirds, orange-crowned warblers, green-tailed towhees and dark-eyed juncos, to name but a few.

WALK #55—SOUTH FORK, ST. VRAIN CREEK

DISTANCE: 4.2 miles

ENVIRONMENT: Forest

LOCATION: Roosevelt National Forest. From the city of Boulder, head west on U.S. Highway 36 (this road actually runs north out of the city). Several miles outside of Boulder you'll see a road taking off to the left, toward Jamestown. You'll reach Jamestown in 8.5 miles; continue west on Boulder County Road 94 for another 4.9 miles to a small road heading north. Turn here, and follow this road 0.1 mile to the trailhead.

As the interpretive sign at the head of this new trail suggests, the splendid little watercourse you're about to follow takes its name from Ceran St. Vrain. A business partner of the famous Charles Bent, who was somewhat of a genius when it came to the art of trading buffalo robes, St. Vrain would gain much of his sterling reputation not as a trader, but as a leader of volunteers who chased down Utes, Apaches and Mexicans for hostilities perpetrated against Americans in the New Mexico Territory. One of St. Vrain's most painful jobs in this capacity was to apprehend a group of Mexican and Pueblo Indian rebels who, as part of a loosely organized uprising in the winter of 1847, broke into the home of his good friend (and then governor) Charles Bent, and proceeded to murder and scalp him in front of his terrified family. St. Vrain and his men wasted no time hitting the war path. Their search soon led them to a group of renegades holed up in the church at Taos Pueblo; a fight ensued, and when the smoke cleared, 150 of the rebels were dead, compared to a mere handful of Americans. The organizers of this hapless rebellion were later run through the motions of a trial. Fifteen were found guilty. All were hanged.

The South Fork of St. Vrain Creek suggests none of this torrid past. In fact, while not necessarily a spectacular route, this trail is easily one of the most peaceful, relaxing forest ambles for miles around. After a spectacular stream crossing the trail will make a gentle descent into a forest of spruce, fir and lodgepole pine, underlain by patches of big whortleberry, buffaloberry, and false Solomonseal. Also easy to spot along much of this walk is common juniper, a mat-like shrub sporting awl-shaped needles, scaly bark and the familiar blue fruits (actually cones) that you see on other, more tree-like species of juniper. True to its name, the common juniper is the most widespread juniper on the continent.

About 0.2 mile in, look to your right and you'll see a hodge-podge of trees that have fallen across and into St. Vrain Creek. There was a time when the Forest Service and other land management agencies spent a great deal of energy clearing away such debris. But now we realize that fallen trees help to create quality habitat, forming pools where fish can rest and feed, as well as small waterfalls that help to aerate the water. In fact, in another 0.75 mile or so you'll arrive at the start of an 800-yard stretch of a fisheries improvement project sponsored by the Forest Service, Colorado Division of Wildlife and Colorado State University, in which logs have actually been placed across the width of the creek for just such purposes.

While this walk may not offer the wide range of habitats available during, say, a climb up a mountain, it's hardly homogeneous. From 0.5 to 1 mile you'll be passing small, shaded pockets along the trail where moisture hangs on slightly longer than in other places, giving rise to small gardens of bracken fern, an occasional alder and nice tufts of Rocky Mountain maple. This latter tree (here more often a shrub) has an extensive range, growing from the

False Solomonseal

southeast coast of Alaska all the way to southern New Mexico. While it certainly lacks the stature of other maples, in autumn it adds welcome splashes of yellow and sometimes red to the thick green curtain of the coniferous forest. In spring the show continues on a more subdued scale, as the tree's branches become dotted with the deep red hues of winter buds.

Continue on past harebells, fireweed and false Solomonseal, as well as splashes of wild rose, current, raspberry and kinnikinnick. At about 1 mile, just beyond the first of several trailside signs informing you of the fisheries-improvement project mentioned earlier, you'll come upon one of the largest, most beautiful blue spruce you will ever see in the backcountry. Naturalist Donald Culross Peattie once likened the color of this tree's new growth to "blue moonlight." Indeed, in the wild there is something almost magical about both the symmetry and cast of the blue spruce, something that can stop you in your tracks, as if you were seeing the beauty of a tree for the very first time. It's little wonder that Colorado, where blue spruce is most at home, selected it as its state tree.

Our turnaround is a small jeep road that crosses the creek and comes into the trail from the right at about 2.1 miles. If you haven't paid much attention to the bird life of the forest, keep your eyes and ears open on the way back to the trailhead. More than likely you'll be treated to the sights or sounds of mountain chickadees, dark-eyed juncos, yellow-rumped warblers, ruby-crowned kinglets, brown creepers, robins and even an occasional blue grouse.

Yellow-rumped Warbler

WALK #56—WATERTON CANYON RECREATION AREA

DISTANCE: 4.4 miles
ENVIRONMENT: Mountain
LOCATION: Near the eastern edge of Pike National Forest. From Denver, head south on Wadsworth Boulevard (Colorado Route 121) to Interstate C-470. Continue south for 4 miles, and go left at the sign for Waterton Canyon/Roxborough State Park. A hundred yards from this turn, make a right at the Waterton Canyon entrance sign, and follow this road to the parking area. *Note:* While our walking route—actually a small portion of the Colorado Trail—is closed to private cars, there will be an occasional Denver Water Department vehicle using it; do keep an eye out for such traffic.

Despite the enormous growth that has occurred along the Front Range in the past 20 years, Denver is still blessed with a wonderful variety of places to go to let the mountain winds blow the metropolis out of your hair. One such place is Waterton Canyon, a trail perfect for either a quick, easy stroll, or a full-fledged hike along the Colorado Trail deep into the craggy foothills of the Pike National Forest. While the accessibility and ease of this trail can cause it to be somewhat crowded on weekends, rest assured that there's more than enough canyon, mountains and cool South Platte River water for everyone.

I found that it took about 0.25 mile of walking on this road (actually the bed of the Denver South Park and Pacific Railroad, built in 1877) before suburbia began to fade, before the South Platte canyon started to really capture my fancy. The noise of engines starting and doors and trunk lids slamming yielded to the singing of birds; picnic tables started to appear, the first of which were nicely placed in the fluttering shade of a fine grove of Frémont cottonwoods. John Frémont, the explorer whose name graces this particular species of cottonwood, referred to it on occasion as "sweet cottonwood," very likely because his horses found the inner bark to be tasty fodder at the end of a hard day of riding. This is the common cottonwood throughout much of the Southwest—along the Colorado River in the haunting depths of the Grand Canyon, rimming water holes on the high plateaus of eastern New Mexico and huddled against the thin, sandy ravines that drain the northern deserts of Baja, California. There was a time when travelers in the southwest deserts would look down from a high mesa and rejoice to see a grove of Frémont cottonwoods, since the tree is a reliable indicator that permanent water isn't far away.

Continue down the wide, meandering roadway, past clusters of rabbitbrush, yarrow, Gambel oak and smooth sumac, until at 0.5 mile you reach a large grove of box elder trees on the right. Box elder is closely related to maple, as you may guess from the pairs of pale yellow, winged seeds that hang from its branches. The leaves of this particular variety of box elder are rather thick and light green above, and form three, deeply lobed leaflets. In the West this short-lived, but very tenacious tree has long been welcomed for its shade, and Indians along the Missouri River tapped it to make sugar. And, in a land that tends to be short on fall colors, box elder can certainly hold its own. In the East, however, the box elder is considered a rather scrawny resident of riverbanks, a weed among trees, barely fit for consideration. Even the name of box elder isn't something it can claim for its own, part of it coming from the fact that the light-colored wood looks like that of the boxwood, and the other from the leaves, which resemble those of the elder.

In about 0.7 mile a service road will come in from your left, and shortly afterward, you'll have the pleasure of meeting the South Platte River, fresh and cool after its dash from the mountains near South Park. This river has certainly seen its share of western history. It served as a pathway for the first American to reach the central Rockies, a Kentuckian named James Purcell, who in 1805 hustled upstream along the South Platte all the way to South Park with an angry band of Sioux hot on his trail. In November of the following year, Zebulon Pike made his way up along the frozen banks of the Platte on an almost desperate search to find the source of the Red River. From South Park, Pike and his men traveled through the frigid mountain cold, spent the most dismal Christmas imaginable and finally stumbled east through the rugged Royal Gorge country, emerging beaten and battered along not the Red but the Arkansas, at nearly the same spot that he had begun his trek in the first place. A half century after Pike's fiasco, miners would pour up the South Platte in Colorado's first gold rush, some of them finding a fair quantity of the precious metal in the vicinity of South Park.

The road continues ever deeper into the steep, rocky walls of a fine sedimentary canyon. This country is home for a number of bighorn sheep, which can sometimes be seen resting in a small, grassy bowl on the right at about 1.5 miles. Bighorn are perhaps best known for the fierce, head-to-head sparring matches that take place between males in the fall to establish social rank and breeding privileges. What keeps these creatures from knocking themselves senseless is a unique double cranium; there is not one, but two plates in the front part of their skulls, each separated by an inch or so of porous material that helps absorb the shock of battle. While the sheep you see here can seem docile to the point of being tame, it's important to keep a respectable distance. Bighorn react poorly to strains of any kind, and in certain cases undue stress may make them vulnerable to disease.

You can continue to walk this path for many miles, each turn of the road offering more and more glimpses of the rugged mountain country to the west, as well as fine opportunities to rub elbows with 1.5-billion-year-old metamorphic rock. (As you look up the canyon, notice the difference in how much vegetation grows on the north-facing slopes of this canyon, compared to the south-facing slopes.) As for roadside plants, once you cross under a water-diversion pipe, look for mullein and Gambel oak, as well as the occasional prickly pear. For those keeping track of mileage, you'll come to a small check dam at about 1.9 miles, and 0.3 mile later, our turnaround point, near a highway pedestrian caution sign. For those who feel somewhat more ambitious, an especially fine walk or bicycle ride can be had by following this road all the way to Strontia Springs Dam, located 6 miles from the parking area.

WALK #57—SAINT MARY'S FALLS

DISTANCE: 4 miles
ENVIRONMENT: Forest
LOCATION: Pike National Forest. In Colorado Springs, take Cheyenne Boulevard to North Cheyenne Canyon Road. Follow this for approximately 3.4 miles to an intersection with High Drive and Gold Camp Road. Turn left onto Gold Camp Road and park in the designated area. *Note:* Because of unstable road and tunnel conditions, Gold Camp Road has been barricaded; you'll have to walk roughly 0.8 mile down it to reach the trailhead.

The 0.8-mile stretch of closed roadway you'll be walking to reach the trail to Saint Mary's Falls is actually part of the old Short Line Railroad. Today it is a forlorn, neglected-looking thoroughfare, portions of it covered by slides, and several of its tunnels in imminent danger of collapse. But there was a time not so very long ago when this route was thoroughly steeped in commotion, as tons of ore and scores of miners, bankers, dance-hall girls, shopkeepers, carpenters, entrepreneurs, honest men and general n'er-do-wells made their way to and from Colorado Springs and the fabled gold camp of Cripple Creek. Built in 1900 as a competitor to the Midland Terminal Line, which reached Cripple Creek by circling Pikes Peak to the north, the Short Line was considered to be among the most beautiful railroads in America.

From a point about 5 air miles southwest of where you're now standing, near Penrose-Rosemont Reservoir, passengers could look out on a dazzling tapestry of western scenery, from the ramparts of the Continental Divide to the west, eastward across a long reach of prairie to the Kansas state line. Like so many others, when Vice President Teddy Roosevelt decided to take a ride on the Short Line, he could hardly believe his eyes.

"Bully!" he exclaimed. "This is the ride that bankrupts the English language!"

Cripple Creek was actually one of the last places in Colorado to feel the fire of gold fever, though this was certainly not due to any lack of trying. Discovery of gold in 1858 in the Cherry Creek area to the north touched off a mining stampede. The swell soon came to be known as the Pikes Peak Gold Rush, primarily because it was Pikes Peak that served as a beacon to the swarms of hopeful miners drifting westward across the plains. As the months went by there were scores of men scouring the steely gray flanks of Pikes Peak looking for gold. Not only did these men fail to find any of the precious metal; they didn't even find the veins of quartz that miners usually relied on to tell them that a place might be worthy of a closer look.

It was more than 30 years after the Cherry Creek discoveries were made that hints of gold were finally uncovered near Pikes Peak, in pieces of rock known as sylvanite. The find was made by a man named Crazy Bob Womac—crazy because he had spent 16 years looking for gold in a place where everyone was sure there was none. When the Cripple Creek mining district was formed in 1892, it produced $500,000 worth of gold; eight years later, that figure had jumped to $18 million. When it was all said and done, an incredible $400 million worth of gold was pulled from these mines, more by far than any other district in Colorado history. Sadly, the man who started it all—Bob Womac—sold out his claims early on for a few hundred dollars. In the year that Womac died, nearly penniless, $11 million worth of gold was plucked from the Cripple Creek mines.

About a mile from where you parked your car and began walking along Gold Camp Road, a signed trail will take off on your left, climbing up and over a tunnel toward Saint Mary's Falls. For the most part the path climbs steadily through a forest of ponderosa pine and Douglas fir—two trees that are very much at home in this well-drained granitic soil. Because of the loose, unstable nature of decomposed granite—the same condition that caused the slides visible along the roadway—sturdy shoes with good treads will make this walk much easier. Buffalo Creek will be gurgling by your side for much of the walk, in places framed by fine stands of aspen, as well as enough wild roses to drench the early-summer air with waves of perfume. People in Europe and America have long used the red fruits of the rose, sometimes called "hips," as a source of vitamin C. Unable to import citrus during World War II, the British government organized the collecting of tons and tons of rose fruits, which were then made into something called National Rose Hip

Syrup. Interestingly, Native Americans were only inclined to eat rose hips as a last resort against starvation. More common for them was to drink a tea made from the roots or stems for stomach disorders, or to make an astringent wash from the petals for sore throats or inflammation of the eyes.

As you make your way up the trail, watch for harebells, fireweed, mountain maple, wild lily-of-the-valley, narrowleafed yucca and kinnikinnick, the latter plant forming beautiful evergreen mats at the feet of ponderosa and Douglas fir. At about 1.7 miles you'll come to an intersection; turn right here away from the creek, following the sign toward Saint Mary's Falls. A short distance past this intersection you'll be afforded an outstanding view of Colorado Springs and the Broadmoor Hotel at the foot of South Cheyenne Creek Canyon, and beyond that, the wide, grassy wash of the Great Plains. (The beautiful Broadmoor Hotel, by the way, was built largely on revenues from copper mining; those mining efforts were largely staked, however, with income made from Cripple Creek gold.)

At 0.2 mile from the last trail intersection you'll reach another junction; stay left, and continue another 1,000 feet or so to the base of Saint Mary's Falls. From this point the falls appear as a frothy, 125-foot cascade of white water, framed by a dark jumble of rocks, as well as a pleasant weave of wild rose, raspberry, yarrow and water birch.

Northeastern Colorado

WALK #58—CROW VALLEY PARK

DISTANCE: 0.1 mile
ENVIRONMENT: Prairie
LOCATION: Crow Valley Recreation Area. Heading east on Colorado Highway 14, turn north just outside the small town of Briggsdale, onto Weld County Highway 77. Follow signs for Crow Valley Recreation Area, the entrance to which turns off to the left about 0.2 mile north of Colorado 14. Head west through the park into the campground; our walk takes off beside camping unit 4.

This quiet little park is one of those pleasant jewels that drifting vacationers hope to find, but almost never do, along main thoroughfares of travel. While much of it is nicely manicured—the "state park" look—a tiny slice of moist prairie thrives directly adjacent to the campground. Make no mistake; there are more than a few introduced plants mixed in with the natives. Yet this shortest of all our walks will provide you with a good opportunity to learn a few of the plants that you'll see on other, more remote forays in the Pawnee Grassland. (See the Pawnee Buttes walk, page 183.) The Pawnee Indians, for which this grassland is named, were among the first Native Americans of the past 300 years to establish themselves on the prairie. They came at a time when bison and pronghorn thundered across this gentle landscape by the millions, and great flocks of migratory birds darkened the skies each autumn.

Threats to this delicate balance between the Pawnee and their homeland did not come so much from other tribes (Sioux poured through these lands early in the 19th century, pushed out of Minnesota by the Chippewa), but rather from the storms of Europeans who decided to "go West." Hundreds of thousands of pioneers rumbled through this country in wagon trains bound for the Pacific coast in the 1850s and 1860s, wiping out a good share of Pawnee grass and game in the process. Much later people came looking to be farmers, each determined (with the blessing of the U.S. government) to put this land into more "productive" use. Watching his former hunting grounds being sliced by the blade of a plow, one dismayed Pawnee chief made the comment that grass was "no good upside down." This was a rather prophetic remark, considering the fact that just a few decades later the great drought arrived, turning these tended fields into nothing but barren sand and blowing dust.

Our short little stroll takes off from behind camping unit 4. Once past a beautiful weave of willow, the path drops down off a small bench into a congregation of young cottonwoods, thistle and curly dock. This latter plant is one of the most common in the entire world, easily identifiable by its curly leaf edges. Curly dock (sometimes called yellow dock) has had a rather long history as a medicinal plant, primarily used for the treatment of indigestion and constipation, but occasionally as a remedy for acne, as well. Before more modern therapies came along, it was also used to treat intestinal cancer.

On the left at 30 to 40 yards you'll see a collection of Rocky Mountain juniper and Siberian elm, as well as a fairly lush carpet of smooth brome grass. Both the elm and the brome grass were brought into the plains area long ago as part of the effort to retard soil erosion. Even today, brome, with its ability to form sod quickly, is one of several species used by highway departments to stabilize disturbed road corridors.

As the trail makes a turn to the left, you'll be walking through a mixture of western and crested wheat grasses, the latter of which is yet another non-native species, this one brought in from Asia to stabilize soils abused by farming and overgrazing. Farther down the path are the very delicate fronds of switchgrass, and the distinctive low, curly, mat leaves belonging to blue grama.

In a short distance the path makes another turn to the left, heading back toward the campground. The small depression on your left contains willow, curly dock and evening primrose. Once the beautiful blooms of primrose have withered away, the seeds of

Western Kingbird

Western Meadowlark

the plants provide an important source of food for wildlife. Also nearby is milkweed, a species that certainly deserves more than a little admiration. The beautiful monarch butterfly depends entirely on milkweed leaves for its sustenance, and Thomas Edison used the sap of milkweed to make a primitive form of rubber. But, perhaps most astounding of all is what milkweed provided for us during the Second World War.

Up until the early 1940s America used tremendous amounts of a fibrous seed from the silk cotton tree, which grew on the East Indian islands, to fill life vests for our fighting Navy men. But in 1942 these islands were captured by the Japanese, leaving us in a major pinch for flotation material. Milkweed to the rescue! It was found that less than 2 pounds of milkweed floss could keep a 150-pound man afloat for two days. Prodded into action by the Department of Agriculture, thousands of school children and Boy Scout troops set out across the American countryside, filling onion sacks with pods and sending them off for processing to a plant in Petosky, Michigan. Before they were finished, these young pickers had harvested 25 million pounds of pods—enough for more than a million life vests.

As you continue along this depression, keep your eyes open for western kingbirds, horned larks, shrikes, western meadowlarks, vesper and lark sparrows, as well as the beautiful lemon-colored plumage of the American goldfinch. The path will pass near a cluster of old elm trees on your right, and then exit adjacent to camping unit 5.

WALK #59—PAWNEE BUTTES

DISTANCE: 4.2 miles
ENVIRONMENT: Prairie
LOCATION: Pawnee National Grassland. Head west out of Briggsdale on Colorado Highway 14 for 13 miles to Weld County Road 103. (This is the "Keota Turnoff.") Follow Weld County 103 north for 4.8 miles, following the signs for Pawnee Buttes. You'll be going north for 3 miles on Weld County 105 to a "T" intersection with Weld County 104. Head east on 104 for 3 miles, then go north on Weld County 111 for 4 miles to the Buttes Trailhead turnoff. Our trailhead is 1 mile from this last intersection.

It's little wonder that the director of the movie version of James Michener's epic *Centennial* chose this place to film wagons rolling into the wild frontier. This is still a remarkably uncluttered slice of Colorado prairie. The songs of early America seem fresh and crisp here, and they riffle through your hair and past your ears, carried in the strong arms of the western wind.

Though they rise only 250 feet above the grassy valleys below, the Pawnee Buttes themselves surely must have seemed like giants to those who had jostled in their wagons across half a continent. To some they were warm portals of welcome; to others, troublesome reminders that not far beyond were the ramparts of the Rockies.

Our walk begins with a gentle descent to the east down a shallow ravine peppered with yucca, western wheatgrass and cheatgrass. While the first two of these plants are natives, cheatgrass was introduced more than a century ago, and, with its remarkable ability to take over abused soils, it is absolutely flourishing on the prairies of the West. Unfortunately for the cattle industry, which has inadvertently brought about the rapid spread of cheatgrass, the plant has very little value as forage.

Down the trail 0.2 mile you'll come to a beautiful, flat plain rich with blue grama, an important sod builder and valuable forage plant on the prairies of the West, and now the state grass of Colorado. From this plateau the view is indeed a grand one, the Great Plains tumbling off to the east for mile after mile, finally becoming lost to vision in a melt of summer sky. It was on the distant shore of this great sea of grass in 1853 that a bizarre event took place in Westport, Missouri, the jumping-off place for the Santa Fe Trail.

Living at the edge of the frontier provided the citizens of Westport with more than their share of excitement. Yet, no one was ready for the stir that a former sea-faring captain named Zeb Thomas caused when he came rolling down Main Street that sunny spring morning on a wagon powered not by horses, but by sails. His intention, as he revealed to a full house of curious residents at a local tavern, was to launch an entire fleet of these prairie clippers on the rolling grasslands between Westport and Santa Fe. With their great speed and lack of any need for fuel, explained Thomas, windwagons would make the road to riches one smooth sail. All he needed to get started was a few partners— a few partners with money, that is.

"Windwagon" Thomas didn't wait for the hoots and hollers of laughter to die down. He stormed out of the tavern, climbed aboard his prairie schooner, and announced that he was off to Council Grove, Kansas. When he returned from the 300-mile trip six days later, armed with a letter from a prominent resident of the city as proof of the trip, suddenly there was a shortage of laughter and an abundance of investors. Showered with all the money he

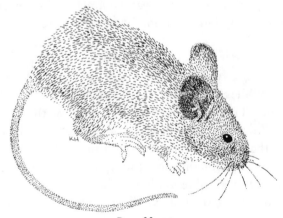

Deer Mouse

could use, Thomas wasted no time in getting down to the business of building the first freight-hauling windwagon. And what a vessel it was, measuring 25 feet long and 7 feet wide, sporting wheels twice the height of a man. As the partners stood by, grinning at the thought of how much cargo a fleet of these clippers could carry, Admiral Thomas prepared the sleek craft for its maiden voyage.

Things started off well enough. But then the wind picked up a little. And then it picked up a little more. Soon Thomas and his rather inept crew of landlubbers began cruising at a much higher speed than they had ever intended. And then, as luck would have it, there was that blasted dip in the prairie. Unable to get the boom down in time, the windwagon drove hard into the side of the ravine, pivoting it into the air and smashing it on its side in a flurry of splinters, tossing the good Admiral Thomas onto his head in the process. With a blue streak of curses that only a New England sailor

Swainson's Hawk

could muster, Thomas got up and stomped away. Later that evening he loaded a few belongings into his smaller, still intact windwagon, and sailed out of sight, never to be heard from again.

Shortly after passing through a fence at 0.5 mile, the trail begins a descent through a lovely huddle of miniature shale pillars, framed on either side by large, buff-colored sandstone buttes. Look for creepers here, sinking their roots deep into the dry ground. As wind and water carry away the surrounding soil, the patches protected by these plants are left standing as sandy pillars, looking from a distance like huddles of green stumps. (A larger feat of erosion, conducted by great rivers of glacial melt water that coursed through the area following the last ice age, is what left the Pawnee Buttes standing far above the surrounding landscape.) Watch along this stretch for little bluestem grass, the seeds of which provide an important source of food for wintering birds. Speaking of birds, the rock spires around you form an important nesting area for several raptors; turn your eyes skyward occasionally, and you may glimpse a soaring prairie falcon or golden eagle. It's important that you stay on the trail here, so as not to disturb nesting birds in any way.

The path continues into a ravine with squawbush and Rocky Mountain juniper, then climbs back up onto a flat dappled with needle and thread grass. After passing a large butte on the left, at 1.5 miles you'll come out on a road with a view of a teapot-shaped butte ahead and slightly to your left. Follow the road to our turnaround point at the base of this massive monument. (You'll be crossing private land between the buttes; please stay on the trail, and keep the area free of both fire and litter.)

Sit for a few minutes with your back against these warm brown walls, letting the prairie winds blow this airy, silent scene into your consciousness—the ripple of grass, the wash of rock and sky. While I was here I had the distinct feeling that in some small measure this was still the West of old, a priceless launching pad for the spirits of yet another generation.

Southeastern Colorado

WALK #60—PICTURE CANYON

DISTANCE: 3.2 miles

ENVIRONMENT: Prairie

LOCATION: Comanche National Grassland. Take Highway 287/385 south out of Springfield, Colorado. Turn right (west) just past mile marker 13, at a sign marking the turn for the Picture Canyon Picnic Area. Following the signs for Picture Canyon, proceed west for 8.2 miles, turning left just past a cattle guard onto County Road 18. Go south for another 8.2 miles on this road. A small house will be on your left, with a two-track dirt road on the opposite side, heading west. Take this small road across a cattle guard (0.4 mile) which marks the boundary of the national grassland. Just past this is a fork in the road; park here and begin walking along the left branch. *Note:* A new picnic area has been constructed farther down the road near the mouth of Picture Canyon; those looking for a shorter walk can begin there.

The former secretary at the Comanche National Grassland office in Springfield was just a young girl when the first terrifying storm of the dust bowl unleashed its dark, gritty fury onto this shortgrass prairie. "We called them the black days," she says of the three-day ordeal. "My older brother was out riding broncs at the rodeo arena when it hit. All the people there just sort of huddled together, thinking that it was the end of the world. Some were crying. A lot were praying." Dust was so thick that it was hard to see your hand in front of your face. Men went around with wet kerchiefs held against their noses and mouths, choking and coughing as they called out the names of brothers or fathers or ranch hands lost in the storm. The nostrils of the range cattle clogged, and many ended up dead in piles of dust. "For days we had to keep covers on all our food," recalls the secretary. "When it came time to eat we'd stick our hands underneath and grab whatever we could."

Here too, in Picture Canyon, the dust sifted down day after day. Despite the overwhelming odds against them, some of the ranchers in the area were able to hang on, a fact that to this day is a source of immense pride for them. But for others it was too much. When government agents came in offering to buy this land from homesteaders in order to remove it from further agricultural use, they found that a great many of the farms and ranches had simply been abandoned, more than a few with pictures still hanging on the walls, with cribs and dressers and wooden dolls, all left to the raging prairie winds.

The road begins in typical eastern Colorado grassland fare, with clumps of blue grama, buffalo and cheatgrass dotting the landscape, as well as snakeweed, narrowleaf yucca and the sticky yellow heads of gumweed. There is a peaceful tranquility to this walk, as you slowly curl southward toward the mouth of the canyon, carved flat and wide out of the warm, brown sandstones and shales. Later, on the right side of the road you'll see erosion-resistant cap

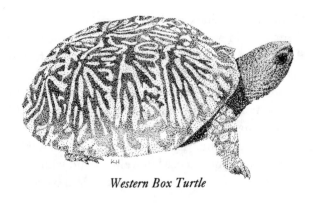

Western Box Turtle

Buffalo Grass

rock sitting on top of the sandstone, a feature which offers protection from the ravages of the weather. In places these cap stones sit atop striking collections of towers and parapets, a medieval fantasyland, complete with clusters of junipers huddling like green-robed monks in the castle wings.

At 1 mile you'll cross a wash, its surface wet during enough of the year to give rise to moisture-loving plants like willow. Also in this area are blue flax, blazing star and wild prairie rose. Start listening at this wash crossing for the sad lilt of the mourning dove, and, to a lesser extent, the cricket trills of the rock wren. This latter bird has the strange habit of constructing a pathway of small stones leading up to a well-hidden nest.

In 1.6 miles the road will fork. Stay left, and work your way to the base of a long cliff. Here in this pocket is a small supply of permanent water, giving rise to a tremendous collection of plant life. On the lower walls of this canyon face is an expansive panel of rock art. Though the subject is very controversial, some researchers claim that the vertically incised lines you see here are actually Ogam, an ancient language thought to have originated in the British Isles. If this is true, then the "words" you see on these rocks may well have been inscribed by a Celtic traveler some 1,500 years ago.

While you're studying the possibilities of this rock panel, notice the rings of mud from old cliff-swallow nests, as well as the frequent signs of woodrats in the narrow, protected crevices. Woodrats (or packrats) are incurable collectors, creating gargantuan nest areas filled with everything from barbed wire to pieces of Indian pottery, shotgun shells to bits of handkerchiefs, rope and leather gloves. Woodrats store large quantities of leaves to sustain them during the winter months. The notion that these animals "trade" an item for one that they take is somewhat misleading; in fact they load themselves up with so many treasures that they usually have to abandon one in order to gain the other.

The Comanche National Grassland has started to develop a comprehensive trail system through other parts of the reserve, including plans for a fine interpretive path that will give visitors a good look into the region's history. If you'd like to spend more time in this beautiful area, call or stop by the grassland office in Springfield for additional suggestions on where to go.

Broom Snakeweed

■ NEW MEXICO ■

NEW MEXICO
...

Shiprock
Farmington 64
Clayton
64
56
Taos
84
77
74
666
61
44
75
Los Alamos
72 73
62 63
64 68 69
70 71
76
25
Gallup
67
Santa Fe
Thoreau
Las Vegas
Tucumcari
Albuquerque
65
40
40
666
Santa Rosa
25
60
285
Socorro
380
Roswell
70
380
Truth or
Consequences
White Sands
Nat'l Mon.
25
285
78
Alamogordo
54
Carlsbad
Caverns
Carlsbad
80
Las Cruces
Nat'l Pk.
79
70
81
Deming

Chaco Canyon

WALK #61—PEÑASCO BLANCO

DISTANCE: 4.4 miles

ENVIRONMENT: Desert

LOCATION: Chaco Culture National Historic Park. Chaco Canyon can be reached either from the north or south along dirt roads, either of which can be dangerously slippery when wet. For this reason it's advisable to contact the monument for current road conditions before making the trip. If you're coming from the north along New Mexico Route 44, head south on New Mexico 45 at the small village of Nageezi. In 13 miles take a left onto New Mexico 57, and continue south. You'll enter the park after descending a steep grade, at the bottom of which is Casa Chiquita ruin on the right, where this walk begins. Coming from the south, exit Interstate 40 onto New Mexico 197 at the town of Thoreau. Continue for approximately 40 miles and turn north on New Mexico 57, reaching the park visitor center in 21 miles. From the visitor center, head northwest through Chaco Canyon, following signs for Chetro Ketl and Pueblo Bonito. Continue a short ways past the parking area for these two ruins, to an intersection with a road coming in from the northwest. Turn right here and proceed for about a mile to the parking area for Casa Chiquita, on the left.

This walk takes off to the northwest along a service road adjacent to Casa Chiquita, or "Little House." Compared to "great houses" like Pueblo Bonito and Peñasco Blanco, this ruin is aptly named. Archaeologists think that the almost square structure, still unexcavated, was built sometime between A.D. 1100 and 1130. Some of the room rows were two and even three stories tall, built around an elevated round room. Even on this small scale, the amount of work involved to build this type of structure was considerable. The walls consist of an inner core of small stones, covered inside and out with thick veneers of quarried sandstone, carefully shaped into easy-to-fit blocks. One architect has speculated that the construction of Pueblo Bonito, the magnificent "great house" located about a mile southeast of here, may have required as much as 100-million pounds of stone veneer! When you also consider the fact that thousands of ponderosa pines had to be harvested for roof beams, perhaps carried here from the distant mountains, the achievement becomes downright incredible.

Leaving Casa Chiquita, the service road (actually an old wagon road) continues to the northwest along Chaco Wash, through a weave of black greasewood, four-wing saltbush, amaranthus, rice grass and broom snakeweed. Each of these plants played a significant role in the lives of those people who once made their homes in these canyons. The leaves and spring shoots of four-wing saltbush, a member of the goosefoot family, were eaten regularly, and the seeds ground into meal. Some Navajo people still make a beautiful yellow dye from the leaves and twigs of this plant, and also mix ground seeds with water and sugar for a drink called pinole. Likewise, the seeds and leaves of the black greasewood were also edible, and the wood was commonly used as fuel. Broom snakeweed, the tall, spindly green plant with thin leaves and clustered yellow flowers, derives the second half of its name from

Four-wing Saltbush

Indian Rice Grass

the fact that Navajo people use it to treat sheep that have been bitten by rattlesnakes. The plant's leaves are ground and boiled into a poultice, which is then applied to the bite.

About 0.2 mile into the walk the trail comes close to Chaco Wash, where you'll see several beautiful Frémont cottonwoods, named for the famous explorer John Frémont. Pioneers crossing the parched terrain of the Southwest always rejoiced at seeing this tree, because it meant that permanent groundwater was not far from reach. Hopi Indians still use the roots of this tree to carve their beautiful Kachina dolls.

At 0.75 mile, just before a side wash comes in from the right, are a couple of nice petroglyph panels 20 to 30 feet up on a northwest-facing cliff. Here you can see various geometric designs, bighorn sheep and also a human-like figure, facing forward, squatting with his hands out in front of him. Researchers have documented Indian rock art in Chaco Canyon which may stretch back 2,000 years, beginning with simple hand prints and birds and plants made by the early basketmakers. Besides images and symbols from 200 years of Navajo occupation, the walls also hold records of visits from the U.S. Cavalry, cowboys and sheepherders who passed through here in the first half of the 20th century. Though they might not seem so, these petroglyph etchings (as opposed to pictographs, painted with dyes) are quite fragile; touching them dislodges the sand grains and hastens their demise.

In another 0.3 mile you'll cross Chaco Wash, profuse with tamarisk, a tall, feathery tree with juniper-like leaves. Tamarisk was introduced from the Mediterranean (its name may derive from the Tamaris River in Spain) in an effort to control severe soil erosion caused by years of overgrazing. To that end it has proven to be very effective. Unfortunately, tamarisk is remarkably adept at taking over entire landscapes, using great amounts of groundwater which is then unavailable for other native plants. Once entrenched, the plant is almost impossible to eradicate. Willows are the other common plant in this wash. Anasazi commonly used willow for sleeping mats; in addition, archaeologists have found several burials placed on top of mats woven from this species.

Once out of the wash you'll come to a trail junction at the foot of a mesa. The fork heading west leads in 0.25 mile to a rather famous pictograph known as the "Supernova." Though no one knows for sure, many archaeologists believe that the art panel is a record of a great supernova that occurred during the summer of 1054. (We know the date of this celestial event from having read about it in ancient Chinese records.) The trail to Peñasco Blanco climbs the mesa, and is well marked by a series of rock cairns, which are small piles of stones placed as guide posts along the trail.

Peñasco Blanco, which means "white rock point," is located on a rocky spur atop West Mesa, and offers sweeping views down Escavada and Chaco washes. This unusual oval structure, still unexcavated, consisted of more than 160 rooms and four great kivas (round rooms perhaps used for social and religious rituals)—two in the structure's plaza and two more just outside the building. It is thought that construction began on Peñasco Blanco around A.D. 900 and continued in five stages through about 1120. (A great kiva located near this site, however, dates back 400 years earlier, between A.D. 516 and 557.) To the northeast is a unique terrace, upon which lie the ruins of a small, L-shaped building, perhaps a storage unit of some type, as well as a slab that one early archaeologist thought might be a calendar device. Could this great house, which lies along one of Chaco's famous prehistoric roads, have served as the controlling governmental unit for the communities that lay beyond? What a fantastic thought to spend a lifetime wandering these lonely canyons and mesa tops, walking these prehistoric roads, probing these remarkable buildings. What a challenge to try to piece together the fantastic social system that existed here, a system so complex that several 19th-century writers suggested that it could only be the work of the ancient Greeks.

WALK #62—TSIN KLETSIN

DISTANCE: 3 miles
ENVIRONMENT: Desert
LOCATION: Chaco Culture National Historic Park. Chaco Canyon can be reached either from the north or south along dirt roads, either of which can be dangerously slippery when wet. For this reason it's advisable to contact the monument for current road conditions before making the trip. If you're coming from the north along New Mexico Route 44, head south on New Mexico Route 45 at the small village of Nageezi. In 13 miles take a left onto New Mexico Route 57, and continue south for 15 miles into the park. A short distance after taking a right turn on a one-way loop road (just past Pueblo del Arroyo), you'll come to a parking lot for Casa Rinconada on the right side of the road. Our walk begins from here. Coming from the south, exit Interstate 40 onto New Mexico Route 197 at the town of Thoreau. Continue for approximately 40 miles and turn north on New Mexico 57, reaching an intersection just west of the park visitor center in 21 miles. Take a left at this intersection (onto a one-way loop road), and continue around the loop past the parking area for Chetro Ketl and Pueblo Bonito. Soon after the road makes a horseshoe turn to the left, heading back toward the southeast, you'll come to the Casa Rinconada parking area on the right. Park here.

The walk to Tsin Kletsin, which means either "black wood" or "charcoal place," is a journey not only through a superb collection of archaeological wonders, but into one of the most expansive, haunting desert views to be found on any trail in the park. Keep in mind that this walk can be a bit of a scorcher in the summer. During these months plan to leave early in the morning, when the coo of mourning doves and the whistle of canyon wrens run thick off the rock walls, or late in the evening, as the last light of day seeps off the stony fingers of West Mesa.

Before ascending the northern flank of South Mesa the trail meanders past the ruins of Casa Rinconada, which means "the house in the corner." A short distance from the parking area the path makes a quick climb to the edge of a large circular chamber. This is a superb example of a great kiva—the largest in the park, and one of the finest to be found anywhere in the Southwest. Though the functional extent of great kivas is not known, they are generally thought to have housed special social gatherings, and were places where important religious ceremonies were performed.

The room against the north side of the kiva may have served as both an entryway and storage area for religious items. Some researchers feel that the covered sub-floor passage from this room to the chamber allowed for entry into the kiva as if from within the earth. Such a ceremonial maneuver has a firm link to the rituals of modern Pueblo cultures, who are more than likely the descendants of these Anasazi, or "ancient ones." To modern Pueblos, kivas represent the underworld out of which their ancestors first emerged onto the face of the earth. Their kivas, just like this one, have a symbolic hole known as the *sipapu* (see-pah-pooh), which represents this sacred place of emergence. It's been suggested that tower kivas, two of which existed at Tsin Kletsin, were simply kivas built atop one another, each level perhaps representing a

Turkey Vulture

Roadrunner

former stage of the underworld that the ancient ancestors once passed through.

Leaving the complex of Casa Rinconada, the path soon begins a moderately steep, but fairly short climb up to the top of South Mesa. Partway up you'll pass through a very narrow slit in the sandstone, riddled with small pockets and passageways carved in the rock by the relentless beat of wind and water. Soon after this section you'll leave the well-worn path behind. Much of the rest of the journey is accomplished by following a series of rock cairns, which are small towers of piled stones used to mark the way.

The vegetation is fairly sparse on this parched, windswept mesa, consisting predominantly of grasses, broom snakeweed, cliffrose, four-wing saltbush and, in about 0.75 mile, a smattering of juniper. The bark of cliffrose, by the way, was commonly used by the Anasazi to make both baskets and sandals; juniper is still used by modern Pueblo Indians for an array of religious and medicinal purposes.

In 1.5 miles you'll reach the ruins of Tsin Kletsin, an unexcavated structure that was probably built during the early 1100s. It consists of a central block of rooms, an L-shaped wing to the west and an arc of rooms to the south enclosing a large plaza. Of particular interest to archaeologists is Tsin Kletsin's unique line of sight to other ruins in the Chaco complex. From atop the highest tower could be seen the great houses of Kin Kletso, Peñasco Blanco and the Pueblo Alto complex, as well as several "outlier" structures. Moving this site a short distance in any direction would eliminate these sight lines. Could it be, as several researchers have suggested, that the Anasazi constructed an ingenious system whereby the entire complex could be alerted to a stranger's approach?

The view from atop this mesa is absolutely haunting, the long, lonely roll of high desert stretching almost beyond what the mind can comprehend. Only far, far to the north is there any significant uplift—a thin crest of Rocky Mountains painted lightly on the distant horizon. All else, it seems, has been reduced to sun, stone and silence. Yet strangely, when one stands at Chaco, on the crumbling threshold of one of the greatest civilizations North America has ever known, it seems as if the Anasazi never really perished at all. Perhaps they are out there still, dancing, singing, riding like turkey vultures on the warm desert winds.

WALK #63—WIJIJI

DISTANCE: 4 miles
ENVIRONMENT: Desert
LOCATION: Chaco Culture National Historic Park. Chaco Canyon can be reached either from the north or south along dirt roads, either of which can be dangerously slippery when wet. For this reason it's advisable to contact the monument for current road conditions before making the trip. If you're coming from the north along New Mexico Route 44, head south on New Mexico Route 45 at the small village of Nageezi. In 13 miles take a left onto New Mexico Route 57, and continue south for 15 miles into the park. Coming from the south, exit Interstate 40 onto New Mexico Route 197 at the town of Thoreau. Continue for approximately 40 miles and turn north on New Mexico 57, reaching the park visitor center in 21 miles. From the visitor center, head east toward Gallo Campground, continuing past the campground turnoff to the Wijiji parking area on the right.

It's a stretch of the imagination to consider that this haunting collage of quiet, windswept desert washes was once the scene of one of the most extraordinary leaps of cultural development on the North American continent. In barely 30 square miles, more than 2,400 archaeological sites have been identified, ranging from 2,000-year-old baskets and sandals found in Atlatl Cave, to the imposing "great houses." One of these great houses (Pueblo Bonito) was a four-storied architectural masterpiece of more than 800 rooms spanning nearly two acres. Such architectural scope was virtually unknown in the United States until after the advent of structural steel.

But beyond the actual sites themselves, what is really most appealing about this entire 25,000-square-mile region is the sense of mystery that still pervades the entire notion of the "Chaco Phenomenon," a term often used to emphasize the remarkably complex developments that mark the area's peak habitation period during the 10th, 11th and 12th centuries. How could such a dry, fragile environment support the kind of numbers that the great houses seem to suggest once lived here? And, if this was such a populated area, why have so few human burials been found? In a culture that had no wheeled carts, what was the purpose of having half a dozen major road systems, many nearly 40 feet wide and stretching straight as arrows across the landscape for more than 50 miles? After having spent 300 years establishing such a fantastic place, why, during the mid- to late 12th century, did the people suddenly begin drifting away? Walking to Wijiji (a Navajo word for the greasewood that grows in the area), it's exciting to ponder these questions. Who knows? With so much of this cultural puzzle still unsolved, some of the answers might well lie with you.

This walk runs along an old ranch road on the north side of Chaco Wash, and is especially beautiful early in the morning, when the first shafts of sunlight flood the rocky tongues of land lying between Wijiji and Chacra mesas. Canyon wrens flit among the boulders, their crystal-clear, down-the-scale whistles dripping off the warm, brown canyon walls. Also here are mockingbirds and loggerhead shrikes, the latter of which routinely store their excess catches of insects and small birds and mice by impaling them on thorns, yucca leaf tips, barbed wire and other pointed objects.

There's also an interesting mat of vegetation in this area, one that has changed considerably in the past 40 years. In 1920, an

Canyon Wren

archaeologist excavating Pueblo Bonito made the rather extraordinary claim that Edward Sargent, the bad-boy kingpin of early 20th-century ranching, was running close to 60,000 sheep in this fragile desert ecosystem. Besides the sometimes violent techniques he used to run off the Navajo people who had been here for two centuries before him, Sargent's operation proved to be an absolute disaster for the resource. Where fine grasses once grew, suddenly there was only black sage and Russian thistle. It was not until the mid-1940s, when Sargent lost his grazing lease and the entire monument was finally fenced off, that the land began to recover. (It must be remembered that, after more than a century of heavy grazing, very little of the American Southwest looks the way it did to early explorers.) The abundance of rice grass in Chaco Canyon is testimony to the fact that, if given half a chance, the land does indeed begin to heal itself.

Wijiji ruins lie 2 miles into the walk on the left side of the road. This structure contained 103 rooms at floor level, but most of the building was two and in some places three stories high. Built around A.D. 1110–1115, it may have been one of the last "great houses" to be constructed in Chaco Canyon. Speaking about the symmetry of the structure, Archaeologist Stephen Leksen has called Wijiji "the most perfect of any Chacoan ruin." This, he goes on to say, suggests that the building of Wijiji did not occur in several stages over many years, but was most likely a single construction event. The masonry here is strikingly uniform, the thin sandstone

Loggerhead Shrike

slabs having been quarried from the top of the cliff located behind the ruin. The opposite rows of holes you see in some of the rooms were anchoring sockets for roof beams. If you look carefully, you'll also see a row of these anchor holes high up along a cliff wall behind Wijiji. A series of portals on the north exterior wall of the ruin, of which two remain today, have never been explained. Oddly, Wijiji shows no signs of having had an enclosed plaza. Since this was the architectural fashion of the day, some archaeologists suspect that Wijiji may have never been finished.

Two fine rock-art panels lie on the cliff immediately behind Wijiji. The closest one, slightly west of the ruins, has a fascinating array of petroglyphs. (Petroglyphs are etchings in rockfaces, whereas painted images are known as pictographs. Do not touch these rock panels in any way, since this hastens their decay.) Spirals, horned animals and figures resembling humans—some of which were etched in this stone a thousand years ago—are common themes throughout the park. The finer, more deeply incised images, particularly those depicting plants, are thought to have been done by Navajo people in more recent times.

North–Central New Mexico

WALK #64—PONDEROSA

DISTANCE: 1.8 miles

ENVIRONMENT: Forest

LOCATION: Santa Fe National Forest, west of Las Alamos. The trailhead is located on the north side of New Mexico Route 4, west of Las Conchas Campground, and 0.35 mile east of mile marker 35. This small, grass-covered pathway, actually a cross-country ski trail, is visible from the highway behind a Forest Service gate. A small pull-off area is located immediately adjacent to the trail.

I must admit that I have a strong love affair going with the ponderosa pine, certainly one of the most stately trees of the entire Rocky Mountain chain. In California it shares the stage with Jeffrey pine, but here it is the only cinnamon-and-sugar-colored giant standing guard over the drier, grass- and oak-covered mountain slopes found between 4,000 and 8,000 feet. I can still see the movie cowboys of my boyhood shuffling their horses through the ponderosas, and more than once, usually around sunset, I swear I've spotted Hoss Cartwright's big white hat disappearing just over the next ridge.

Almost as soon as you pass through the gate adjacent to the highway you'll be in an almost magical slice of forest. The leaves of aspen and tall, slender meadow grasses wave in the wind, while a fine mat of scarlet gilia, harebell, asters, lupine and yarrow lends splashes of color to the soft green conifer blanket. Incidentally, the yarrow you'll see growing along this pathway—the plant with clusters of tiny white flowers and fern-like leaves—is one of the most heavily used medicinal plants in the world. Even its genus name, "Achillea," is a reference to the Greek warrior Achilles having supposedly used a relative of yarrow to stop bleeding in the wounds of his soldiers at the battle of Troy. In old Europe the plant was known as "soldier's wound wort." (Science long ago verified that the alkaloid present in yarrow does in fact reduce the clotting time of blood.) Native Americans also used yarrow in this way, as well as to help break fevers and treat aching muscles.

At 0.25 mile into the walk you'll reach another gate. The ski trail, which in national forests is marked by blue diamonds, takes off to the left. We'll continue straight, however, climbing gently through an area that was burned by a forest fire more than a quarter century ago, and was then replanted with ponderosas in 1962. While these trees have certainly done well, they are nonetheless a long, long ways from reaching the giant proportions of the timber you saw along the first stretch of trail. A quarter century is actually a drop in the bucket when it comes to forest growth, a ponderosa grove taking more than 10 times that long to reach full maturity. In this sense the growth of a forest can provide some sobering thoughts about time, making us at least halfway conscious of such notions as centuries and millennia, if not the slow, thick flow of eternity itself.

In less than 0.1 mile from this second gate you'll reach a "T" intersection. Take a left here, but before you do make sure you take notice of where you've come from; this is an easy path to miss on the way back. Not all of the large ponderosas on the land you're walking on were killed by the Las Conchas fire. Many were removed because they were badly infested with a parasite known as dwarf mistletoe, which, if not eradicated, could have easily been spread to the young planted trees. You can recognize dwarf mistletoe by its yellow or orange blooms lining the branches of a ponderosa, or, more commonly, by the disfigurement it brings to the tree. Mistletoe sinks a vast network of roots beneath the bark to collect the nutrients it needs, in the process severely interrupting normal growth patterns. Large swelled areas, and clusters of stunted branches known as "witches brooms," are common indicators that the parasite has gained a firm hold. It may take 15 or 20 years for the ponderosa to die, its death often the result of attacks by insects or other infections that gain access to the weakened tree.

A short distance from the last left turn, past some beautiful New Mexico locust trees, you'll reach another fork in the road; stay to the right, on the fainter of the two paths. At this junction you'll have a fine view of the high peaks and ridge lines to the north that make up a small part of the Jemez Mountains, a name derived from a Tanoan Indian word for "the people." This beautiful quilt of high country also happens to embrace the Valles Caldera, the sunken remnants of a crater that, 1.2 million years ago, spewed enormous quantities of magma and ash across the landscape, some of it reaching as far as present-day Kansas. This nearly perfectly circular crater, more than 13 miles across, is located immediately to the north of where you now stand. You can get a fine view of a small portion of it by driving east a short distance on New Mexico 4 (the road you parked on).

Continue walking west through huddles of young aspen and ponderosa, the former straining to claim their place in the sun before one day being edged out by conifers. The road soon begins a gentle descent, and, at 0.9 mile, again enters the mature forest. This is our turnaround point. If you wish, however, you can keep going, as this road continues to amble through the ponderosas a bit longer before it rejoins the fast lanes of Route 4. If you have the time, I'd highly recommend taking a walk on the East Fork Trail, which winds along the beautiful East Fork of the Jemez, now a Wild and Scenic River. To reach this trailhead from where you're now parked, drive west on New Mexico Route 4 for a couple of miles to a newly developed turnout on the right with parking, picnic tables and a restroom. The number of this trail is 137.

WALK #65—SOUTH CREST–SANDIA SUMMIT

DISTANCE:	1.2 miles
ENVIRONMENT:	Mountain
LOCATION:	Cibola National Forest. From the east edge of Albuquerque, head east on Interstate 40 for approximately 10 miles to the intersection with New Mexico Route 14 (exit 175). Follow New Mexico Route 14 north for just under 6 miles, and turn left, following the signs for Sandia Crest. The trail leaves from the south end of the lower parking area, which is about 14 miles from New Mexico 14.

There are very few places you can drive to that will provide such magnificent views as does the Sandia Crest. To the west the world drops like a stone, first through a jumble of granite pinnacles peppered with conifers, then past rocky ledges and chestnut-colored fields of scree, onto sweeping alluvial fans and finally leveling out onto the river-valley floor, nearly 4,000 feet below where you now stand. In the distance is the great sweep of the Rio Grande, drifting ever southward on what may be the greatest, most sun-drenched run of river to be found anywhere in the American Southwest. Along this stretch in 1540 strode Coronado's ruthless explorers, slowly making their way northward to Pecos. There they would meet a captive of the Pueblo Indians who would tell them of a city of gold lying far to the northeast, a tale that in the following spring would lead Coronado, a willing believer, on the wildest goose chase of his career.

As you make your way southeast along the rimrock from the parking area, watch for interpretive signs identifying several common plants, including limber pine, snowberry and lichen. (Note that just south of the concrete walkway and the observation platform, the Crest Trail takes off to the east; you want to continue straight ahead along the rim, following what is known as the Crest Nature Trail.) You could hardly be in a more different world than what you left behind at the base of the Sandias. Piñon and juniper, yucca and prickly pear have been replaced by the sentinels of the high country—limber pine, Engelmann spruce and corkbark fir. This latter tree is a subspecies of subalpine fir, and can be recognized by its short, bluish needles and thick, corky bark.

The magnificent granite towers and buttresses rising below you and off to the west were created as great slabs of rock weathered and finally peeled away along vertical fracture lines. As staggering as it is to comprehend, it took more than a billion years for these granite slabs to form inside the earth, reveal themselves through erosion and then become covered once again by sediments laid down in ancient seas. Elements of those ancient seas can be found all along the upper reaches of the western crest of the Sandias, most notably in the bed of marine limestone lying beneath your feet.

Climb the stairs at 0.2 mile and take a right, and in a very short distance you'll rejoin the Crest Trail; turn right again, following the Crest Trail to the Kiwanis Cabin, a stone shelter built in the late

1930s by the Civilian Conservation Corps. (The Kiwanis Club had erected a log structure here some years before the CCC effort, but it burned to the ground.) From the cabin you can see the upper terminal of the famous Sandia Peak Tramway, lying just 0.7 mile to the north. If you haven't taken this ride, put it at the top of your "to do" list. The feeling one gets hovering over sheer ledges and mammoth tongues of granite, the latter poking out of the earth like the teeth of some primordial beast, is one not soon to be forgotten. For those interested in geology, the tram provides a wonderful study of the western flanks of the Sandia Uplift, taking you from the granite core of the mountain to the limestone cliffs that cap its upper reaches. The brush-covered slopes you see are hiding what's known as the Great Unconformity, which is the boundary between the two formations. On a clear day, from either the Kiwanis Cabin or the upper tramway terminal you can see Mt. Taylor and Cebolleta Mesa far off to the west, 67 and 86 miles away, respectively; to the southwest lie the beautiful, lonely Magdalena Mountains, more than 90 miles distant.

As you leave the Kiwanis Cabin, head downhill away from the rim and slightly back to the north. Within a few hundred feet, still in the trees, you'll come upon the old road that once served the cabin, now a hiking trail in the summer and a cross-country ski route in winter. Turn left here. This road will continue along the upper reaches of Kiwanis meadows for a short distance (meadows, incidentally, that make idyllic lunch spots), from which you can look off into the Sangre de Cristo Mountains and beyond to the Pecos River country far to the east. Eventually the road makes an abrupt dive into a thick, dark spruce-fir forest, much of it peppered with New Mexico maple, snowberry and wolf currant. In places there are aspen trees leaning their supple, white branches over the road, looking every bit as lovely as the New England birches that so pleased poet Robert Frost. During autumn the contrast between the golden aspen leaves and the dark, shadowy branches of Engelmann spruce and corkbark fir is absolutely spectacular.

In 1.2 miles you'll find yourself entering the lower reaches of the Sandia Overlook parking area.

WALK #66—SOUTH CREST TRAIL

DISTANCE: 1.4 miles
ENVIRONMENT: Desert
LOCATION: Cibola National Forest, Canyon Estates Trailhead. From the eastern edge of Albuquerque, head east on Interstate 40 for approximately 10 miles to the Tijeras exit. Near the bottom of the exit ramp, take the left fork, observe the stop sign and then turn left, back under the interstate. Once under the freeway, bear to the right on a marked dead-end road, following it for 0.6 mile through a residential area to a small trailhead parking lot. *Note:* Near the underpass there is also a dirt road heading east, with a "No Outlet" sign; don't take this by mistake.

Although this walk covers only a tiny segment of the 16-mile South Crest Trail, it traverses a classic mix of lower-Sandia plant life; in addition, near the turnaround you'll have the pleasure of seeing the special kind of beauty that can rise in shaded ravines, along slow, cool seeps of spring water. Anyone seeking a short, relaxing walk, or who simply wants to get a bit more familiar with some of the more intriguing regional vegetation and bird life, would do well to head up the South Crest Trail.

Our walk begins in a fine mix of one-seed and Rocky Mountain juniper, prickly pear, piñon pine, mountain mahogany, shrub live and Gambel oaks and broom snakeweed—the plants that, from a distance, bleed together to wash the New Mexico hillsides in those beautiful shades of light to dusky green. Those of you trying to master the various kinds of oak that grow in this area should be aware that these species cross-pollinate rather freely. Because of this, you may well find the leaves of several different species on the same tree!

At about 0.4 mile into the walk, just before the trail crosses a shallow wash, are several nice cholla cacti. If there happens to be a dead cholla nearby, take a closer look at the curious skeletal frame of this plant, a kind of tinker-toy construction made up of hollow, woody tubes pierced by diamond-shaped holes. The branches of most chollas are quite sturdy, and have long been used not only ornamentally, but also as walking sticks, hence one of this cholla's common names, "walking-stick cactus."

Immediately after the wash is a beautiful garden of plants, most notable globemallow, Apache plume, squawbush (so named because Indian women long prized it for basketmaking) and the long, sinewy branches of canyon grape. The tart fruit of this latter plant has long been used for making jellies and preserves; various pueblo cultures actually cultivated canyon grape, harvesting the fruits in July and August and then drying them for later use. This particular stretch of trail, like much of it ahead of you, is also home to a much less coveted plant—poison ivy. Indeed, there are places where the shiny, three-part leaflets and clusters of ivory-colored fruits can be found in abundance, especially on disturbed soils. While birds eat the fruits of poison ivy, most people have some kind of moderate to severe skin reaction if they come into contact with even minute amounts of the plant's toxic urushiol oils. Admire it, especially when in fall it begins to lend gorgeous splashes of scarlet to the woods, but avoid getting too cozy. (Even burning poison ivy is dangerous, as the oils present in the smoke can cause severe irritation of the eyes.) Also, keep in mind that the toxicity of these oils lasts a very long time; in fact, they can survive intact on unwashed clothing and pet fur for months, if not longer. If you do happen to brush up against poison ivy, wash the affected area repeatedly with a strong soap.

At about 0.6 mile the trail will turn west toward the mouth of a lovely shaded ravine. Less than 0.1 mile from this point you'll come upon a perfectly wonderful little oasis, small seeps of water giving rise to a cool tapestry of box elder, canyon grape, juniper, chokecherry, globemallow and the beautiful Gambel oak. The sweet acorns of this latter tree are prize by many forest residents, especially squirrels.

This refreshing little sanctuary is the perfect place to relax on a hot summer day, serenaded by the quiet ooze of water over the rocks, and the whisper of leaves overhead. Also, if you're looking for a bit of color in the fall, you could do worse than to find yourself right here, surrounded by red-tinged oak and poison ivy leaves, and the soft, pale yellows of chokecherry and box elder.

WALK #67—TENT ROCKS
(Area of Critical Environmental Concern)

DISTANCE:	1 mile
ENVIRONMENT:	Desert
LOCATION:	North-central New Mexico, Bureau of Land Management. Head north out of Albuquerque on Interstate 25 for approximately 30 miles. Turn off at the Cochiti Dam exit, head west on New Mexico Route 22, and follow the signs 14.2 miles to Cochiti Pueblo. Turn right at the pueblo water tower, which is painted like a drum, onto Forest Road 266. Follow this road for 6 miles to the parking area for Tent Rocks, on the right. *Note:*All roads and washes leading up to the rock formations are closed to vehicular traffic.

In few places is the ancient fury of the earth more uniquely preserved than in the bizarre collage of buff-colored cones and hoodoos known as Tent Rocks. In fact, so thoroughly distinctive are these formations that for years they have served as favorite backdrops for Hollywood westerns, including *Silverado*, *Young Guns* and *Lonesome Dove*. Indeed, wrapped in the quiet of these rocky folds, nothing moving but a lone hawk hanging on the hot winds of summer, it's easy to imagine that the Old West is still very much alive and well.

Had you been here a million years ago you would have found yourself in the middle of a tremendous volcanic storm, as the mighty Valles Caldera to the northwest spewed ton after ton of fiery ash and rock over the New Mexico landscape. When the smoke finally cleared, debris lay over hundreds of square miles, and in some places, had accumulated to depths of 400 feet.

These layers of debris, composed primarily of pumice and a mixture of volcanic ashes known as tuff, formed the medium from which wind and water would sculpt the Tent Rocks over thousands of years. A key characteristic to note about these formations is that most of the soft, cone-shaped mounds of tuff are capped by hard, erosion-resistant volcanic rock. Many of these mushroom-shaped cap rocks look so precariously balanced that standing here in a good wind, I half expected several of them to topple off of their puny perches. Without these protective caps there would be no Tent Rocks as we see them today, since the underlying tuff would have long ago eroded away. (You can see that a few of the cones farthest away from the cliffs have already lost their caps, and are in various stages of rapid decay. The delicate nature of this rock is why the Bureau of Land Management has asked that you not climb on them.)

At the parking area for Tent Rocks is an interpretive sign highlighting the geology of these formations. Immediately behind this sign is a primitive trail that you can follow up to the base of the rocks. The trail is framed with vegetation typical of this stretch of high desert, including one-seed juniper, piñon pine, Apache plume, paintbrush, rabbitbrush, narrowleaf yucca and trailing four o'clock.

At the first fork in the wash, keep to the right, climbing up to the base of the Tent Rocks. From here you'll have a fine view of Cochiti Pueblo, as well as the jumble of mountains and mesas to the south and east. In certain parts of the United States, in particular the Northeast, much is made of the chance to sample slices of history 300 years old. But Cochiti Pueblo has been in its present site for more than 700 years! Before that the people lived in a vast network of cliff dwellings and pueblos to the north, at what is today Bandelier National Monument.

In the beginning of the 17th century, both the Spanish government and the Catholic church were more than a little eager to maintain a presence in this part of the Southwest—the former in order to keep foreigners well away from the rich Mexican silver mines, and the latter to continue the already well-entrenched business of saving souls. While the Franciscan fathers strenuously objected to the stealing of Pueblo people like the Cochitis to be used as slaves in the silver mines, they also had no tolerance for any culture that would not abandon its former religious practices for Catholicism. Those who continued to dabble in traditional worship were often whipped, or in the case of shamans or medicine men, hanged for being servants of Satan.

Years of such oppression eventually led to a fierce Pueblo uprising in the summer of 1680, a battle in which the Cochiti people played an important part. As the Spaniards fled southward, the Indians wasted no time in ridding the land of all sign of their presence; at Cochiti Pueblo, the people burned the mission church to the ground. Legend has it that at the start of this uprising, a wounded priest fell to his knees at the foot of the mountains east of here, and prayed to God for a sign of the future. At that moment the mountains above him turned a brilliant red. It was the blood of Christ, the priest concluded, the Sangre de Cristo. This vision supposedly assured the Spaniards that the Catholic church would one day return, which it in fact did a dozen years later; what's more, an arm of the southern Rocky Mountains—the Sangre de Cristo Range—was given the name by which it is still known today. (Many historians discount this tale, saying that name originated with a group of religious zealots called the Penitentes, who lived in the area during the early 1800s.)

When you reach the base of Tent Rocks, work your way northwestward along the face of the Tents, taking time now and then to wander back into the twisted clefts and ravines. One plant commonly seen in these ravines, as well as growing from cracks in the cliff face, is greenleaf manzanita. The word *manzanita* means "little apple," and the spring crop of urn-shaped, white to pink flowers is indeed followed by fruits that taste more than a little like apples. Manzanita fruit has long been an important staple of the American Indians of the Southwest, especially in California, where several varieties of the plant grow in profusion. Herbalists today continue to relish a cider made by scalding the fruit, pulverizing it and then adding equal amounts of water. Those who would try such fare, however, should keep in mind that for some people manzanita fruit leads to serious constipation. (Those interested in harvesting manzanita fruits should do it in locations less visited than Tent Rocks.)

When you've finished your trek along the face of the Tent Rocks, you can either return the way you came, or drop down and return via the road. Whatever route you choose, keep your eyes on the sky for glimpses of a red-tailed hawk or an American kestrel, both of which are commonly seen soaring above Peralta Canyon. Though the American kestrel was for years known as a sparrow hawk, that was a misleading name, since this smallest of the falcons feeds on mice and insects far more often than it does sparrows. When hunting, the kestrel may hang almost completely motionless in the air, floating as if by magic in the blue New Mexico sky.

WALK #68—APACHE SPRING

DISTANCE: 3 miles
ENVIRONMENT: Forest
LOCATION: Santa Fe National Forest. The trailhead for this walk is located on the south side of New Mexico Route 4, 1.7 miles west of the point where the route splits, one going to Los Alamos, the other going to Bandelier National Monument. (Also located at this road split is Ponderosa Group Campground.) The trail is along a fire road, closed off by a gate a short distance from the highway. Because thick timber makes the trailhead and small parking area very difficult to see, I recommend pulling off of the highway 35 yards east of the trail, where Forest Road 181 takes off to the north.

Just a few miles south of this beautiful forest the land dances to a much drier song. In fact, standing down there in that landscape of sheer rock, surrounded by pastel canyons that have been carved from volcanic ash and pumice, it is almost impossible to imagine that such a rich forest could be so close at hand. For many creatures, life in the West flows with the rise and fall of mountains. Plant communities change quite rapidly as you climb, a thousand vertical feet of mountain being equivalent, as far as the vegetation is concerned, to a northward trek of several hundred miles. The ancient Indian peoples in the Bandelier region knew this well. They chose to live in the lowlands for the warmth and longer growing season such regions offered, but regularly came to these mountains to hunt large game, to gather the nuts of the pines and oaks and to harvest the sturdy logs of ponderosa to use in construction.

Our walk begins in a fine collection of white fir, aspen, ponderosa and a smattering of Gambel oak. These last two trees, by the way, were very important to early peoples of this region, the former providing seeds which could be ground into bread, while the latter produced acorns that were less bitter-tasting than those of other oaks. (All acorns, however, were leached in water to remove tannic acids before using them in mush, breads, etc.)

Because the ponderosa dominates the show here, this is a perfect chance for you to get to know this stately giant a little better. Its rough, cinnamon-colored bark is assembled in layers of a thousand shapes, like the pieces of an impossibly complicated jigsaw puzzle. All sorts of imaginary creatures can be found clinging to one of these trunks. Some of the larger ponderosas in this forest may be over 350 years old, having begun their stretch toward the sky about the same time a fellow named Rembrandt was busy creating masterpieces.

At 0.25 mile the road makes a smooth right turn. Before you is one of the finest mixed-conifer meadows you're ever likely to set eyes on. At the east end, an old logworm fence snakes through the tall grass, with a pair of absolutely remarkable white firs standing sentinel on either side of the road, the two bluish green skyscrapers forming a striking portal to the meadow beyond. You may see red squirrels, or at least hear their incessant chattering here, as they go about the business of collecting nuts, as well as the occasional bird egg.

At 0.5 mile you'll reach a road junction. Our route, which may or may not be signed, is the more well-worn path taking off to the right. While on the out-bound walk this junction shouldn't cause any particular problems, be careful on your return that you don't let a pleasant forest stupor cause you to miss the proper route. With this turn you'll have gained a drier, more exposed ridge sporting a more homogeneous growth of ponderosa, as well as a couple of beautiful stretches of New Mexico locust. In early summer this latter plant produces soft, satiny clusters of light pink flowers that can halt the most hurried traveler. These blooms, as well as the seeds that come on during autumn, were common sources of food for Native Americans of the region.

By the time you've walked a mile you can see a few signs of the 1977 La Mesa fire, a violent, man-caused inferno that took 2,000 firefighters eight days to control, but not before it burned more than 15,000 acres of forest. Throughout the 20th century firefighters suppressed nearly every forest fire they could get their hands on. This aggressive policy actually resulted in a tremendous buildup of deadwood. If a forest then did catch fire under dry conditions, like this one did, there was simply no stopping it. (Firefighters reported flames in the La Mesa fire of 150 feet!) To avoid such disasters happening again, today's foresters carefully burn accumulated downfall. This also tends to return valuable nutrients to the soil, and promotes the growth of ground plants that produce good graze for wildlife.

This does not, of course, excuse careless handling of fire by man. Controlled fires and haphazard burns with no supervision are two very different things. Being careful with fire seems especially appropriate in New Mexico. In case you didn't know, south of here in the Lincoln National Forest, a small bear was rescued in 1950 when a 17,000-acre forest fire obliterated his home in the Capitan Mountains. After being treated in Santa Fe for severe burns, the little bruin went on to some rather great things, most notable of which was his being christened with the name "Smokey the Bear" (yes, Virginia, there really *is* a Smokey). The scars from Smokey's fire are still visible today, as will be those from this one, for several generations to come.

Pass a roadside strewn with asters, gilia and harebells, and then begin a descent in 1.3 miles that leads to the boundary of the Bandelier Wilderness. From this point make a gentle fall on a forest trail for 0.1 mile, keeping your eyes out at the bottom of the ravine for a very faint pathway taking off to the left. This leads in 40 yards to Apache Springs, surely one of the finest, most relaxing little pockets of greenery to be found anywhere in the state. Surrounding the old

Abert's Squirrel

stone catch basin, which was built by the Civilian Conservation Corps in the mid-1930s, is an absolute wonderland of sights, sounds and smells. There are currants and raspberries, fir and oaks, alders, elders and aspen. Lavender sticky geraniums line the gentle flow of spring water; soft green Rocky Mountain maple leaves shimmer in the afternoon sun. This entire setting, the result of just the right amount of water in a fold of land that has the proper soil and exposure, is a real work of art—that will sustain you for many daydreams to come.

WALK #69—TYUONYI OVERLOOK

DISTANCE: 2.4 miles
ENVIRONMENT: Forest
LOCATION: Bandelier National Monument. Go to the monument, which is located south of the city of Los Alamos. Just past the entrance station, turn right into Juniper Campground. Continue to the campground amphitheater parking lot, located on your left. Our trail takes off from the far side of this parking lot. (The Frey Trail also takes off from here; watch the signs to make sure you're on the right path. Basically, you'll be walking toward the amphitheater. When the trail forks, stay left, and make a horseshoe turn to the left onto the Tyuonyi Overlook Trail.)

This enchanting national monument bears the name of Adolph Bandelier, an ethnologist who spent much of the late 1800s in this area exploring possible connections between Pueblo Indian cultures and the great Meso-American civilizations far to the south. This region of New Mexico contains a plethora of ancient ruin sites, from faint cave remnants west of the Rio Grande River that date back nearly 4,000 years, to the more common stone structures you'll see along this walk, most built between A.D. 1100 and 1500. No one really knows how many archaeological sites Bandelier contains; conservative estimates put the number at about 5,000.

This is a fine, relaxing walk across a finger of the Pajarito Plateau, a small part of the one-million-year-old, 2,000-square-mile volcanic field that forms the fabric from which much of this part of the New Mexico landscape is fashioned. It's thanks to such violent, massive, steaming flows of pumice and volcanic ash (tuff) pouring over the land that this beautiful collection of canyons and cliffs exists today—cliffs that yielded easily to the stone scrapers of early residents, who turned their small, natural pockets and caves into rooms for living and storage.

Your trip will be through a lovely forest of piñon and juniper, sprinkled here and there with handsome ponderosa pine. Depending on the time of the year you walk this path, the open areas are likely to be peppered with the blooms of ground plants like aster, paintbrush, groundsel and broom snakeweed. These latter two plants, when seen in appreciable quantities, are indicators of disturbed soil. Look for their yellow cluster blooms along roadways, trail edges and especially where the land has been overgrazed. (Unfortunately, overgrazed land is never hard to find in the West. One can only sit back and daydream about how the land must have looked 200 years ago, when early explorers were praising much of it for its fine grasses.)

Another plant hard to miss here during midsummer to late summer is mullein, the thick, 2- to 4-foot-tall hairy stems that dot many of the open areas near the trailhead. This biennial was introduced from Europe, and now blankets much of the North American continent. Though not particularly attractive, mullein has an impressive record of use by man. Leaves were sometimes smoked as a tobacco substitute, but unlike tobacco, the leaves of mullein contain elements that Native Americans found to be quite effective in soothing irritated tissues. Some of these chemicals are now found in modern skin-softening lotions. Mullein is at its best in sandy or rocky areas, where few other plants can survive.

Soon the open spaces become fewer, and the path begins meandering through a classic piñon-juniper forest, sporting an occasional ponderosa and mountain mahogany. Piñon, which produces delicious nuts, and juniper form an extensive forest belt between 4,000 feet and 6,500 feet. Stretching for nearly 40,000 square miles, the "p-j" forest can be found from New Mexico and Colorado, south into Texas and Mexico, west into Arizona and Nevada and east to Oklahoma. As you may already know if you've spent much time in this type of forest, these two trees have an uncanny way of growing on you. You never know what beautiful surprises lie waiting around the next tree—a prickly pear with delicate yellow flowers, or a yucca flying a stout staff of rich creamy-white blooms. Birds and small mammals consume the "fruits" (actually cones) of the juniper, while mule deer can often be seen grazing in their protective cover.

Keep going past a partially excavated habitation site, and, about 0.1 mile later, a circular "shrine" thought to have been a place of worship for the early residents of the Pajarito Plateau. Just past this shrine site the trail ends on a promontory, with wonderful views of Frijoles Canyon below, dominated by the long, green fingers of cottonwoods lining El Rito de los Frijoles, and the remarkable ruins of Tyuonyi. This fascinating structure, which contains 250 ground-floor rooms and three kivas, or ceremonial chambers, was constructed in the early 1300s. Adolph Bandelier reported that *Tyuonyi* was a Keres Indian phrase for "place of treaty," which alludes to a long-ago territorial pact between the Keres and their neighbors, the Tewa.

Here at this overlook are one-seed juniper, yucca and beautiful splashes of lichen staining the rocks with delightful colors. Lichen is actually a mix of two plants—an outer coat of fungus forming a protective coating over an inner layer of algal cells.

This is truly a symbiotic relationship where the whole is more durable than the sum of its parts. Lichen can produce food and grow at any temperature over 32 degrees—15 to 20 degrees lower than what most plants can manage. It can store more than its own weight in water, and needs nothing but an occasional splash of dew to keep growing. In short, there is no more hearty form of life to be found anywhere in the American West.

WALK #70—BEAR WALLOW–WINSOR–BORREGO LOOP

DISTANCE: 4 miles
ENVIRONMENT: Mountain
LOCATION: Santa Fe National Forest. From Santa Fe, head east on Artist Road, which becomes Hyde Park Road near the outskirts of town. The trailhead parking area is located just over 8 miles from town, on the north side of the road, opposite mile marker 8. Watch for the highway sign marking "Borrego Trail."

Although this loop trail can be on the busy side, especially on summer weekends, it traverses such an enchanting slice of New Mexico mountainscape that it would be a shame to be in the area and not loose your feet in its cool, green quilt of conifers. Where piñon and juniper were the norm as you made your way out of Santa Fe, here the mountains are draped with white fir, ponderosa, aspen and Douglas fir. The earth is no longer sand-colored but a rich, dark chocolate, nursing a surprising variety of flowers and shrubs. There are small huddles of raspberries, elderberries and strawberries. Oregon grape, kinnikinnick and an occasional Gambel oak hug the drier ground next to the loud red blooms of scarlet gilia. The leaves of Rocky Mountain maple and box elder whisper in the shaded, moist canyons; snowberry, sticky geranium and baneberry listen nearby.

So why this sudden richness, this grand diversity, when hardly a stone's throw away the strings of life are pulled by a much more Spartan hand? For one thing, there is more moisture here. Also, temperatures, as you have probably noticed, are lower. These two factors, one tightly bound to the other, both depend on a common master—the mountains themselves. When air systems being pushed across the landscape reach the high country, there is nowhere for them to go but up. As they climb, they enter cooler and cooler temperatures—roughly three degrees cooler for every thousand feet they ascend. Cool air cannot hold as much moisture in it as warm air can, so as air rises and cools, some of the moisture it contains may well have to be released in the form of rain and snow.

There are many days you can be standing in a sunny New Mexico desert and watch afternoon clouds grow thick and heavy over nearby mountain peaks.

More moisture leads to more bacterial activity in the soil, which means more nutrients to feed more plants. But even in a mountain garden like this one you'll find that plants have evolved into fairly specific niches, composed of complicated combinations of soil and sunlight. An aspen forest eventually loses the race to firs and spruce simply because the latter trees can reproduce well in shade, whereas the aspen cannot. Scarlet gilias grow in open, gravelly areas, but sticky geraniums don't. Ponderosa and Gambel oak do well on dry, exposed ground, which is why you often see them together, but Rocky Mountain maple and box elder wouldn't think of setting up shop there.

As you walk, stop and study the great diversity of plant communities you see here. Notice the effects of added sunlight where trees have been cut for the trail, how stream bottoms compare to south-facing slopes, what plants do well on gravelly or sandy soil compared to those on the acidic floor of the pine forest. Besides being beautiful to behold, you'll find this mountain forest to be an incredible slice of evolution—a design of incalculable complexity.

In 0.5 mile you'll reach our first fork, where the Borrego Trail joins the Bear Wallow. Head left here, following the Bear Wallow on a gentle descent to Big Tesuque Creek. Creamy-white aspen trunks seem to almost glow in the deep greens of the spruce-fir forest. Strawberries and an occasional baneberry line the path, with lavender asters and harebell nodding in the breeze. This latter plant, by the way, shows remarkable adaptability. In moist conditions it grows quite tall and sports numerous beautiful, blue, bell-shaped flowers. Yet if a harebell seed's fate is to end up on a drier, south-facing patch of ground, it makes the best of it by reducing height and leaf size, and keeping the blooms to only one or two.

At 1.5 miles from the trailhead you'll reach Big Tesuque Creek. (*Tesuque*, by the way, is a corruption of a Tewa Indian word meaning roughly "spotted dry place." The name refers to the location of Tewa Pueblo north of Santa Fe, where in places the creek sinks into the sand and then reappears again. Up here in the mountains, though, Big Tesuque runs strong and free.) Immediately after crossing the creek you'll take a right onto the Winsor

Trail. From here the path is pretty much all uphill, so plan to take your time and enjoy the sights along the way.

There are several raspberry plants along this stretch of the walk as well as thimbleberries, mullein, Oregon grape and, in late summer and early fall, the strikingly beautiful blooms of the Hooker evening primrose. This latter plant produces a beautiful, large, yellow blossom that typically blooms in the evening, and will have withered away by the afternoon of the following day. The plant contains a substance that has long been used in the treatment of asthma.

After roughly 1 mile of walking upstream along Big Tesuque Creek you'll come to a trail junction, marked by two wooden posts which may or may not have signs on them. Turn right here toward a crossing of Big Tesuque. This is the Borrego Trail, which as late as the 1930s was a primary route for trailing sheep to market in Santa Fe from settlements to the north. Some of the large aspen you'll pass on this part of the walk still bear inscriptions of the shepherds who routinely made this trek. This region is woven with one of the most engaging historical fabrics to be found anywhere in the United States. Santa Fe itself was established by Pedro de Peralta in 1609, just two years after the fledgling colony of Jamestown was established in Virginia. (Albuquerque was still a hundred years away.) Santa Fe was considered a villa (a larger version of a pueblo), established by the acting provincial governor. There was no ownership of land; each person was allotted a house lot and enough acreage for a small farm, all by favor of the king. Lands immediately surrounding the villa were considered common areas.

It was more than two centuries following Santa Fe's founding, after a troubled Spain finally let loose of the lands that would become an independent Mexico, that traders began pouring into the region from the edge of the American frontier with tools, shoes, fabrics and woolens—much to the delight of Santa Fe residents. It was one of these commercial wagon trains, rolling over what would become the famous Santa Fe Trail, that brought a 16-year old boy named Kit Carson to Santa Fe in 1826.

Again, the majority of your walk along the Borrego Trail is indeed a climb, so slow down your pace and really enjoy this beautiful forest community. Steller's jays, mountain chickadees, hermit thrushes and western tanagers will be cheering you on.

WALK #71—ASPEN VISTA

DISTANCE: 1.6 miles
ENVIRONMENT: Mountain
LOCATION: Santa Fe National Forest. From Santa Fe, head east on Artist Road, which becomes Hyde Park Road near the outskirts of town. We'll be walking along a dirt road that takes off from Aspen Vista Picnic Area, located on your right, just past mile marker 13. (This is actually a service road leading in 6 miles to a microwave station at the top of Tesuque Peak; a sign at the beginning of the gated road reads "Not for Public Use." This does not, however, pertain to people on foot.)

The name of the picnic area from which this walk begins aptly describes the trail itself—aspen, and more aspen. To meander along this road at virtually any time of the year will leave you with a new appreciation for this most widely distributed of all North American trees. Walking it in late September or early October, when trembling leaves are shimmering like gold coins in the autumn sun, can leave you breathless. Before you actually set out, stop for a moment at the picnic area vista point. On a clear day you can see one mountain ridge after another falling away in soft green walls, broken in the distance by a large valley, which is backed by yet another line of mountains so far away that they almost seem painted on the distant sky.

The "quaking" in the name quaking aspen refers to the leaves, which you'll almost never find completely at rest. A flat-tened, slightly twisted stem near the point where it joins the leaf is the cause of this trembling, though other, more colorful explanations abound. One of these, for instance, says that aspen wood was used for the cross of Christ, an event that caused all aspen around the world to begin trembling.

Aspen is commonly referred to as a *pioneer* tree, which means that it is among the first plants to reclaim land that has been disturbed by fire, logging or even avalanches. Aspen produce clones, or suckers, from common underground rootstems. Because rootstems are usually not damaged by whatever disturbance moves through an area, they are always available to send up a new batch of trees as quickly as possible. (This tendency to produce many trees off of a common rootstem is why in the fall you'll often see distinct blocks of aspen turning the same color at the same rate.) Aspen, however, like most pioneer species, are very intolerant of shade. If there is no further disruption of the normal growth cycle, aspen will eventually be replaced by spruce and fir, a few of which are poking their dark green branches up from among this sea of soft white trunks.

During the first stretch of roadway you'll be in a very young aspen forest. But by 0.5 mile into the walk you will have entered a grove of young adults (30- to 40-year-olds)—the age at which such groves become truly places of wonder. Here the lower trunks of the trees are smooth and leafless. After a time they begin growing in more and more open patterns, looking like thin towers of porcelain rising out of a rich, green carpet of grass. There is a strange, eerie complexion to such a woodland; a deep, haunting beauty that stretches on and on, ultimately melting away into a wall of summer shadows.

Aspen, of course, are not the only residents you'll see here. Watch for the large, maple-like leaves of thimbleberries growing along the road, as well as Bebb willow and Rocky Mountain maple. Yarrow, harebell and asters are also in good supply, as are occasional

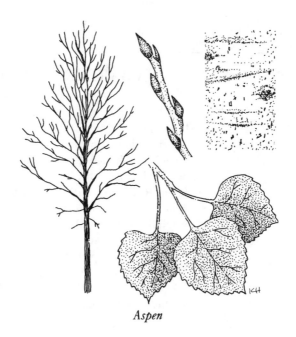

Aspen

red splashes of scarlet gilia, growing in the drier, more open areas along the road.

You'll reach the North Fork of Tesuque Creek in just 0.8 mile. This fine little stream makes a sprightly tumble through the woodland, giving rise to an even greater array of moisture-loving wildflowers. Small paths can be found on either side of the road that meander along the creek into fine pockets of hushed forest.

Yarrow

WALK #72—SANTA BARBARA TRAIL

DISTANCE: 4.4 miles
ENVIRONMENT: Mountain
LOCATION: Carson National Forest. From the intersection of New Mexico Routes 75 and 73 in the town of Peñasco, head south along New Mexico Route 73. South of this intersection 1.5 miles, Forest Road 116 will take off to the left. Follow it southward 4.6 miles to the trailhead, which is adjacent to a campground. There is a large parking area on the left before you actually reach the campground. Park here; our trail (No. 24) takes off opposite this parking area.

These spectacular mountains, running south out of Colorado along the eastern flank of the Rio Grande Valley, have been significant to European man for nearly 300 years. It was the collection of streams and rivulets born within the folds of these peaks that allowed early Spaniards to settle in the region, shaping a string of small corn-, fruit- and grazing-based communities that persist even today. The name of this range is the Sangre de Cristo, or "blood of Christ." One legend says that the range was named by a priest fleeing for his life during the Pueblo uprising of 1680. In the midst of a desperate plea to God for some kind of sign, he supposedly looked up and saw these peaks turning a rich red, a color that immediately reminded him of the blood of Christ. As intriguing as this tale is, many historians say the name didn't show up until the early 1800s, first used by a group of zealous Christians known as the Penitentes. In fact, Penitente Peak is one of the more lovely of the region's mountains, located a dozen miles northeast of the capital city of Santa Fe. Whatever explanation you happen to believe, there's no question that these peaks form one of New Mexico's most magnificent mountainscapes.

Up the trail 0.2 mile the path drops down from its perch above Santa Barbara Campground into a lovely quilt of mountain forest. On the left is an open meadow dotted with asters, harebell, paintbrush, groundsel and fine mats of grass, while the slope on the

Mountain Chickadee

right sports Engelmann spruce, common juniper, white fir and Rocky Mountain maple. The fir and spruce here form what is known as the climax forest, a shade-tolerant mixture of conifers that are ultimately bent on overtaking the smattering of milky-white aspen you see here today.

As you walk along this stretch of trail, keep your ears and eyes open for mountain chickadees, olive-sided flycatchers, mountain bluebirds, pine siskins, gray-headed juncos and ruby-crowned kinglets. Keep in mind that even if you're not able to get clear views of these common birds (often a problem in a conifer forest), you can usually make some good guesses as to their identity by watching their feeding behaviors. Due to their small size, kinglets are able to feed on the very ends of conifer branches. Olive-sided flycatchers, on the other hand, will typically catch their meals of winged insects from the tops of the pines, and not the lower branches. If you don't hear the unmistakable "chick-a-dee-dee-dee," you might recognize a mountain chickadee from its tendency to flit through the tree looking for insects with amazing speed, often hanging upside down in the process.

The beautiful Rio Santa Barbara joins the path about 0.45 mile into the walk. (This stream, by the way, which drains the high Sangre de Cristos to the south, takes its name from a large land grant which was ceded by the King of Spain to 42 petitioners in

False Hellebore

Olive-sided Flycatcher

1796. Much of the private land in new Mexico was obtained in just this way, with many grants still intact.) After joining Rio Santa Barbara you'll find the pathway lined with thimbleberries, ferns and an occasional clump of Oregon grape. This latter plant, especially beautiful when its leaves turn red in autumn, actually grows from a long, sinewy stem running just beneath the ground, hence its species name *repens*, which means "creeping." Native Americans made a beautiful yellow dye from Oregon grape, commonly used for coloring both baskets and clothing.

You'll also see a good collection of willow growing along the stream. This was yet another very valuable plant to Native Americans, who routinely used the inner bark to treat fevers and headaches, and the branches for willow mats and for general construction. The willow is also one of the favorite foods of that spectacular engineer, the beaver. In fact, at just over 0.5 mile you'll spot the remnants of an old willow-branch beaver dam still holding back water. Appropriately, these flooded areas create environments that are perfect for the growth of—you guessed it—more willow.

At 1.2 miles into the walk you'll reach the border of the Pecos Wilderness, a quarter-million-acre slice of mountain country lined with braids of cool streams and shimmering blue lakes. Shortly after entering the wilderness you'll cross the Rio Santa Barbara on a footbridge, entering an even lusher forest corridor, replete with moss-covered rocks and logs, as well as harebell, strawberry and dogbane. The whole feeling changes here, as if the border of the wilderness was some kind of magic gateway. There is an untrammeled, rugged beauty to this stretch of trail; the stream is suddenly framed by towering scarps of sedimentary rock, and giant spruce lie toppled across the watercourse, ever so slowly being turned back to soil by the rains and snows of the high country.

At 2.2 miles you'll reach the junction of the West Fork Trail. Continue past this intersection on the right fork for about 50 yards. Here you'll find a lovely meadow framed to the east by a ribbon of towering fir and spruce, and beyond that, a sheer, soaring ridge of mountain that absolutely sings of the Sangre de Cristo high country. In summer this meadow will be dotted with the white flower clusters of yarrow, the green spikes of false hellebore and the lavender petals of harebell. The stream can be reached by crossing this meadow, descending through a grove of young aspen suckers and dropping down to yet another low bench, perhaps 100 yards from the West Fork Trail. This stream bank is a wonderful rest spot, thick with the sound of bird song and water, as well as the sight of spruce and fir clinging to a ragged jumble of sheer rockfaces. Truly, it is a Rocky Mountain collage of the highest, most unforgettable order.

WALK #73—AGUA PIEDRA CREEK

DISTANCE: 2.2 miles

ENVIRONMENT: Mountain

LOCATION: Carson National Forest. From New Mexico Route 518 west of Tres Ritos, turn south on a dirt road 0.1 mile west of mile marker 51. Just after crossing a bridge over the Rio Pueblo, turn left and follow the road to another bridge, this one crossing Agua Piedra Creek. Park here. The walk begins by heading south through a meadow.

It has been nearly 450 years since Hernando de Alvarado, an officer under the infamous Spanish explorer Francisco Coronado, pushed into this part of New Mexico on his tireless search for the fabled "Quivera." At the time, Quivera was used to denote a region of immense wealth lying somewhere north of Mexico. This was basically an extension of the Spaniards' earlier fantasies about seven golden cities, which in the end turned out to be no more than a cluster of Zuni Indian pueblos located in what is now the state of Arizona. It was south of here about 40 miles, near the town of Pecos, that Alvarado met an Indian whom he dubbed "El Turco," or "the Turk," for his distinctive facial features. El Turco assured Alvarado that such a region of riches did, in fact, exist, but far to the northeast of where he was searching. After a bitter winter spent near present-day Bernalillo, Coronado himself took command of the expedition with El Turco as guide, confident that he was at last on the brink of finding fabulous wealth. As it turned out, El Turco's story was a ruse, likely dreamed up to lure the oppressive Spaniards away from the Pueblo villages. After two months of aimless wandering through the empty Kansas prairie, Coronado caught on. El Turco was ordered put to death, and the Spaniards returned to their New Mexico headquarters. By the following spring the natives had grown truly restless, and Coronado decided it was time to head back to Mexico.

Thanks to short bursts of tenacious resistance by the Pueblo Indians, more than 150 years passed before the Spaniards were able to establish safe, permanent settlements in New Mexico. To meet the needs of settlers who pouring in from the south, a land-grant system was developed. Tracts of varying size were granted either to individuals or groups by the King of Spain, a process conducted by his regional governors. On this road you'll be walking through the old Santa Barbara Grant, made to a group of petitioners in 1796. In the same year, far to the northeast, John Adams and Thomas Jefferson would take on the jobs of president and vice-president of the United States.

After crossing a short stretch of meadow you'll find yourself in a fine forest, a few clumps of mature aspen lending lovely shimmers of light green to the darker, wilder complexion of spruce and fir. In 0.25 mile you'll rub elbows with Agua Piedra ("rocky water") Creek, along which a completely different array of life is found. Here on these cool, moist banks are a few water birch, as well as healthy stands of willow, alder and mountain maple. The seeds of these latter two plants are an important food source for birds, a great many of which can be seen and heard along this drainage in the wee hours of the morning. You can also catch splashes of yellow, purple and pale lavender here in the monkeyflowers, harebells and sticky geraniums that dot much of the stream bank. Sticky geraniums, by the way, are a favorite food of the many deer that make this forest home.

Speaking of deer, a small meadow on the right just past your first stream crossing is a particularly good place to watch these beautiful creatures graze during late evening. Although the number of "points" on a male deer's antlers (which, by the way, are shed each year) is not an exact indicator of how old the animal is, in the early years they can serve as a good guide. Born in June or July, males will show no antlers their first fall. By the second autumn of their lives, two short points may be visible, and by the third, some will show three or even four very light points. For many of the following years, however, the deer may continue to show only those four points, though much more prominently than when they first appeared.

After 0.5 mile you'll see a collection of aspen growing leaves only at their tops, like a cluster of frizzled artist's brushes dipped in green paint and left standing upright. This fairly common phenomenon speaks of the aspen's need for direct sunlight, a preference that eventually will cause them to be replaced by the more shade-tolerant spruce and fir trees growing nearby.

In just over 0.8 mile you'll come to a fork in the trail. Follow the right branch, which will double back along Agua Piedra Creek, now thick with maple, thimbleberry and wild rose. Through the trees you can catch glimpses of a high line of forested mountains to the north, spiked by Gallegos and La Cueva peaks. The term *La Cueva*, incidentally (Spanish for "the cave"), refers to a region southeast of here pocked with shallow caves. An ancient legend says that it was from the mouths of these caves that the Keres-speaking Indian cultures, dating back to the 14th century, first entered this world.

Soon the roadway veers away from the stream, toward our turnaround point in a huddle of aspen sprouting from a thick, lush carpet of bracken fern. The underground rootstems of bracken spread over large areas, a single plant giving rise to several leaf systems. In early autumn, after the first major frost, they will turn a beautiful shade of pale salmon-orange. In large bracken communities like this one, the effect is absolutely magical—a collection of fairy feather-dusters standing at attention, ready to whisk away the aspen leaves that, in a matter of weeks, will begin raining down in showers of gold.

WALK #74—EL NOGAL TRAIL

DISTANCE: 1 mile
ENVIRONMENT: Forest
LOCATION: Carson National Forest. Heading southeast out of Taos on U.S. Highway 64, El Nogal is the first picnic ground you'll come to in the Carson National Forest. Our trail takes off just to the left (east) of the entrance to the picnic area, crossing a wooden bridge over Rio Fernandez de Taos. Once over the bridge, turn left.

For those who are unfamiliar with the classic braid of riparian and piñon-juniper life zones that paint so much of the New Mexico landscape, this small Forest Service trail is a fine place to make acquaintances. The first few feet of the walk are along a beautiful streamside collection of mountain alder and lanceleaf and narrowleaf cottonwood. This latter tree was actually discovered far to the north by Lewis and Clark during their famous trek to the Pacific in 1804 to 1805. All cottonwoods, as well as poplars, willow and aspen, contain varying degrees of chemicals that are closely related to today's aspirin. Indeed, Native Americans have for centuries used teas made from the bark of cottonwoods to reduce fever and inflammation.

The change as you step even a few feet away from Rio Fernandez de Taos (also known as Taos Creek) is a remarkably abrupt one. Where a few feet back the land was thick with trees and grasses, now there is sage and rabbitbrush, along with a few clumps of rice and blue grama grass clinging to the sandy soil. These plants also were, and to some degree still are, important to the Native

Americans who call this region home. Rabbitbrush, for instance (its name alludes to the fact that rabbits find it quite tasty), has been used for centuries to produce a beautiful yellow dye, while its branches were used to weave baskets. The sagebrush you see here has been widely used as both a stomach tonic and as a treatment for worms. This is definitely *not* the kind of sage that has traditionally been used as a cooking herb. Try a few healthy pinches on your next baked chicken, and I guarantee you'll end up ordering out for pizza!

Continuing your climb, you'll soon be at the fringes of a lovely piñon and juniper woodland. These two trees are truly signature species of the southwest uplands. Often found growing in tandem like this, they cover millions of acres in Utah, Arizona and New Mexico. Juniper has been used in sacred ceremonies of regional Indian peoples for centuries. Piñon, on the other hand, is most recognized for its sweet edible nuts, easy to find in local food markets in the fall. Because man was hardly the only creature that relished the nuts of the piñon—deer, jays, squirrels, bears and packrats go out of their way for them—Indian people often collected the cones in late summer before they were ripe, and then heated them in fire pits to melt the binding resin and release the nuts. The gathering of piñons was a major family event; there is

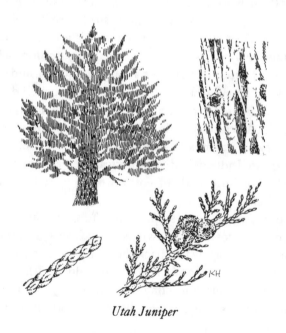

Utah Juniper

some evidence suggesting that entire village sites were located according to their proximity to healthy piñon groves.

On the back side of this loop is a small rest area that affords wonderful views toward Taos and the Rio Grande Valley to the west. From this perch the stage for what has been a staggering amount of history is clearly visible. The Rio Grande, or "great river," has been the site of intrigue from the time that Juan de Onate, leading a sizable group of Mexican colonists, first took possession of its "meadow grounds, pastures and passes" for the glory of the King of Spain in 1598. This is a lonely, hauntingly beautiful river, born in the rugged high country of the San Juan Mountains of southern Colorado. From there it tumbles over 1,800 miles through the length of New Mexico (the only river to do so), along the western edge of Texas and finally into the Gulf of Mexico.

The town of Taos, on the other hand, located just a few miles from where you now stand, is no less enticing. Its name being, perhaps, a corruption of a Tewa Indian word meaning "red willow place," Taos was settled nearly 375 years ago, three years before the Pilgrims set foot on Plymouth Rock. For two centuries the Taos trade fairs were frequented by a variety of Indian, French and, much later, American traders. In the late 1800s and early 1900s this village, like its neighbor Santa Fe, blossomed into a unique haven for well-known artists and writers.

As you make your way westward along this high bench, take a minute to notice the vegetation on the other side of the highway. While of the same piñon-juniper mix, there is obviously a wider spacing among the trees. This is due to the fact that they are growing on a south-facing slope, which offers much greater exposure to the drying effects of the sun. While the same amount of rain and snow falls on both sides of the highway, the one you are walking on is simply able to hold onto it longer, which means that it can support a greater density of plant life. It is in large measure these nuances of exposure, along with the dramatic rise and fall of plain and mountain, that allow the intricate threads of life to weave their magic into this singularly beautiful landscape.

WALK #75—POLICARPIO CANYON

DISTANCE: 1.5 miles
ENVIRONMENT: Forest
LOCATION: Carson National Forest. Heading east on New Mexico Route 518, turn left (east) onto Forest Road 76, 0.4 mile east of mile marker 50. Proceed for 3.6 miles to a small road taking off to the right. Follow this road across a bridge to another road taking off to the left. Turn left and park; begin walking east on this latter road.

I hesitate to even suggest a trail that is also open to all-terrain vehicles. (Woods walking with motorcycles is about as satisfying as waltzing to Muzak.) Yet those who can get on this trail early in the morning, or on an off-season weekday, will find that it traces a most enchanting line through the best of the forested Sangre de Cristo high country.

Our walk begins in a fine spruce-fir forest, with adjacent nooks and crannies peppered with beautiful mature aspen. Right now these aspen are in the glory years that come before they yield the stage to the more shade-tolerant conifers growing nearby. By 0.2 mile into the walk Rocky Mountain maple, common juniper and an occasional blue spruce and alder have joined the scene, along with a lovely quilt of streamside wildflowers, including sticky geranium, false Solomonseal, violets, groundsels, harebells and penstemons.

Such rich forests also give rise to a fine collection of birds and mammals. One of the easiest creatures to spot, or at least hear, in this forest is the chickaree, or red squirrel. (Red squirrels are found from here to Alaska, and east to the Carolinas. In the intermountain West, however, they are not red at all, but rather gray with a slight tinge of rust.) It is most often this industrious little nut lover that you'll hear scolding you as you pass beneath the branches of Engelmann spruce. While you'll have no trouble hearing the chickaree, it's not always so easy to spot. Better to look for the piles of pine cones and scales—called middens—that are its signature. Because many generations of chickarees live in the same place, some of these midden piles may grow to a foot or more deep and be 20 to 25 feet across! Besides being eating grounds, middens serve as storage places where chickarees often store unopened cones in the loose, moist soils; the coolness of the pile helps keep the cones unopened for future meals. Abandoned middens are excellent places to find the small, ground-hugging plant known as kinnikinnick, which Indians mixed with red-osier dogwood bark to make a popular smoking mixture. Chickarees nest in the forks of conifers, or, if possible, in hollow logs and tree holes abandoned by woodpeckers. Young are born in May or early June, and nurse through midsummer.

Of course, where there are chickarees there also will be found those animals who prey on them. In this forest that typically comes down to one of three predators: martens, coyotes or gray foxes. Of these, the marten is the most troublesome to the chickaree, since this beautiful, weasel-shaped mammal is as perfectly adept at

Coyote

maneuvering through trees as is the red squirrel himself. This, combined with the fact that martens will often eat 30 percent of their total body weight each day, hardly makes them a welcome sight for the chattering chickaree. Other mammals in the immediate area include bobcat, striped skunk, raccoon and mule deer; the muddy ground next to Policarpio Creek makes an excellent place to look for their tracks.

Continue climbing gently, through gardens of wildflowers and conifers laced with stringy fronds of goat's beard. You'll find the still pools and shallow rapids of the nearby stream to be perfect places to find dippers, or, as they are known in Great Britain, water ouzels. What these mountain birds lack in color, they more than make up for in charm. The dipper feeds on insects found at the bottom of streams, and to that end spares no effort to obtain them. In deeper rapids and pools you can often see them nimbly swimming with half-outstretched wings, a graceful display that should serve as an inspiration to competitive aqua dancers everywhere. Occasionally the dipper will stop on a rock and—what else?—dip! This unexplainable behavior consists of a delightful series of bobs, making the bird appear to be dancing to some catchy music, unavailable to human ears.

At 0.75 mile the trail climbs up and away from the stream into a fine meadow fringed by mountain ridges clad with dark green

Red Squirrel

Dipper

blankets of conifer. This is our turnaround point. Notice the dramatic difference in vegetation in this more exposed pocket of high country. Here the streamside plants have been traded for those that are satisfied to sink their feet into somewhat drier soil. Besides a wonderful array of grasses, look for yarrow and the beautiful yellow flowers of shrubby cinquefoil, which is an excellent plant to stabilize easily eroded soil. The name *cinquefoil*, by the way, is a French term meaning "five leaves." If you look closely, you'll find they extend in five segments, somewhat like the spread fingers of a human hand.

Northeastern New Mexico

WALK #76—MILLS CANYON OVERLOOK

DISTANCE:	3.6 miles
ENVIRONMENT:	Prairie
LOCATION:	Kiowa National Grassland. From U.S. Highway 56, head south on New Mexico Route 39 for approximately 14 miles. At 0.8 mile south of mile marker 125, a signed road will take off to the west toward the Mills Canyon Campground. Then, 5.4 miles from this turn you'll see a windmill on the right (north) side of the road. Continue past this for 0.6 mile more (a total, then, of 6 miles from New Mexico Route 39) and park. If you look off to the south you'll see a small two-track road heading up the side of a hill on the other side of a wash, perhaps 50 yards from where you're parked. This is our walking road.

Mills Canyon is a beautiful interruption in the otherwise smooth, gently undulating prairie. The old stock roadway leading to the rim, the first 50 yards of which has now been reclaimed by shortgrass, is a classic middle-of-nowhere walk, where the sheer enormity of the land and sky tends to shepherd you into an unhurried cadence, pulling your attention away from any particular destination and into the thick of the journey itself.

This mental drifting is made all the more delightful knowing that you are walking very close to the Cimarron Cut-off branch of the old Santa Fe Trail. Though drier than the original mountain passage to the north, the Cimarron Cut-off was substantially shorter and flatter, two attributes which quickly turned it into a principal travel route. Once you've gained the first ridge on this walk, turn around and look across the vast prairie to the southeast.

What an incredible sight those long lines of blue-painted Conestoga freight wagons must have made, their iron-tired wooden wheels creaking along beneath the weight of brightly colored mackinaw blankets, metal tools and bolts of calico and silk, the sound of the bullwhacker's whip snapping in the hot, dry air.

Two plants you'll see during the short descent to the wash from where you parked are gumweed and snakeweed, the latter with clusters of small, yellow flowers growing on shrubby, narrow-leafed stems, and the former with 1-inch-wide disk-shaped flowers surrounded by sticky, curled green bracts. Both of these plants can thrive on disturbed or overgrazed land. Though snakeweed tends to be somewhat cyclical in nature, an over-abundance of the plant is to some degree a testimony to the general decline in the quality of many lands in this region over the past two centuries, as years of overgrazing destroyed the mat of buffalo and grama grasses that once made up the shortgrass prairie.

Working your way up the hill on the other side of the wash, you'll find a couple places where the road is very faint. Once on top of the ridge, however, the track becomes easy to follow again, and remains so for the rest of the walk. As you move west, the ground becomes dotted with cream-colored blackfoot daisies and the soft lavenders of rough blazing stars. Also noticeable is an increase in the number of piñon pine and both one-seed and Rocky Mountain

Gumweed

Rough Blazing Star

juniper, huddling in greater and greater concentrations until, at just under a mile into the walk, you'll find yourself in a virtual forest of "p-j," as it's known throughout the Southwest. Also growing in this area is wavyleaf oak, with its shiny, blue-green leaves, scattered bunches of blue grama and buffalo grass and several narrowleaf yuccas. Yuccas have evolved an amazing dependency on a certain genus of moth as their sole source of pollination. The moth begins the process by collecting pollen from several yucca plants. She then proceeds to a plant, inserts her ovipositor and deposits her eggs next to the plant's ovary. Then comes the remarkable part. The moth actually places the pollen she collected earlier on the stigma of the flower, thus ensuring that the plant's seeds will grow, which will in turn provide food for the larvae of her offspring. This is surely one of the most fascinating cases of mutual cooperation in all the natural world.

Also growing in the more open areas along this stretch will be a few milkweed plants. These are especially easy to recognize once they acquire pods, which eventually split open on one side to release thousands of silky-winged seeds. Milkweed contains toxic chemicals that are actually related to several of the drugs used in treating heart disease. When monarch butterflies, which eat nothing but milkweed leaves, consume these chemicals, they, in turn, become toxic to any bird that eats them. What a novel way to avoid ending up as an in-flight dinner for some feathered predator!

In 1.8 miles the road reaches the lip of Mills Canyon. Look 700 feet below; you can see the beautiful Canadian River (*Canadian* thought to be a corruption of a Caddo Indian word for "red river"), flowing beneath sheer, crumbling, red- and buff-colored cliffs. It was after trying to find the source of this river system that Zebulon Pike, for which Pikes Peak was named, was interned briefly by Spanish soldiers in 1807. He was later swiftly escorted out of Spanish Territory and turned loose in the middle of nowhere in southeast Texas. Today Mills Canyon seems far removed from territorial power struggles. Somehow it has kept at least a shred of the tranquility that must have been here long, long ago, when Kiowa Indians still led their ponies beneath these warm, brown walls, gathering fish, game and fruits from the rich folds of the earth.

WALK #77—SAND PASTURES

DISTANCE:	4.8 miles
ENVIRONMENT:	Prairie
LOCATION:	Kiowa National Grassland, Unit 3. Head south on New Mexico Route 406 out of Clayton for approximately 0.6 mile south of mile marker 362; turn left (east) onto a gravel road. In 3 miles this road will make a sharp turn to the north, and in another mile make a sharp turn back east. From this second turn proceed east for 2 miles to a smaller dirt track that takes off to the right. Park near this intersection. Walk south alongside this dirt track road, but stay on the west side of the fence, as the road itself is on private property. In 0.6 mile you'll reach a gate in an east-west fence line, with a windmill on your left. From here the walk follows an old roadway running to the southeast; to reach it you'll have to first cross through the gate on the east-west fence, and then cross the north-south fence on your left.

On the whole, managers of the national grasslands tend to meet the couple of hundred inquiries they receive from hikers each year with some skepticism, fairly certain that only a handful of people would really appreciate a day or two ambling across these vast, empty spaces. And with few or no facilities, obscure road systems and the general lack of water, perhaps they're right. Yet I found walking the prairie to be a wonderful experience. Lightly rolling oceans of grass and forbs stretch forever in every direction, stroked by the ever-present fingers of the wind. In spring the land is peppered with the reds, lavenders and lemons of globemallow, daisies and buttercups, while in late summer and early fall it explodes with miles of smiling sunflowers. And all around there is sky. Sometimes it appears soft and tranquil, other times fierce. But always it floods the senses with its sheer enormity. It is the undisputed master of the scene, the caller of the tune to which, season after season, the prairie must dance.

While there are almost no true, native prairie mixes left in this part of the country (or in most other parts, for that matter), this walk does give you a good sense of how diverse grasslands can really be. The sand pastures we'll be wandering through are particularly significant in that they're in very good shape, despite the region having been so thoroughly ravaged just 60 years ago. In fact, this area supports the only bluestem climax community to be found for miles, making it as close to the real "Old West" prairie as you're likely to see.

Lark Sparrow

Our walking road will carry you past a thick mat of vegetation, a clear indication that the 15 or so inches of rain that falls here each year is enough to maintain a rich community of plants. Look for a mixture of side-oats and blue grama grasses, as well as prairie shoestring, snakeweed, groundsel and narrowleaf yucca. As for prairie birds, you should be able to spot rough-winged swallows, brown thrashers, kingbirds, mockingbirds, loggerhead shrikes, lark buntings, northern orioles, horned larks, magpies, western meadowlarks and, if you drive along these roads in the summer, wave after wave of lark sparrows. Grasslands can be especially beautiful to the ear, since the birds who live in these open spaces tend to let loose their territorial songs while flying, something that the birds of the forest rarely do.

There are also plans to reintroduce the prairie chicken. This beautiful bird once numbered in the millions, ranging from Texas into Canada, and eastward all the way to Ohio. Indeed, they were so numerous that early settlers could often bring down several with a single shot. Many are the old reports of the prairie chicken courtship rituals that occurred each year. The birds danced, flashed their tail feathers, inflated orange air sacs on either side of their neck and of course "boomed," producing a low, dull roar that floated through the crisp February air, often being heard a mile or more away. These mating theatrics took place on special stages, or *booming grounds*, which some researchers believe were used over and over, perhaps for several hundred years.

Tahoka Daisy

Common Buttercup

One of the most striking creatures of the western grasslands is the pronghorn, which you may well see grazing on the lands surrounding this walk. To say that the pronghorn is remarkable is a gross understatement. It is the fastest mammal in the Western Hemisphere, having been clocked running close to 70 miles per hour for very short periods. A distance runner as well as a sprinter, it can maintain slower speeds for 15 miles at a time, which tends to leave many of its predators panting in the dust. (Pronghorn fawns can run at speeds in excess of 25 miles per hour when they're just two weeks old!) Pronghorn are able to exist comfortably with little or no water, getting what they need from the plants that they eat. These plants, by the way, tend to include all of those that other animals won't touch, including several thorny and even poisonous varieties. Both male and female pronghorns have black horns, the sheath of which is shed each year. The horns of the female, however, rarely grow more than 4 inches long, while the male's often reach over a foot. In times of danger, the animals stiffen the glistening white hair on their rump patches, an act that serves as a warning to other members of the herd. Pronghorn, incidentally, are often referred to as antelope, which they are definitely not. Unique to North America, they have been given their own family name, Antilocapridae, which translates into "antelope-goat."

As the walk continues, look for fine collections of sand and little bluestem grasses. At 2.3 miles, just before our turnaround point at a windmill, you'll see an old gnarled tree standing stark against a wash of sky, the only one visible anywhere on this rolling sea of grass, shrubs and forbs. This lonely sentinel seems like a perfect backdrop to the tales of heartbreak that occurred on this prairie during the 1930s—hopes and dreams shattered by severe drought, overgrazing and the plowing of thousands of acres that were never meant to sustain intensive farming. In the early 1930s, this area needed 84 schools to serve its ballooning population; today it needs only three. The scant remains of these sad times— abandoned homes, mineral-poor lands over-run with snakeweed, parched windmill towers creaking in the prairie winds—can still be seen along many of the region's back roads. They are a sober reminder of how fragile our dance with nature really is, how easily this intricate tapestry can come unraveled.

Southern New Mexico

WALK #78—WHITE SANDS

DISTANCE: . 7 miles
ENVIRONMENT: Desert
LOCATION: White Sands National Monument. Monument headquarters is located on U.S. Highway 70/82, 13 miles south of Alamogordo. From headquarters, head west into the park on the "Heart of the Dunes Scenic Drive." (At headquarters you can pick up a free interpretive guide to this road.) There are numbered posts along this drive which correspond to the interpretive guide. Our walk is to the Back Country Camp, and leaves from the south side of the road, opposite marker 7.

There is no place in America as unique, as startling in its sheer degree of shimmering vastness, than the White Sands of southern New Mexico. This is the largest gypsum dune field in the world. Driving to the western-most point of the loop road, which you may want to do before you begin this walk, you will feel a tug at your senses in a way that they have never been pulled before. Partway in, a fine layer of gypsum grains begin to scatter across the roadway, lightly at first, but building slowly until they completely obliterate the pavement. When well packed, the grains look remarkably like a sheet of ice; you drive slowly, your foot poised on the brake, thinking that at any minute you might slide off the road. Massive, bright white shoulders of sand rise around you, consuming the view in every direction. It is as if you had slipped through space to another planet, one whose surface is covered by a strange, shifting quilt of warm desert snow. So striking is this dune field, in fact, that it is one of the last earth forms identifiable by astronauts, visible fully halfway from here to the moon.

This 300-square-mile field of sand owes its existence to a complex set of geologic events. The 150-mile-long Tularosa Basin, of which the White Sands is only a small part, began forming hundreds of millions of years ago, when a series of ancient seas invaded and retreated from the area, laying down beds of sediments thousands of feet thick. Some 200 million years later, the same series of uplifts that created the Rocky Mountains also thrust this land skyward. This particular region happened to be bordered by large north-south fault lines, which, much later, allowed it to slowly sink back into the earth, forming a giant, enclosed basin. Because there is no outlet, all the bits and pieces of rock carried by rainwater from the surrounding high country end up trapped in this basin. So far, the rubble has accumulated to a depth of almost 2,000 feet.

To form the sands themselves required first that rain and snowmelt carry down gypsum from the surrounding mountains. Since gypsum is so easily dissolved in water, it poured out of the high country into this basin in great quantities, much of it flowing into the waters of Lake Otero to the southwest. When changes in climate caused Lake Otero to disappear, a massive field of minerals was left, including the selenite from which much of this sand is derived. (Due to impurities, selenite crystals often appear brown; dehydration and abrasion of the surfaces by wind, however, tend to whiten them.)

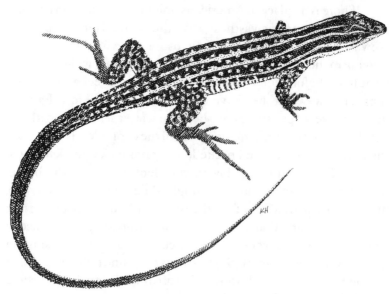

Chihuahuan Spotted Whiptail

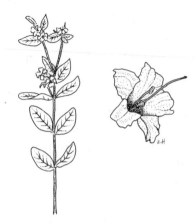

Desert Four O'Clock

All that was required from this point was the arrival of wind—at least 17 miles per hour—to launch these grains into the air. When sand is stopped by a ground object, the grains begin to build higher and higher on the windward side of the obstacle until they have completely covered it. A crest eventually forms on the mound, leaving it looking like a great, white ocean wave frozen in the desert. These crests, in turn, form launching ramps for new sand grains, which blow out over them and fall down the other side. In this way dunes actually move, or *migrate*, along their lee side, which, in this case, is to the northeast.

Because paths, rock cairns and every other conventional system of trail marking would soon be obliterated by the blowing sand, this walk is made by following a series of numbered posts southward. Once away from the road you'll find this to be a stunning, beautiful world. Rubber rabbitbrush and soaptree yucca race the wind to keep their heads above the migrating dunes. Sometimes blowing sand becomes firmly packed into a plant's fine web of roots. When the dune moves on, beautiful gypsum pedestals remain, like those visible to the left a short distance into the walk. Despite the fantastic adaptability of these plants, as well as about 60 other species found here, vegetation living on the dunes owes much of its existence to a strange, little-understood mix of bacteria and algae that thrive in this shifting world. Without them, there would almost certainly not be enough nutrients for these plants to survive.

As you continue south along a high ridge of sand, you'll have good views of the San Andres Mountains to the west, and the Sacramento Peaks to the east. The names of both of these ranges attest to the deep Spanish-Catholic roots of New Mexico. The former range was named for Saint Andrew, and the latter for Holy Eucharist. (Because certain saints are hallowed during different times of the year, the name that a place ended up with often depended on what month it was discovered.)

Near marker post 5 you'll be able to spot several cottonwoods growing in the nearby dunes—rather a surprise, since cottonwoods never grow in places where there is not permanent groundwater fairly near the surface. In fact, in some of the lower areas of this dune field, water may not be more than 3 feet beneath the ground.

After you climb the hummocks behind the designated backcountry camping area, take a minute to sit down and look around you. Note the brown heads of rice grass, and the sweet scent of rosemary mint hanging on the desert wind. A short line of whiptail lizard tracks arcs across the sand, stopping abruptly at the point where a roadrunner suddenly arrived and carried him off for dinner. Every so often the air runs thick with bird song—the loud whistles of a Bullock's oriole, or the fluty melodies of a western meadowlark. Though the White Sands is indeed a harsh place to live, it is hardly devoid of wonders. Here the world has struck a special balance, a carefully evolved, Spartan harmony between an unforgiving climate and the indomitable flow of life.

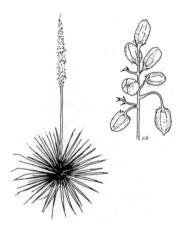

Soaptree Yucca

WALK #79—RATTLESNAKE CANYON

DISTANCE: 1 mile

ENVIRONMENT: Desert

LOCATION: Carlsbad Caverns National Park. To reach Carlsbad Caverns, head south out of Carlsbad on U.S. Highway 62/180 for 20 miles to White's City. Turn west on New Mexico Route 7 and the Park Entrance Road, and proceed for 7 miles. A signed, 9.5-mile scenic loop drive takes off to the west just before reaching the park visitor center. The signed Rattlesnake Canyon Trail is located on the south side of this road, approximately 4 miles from the starting point of the loop.

The vast majority of visitors to this national park head 750 feet straight down, bound for the spectacular medley of limestone chambers that make up Carlsbad Caverns. What most don't realize, however, is that there's also a very engaging world up on top, found in the endless folds of rock and sky, in the yawning plateaus and quiet, hidden nooks of the Chihuahuan Desert.

The Rattlesnake Canyon walk offers a good taste of the rugged drainage systems sliced into this ancient ocean reef, as well as the thin, green cover of plant life that has woven itself across these rocky shoulders. The trail begins with a quick westward descent into a small wash. Following this wash for a short distance, it then crosses over to hug the north face of a large thumb of rock, the wash falling away in a mad tumble toward the bottom of Rattlesnake Canyon. Along this stretch you'll see a fine collection of desert plants, including one-seed juniper, sotol, lechuguilla and New Mexico's state flower, the soaptree yucca

Every one of these plants, as well as dozens of others found in these canyons, was utilized by the people who lived here long ago. One-seed juniper provided good firewood, and the shreddy bark of the tree was used in making mats, sandals and even cloth. You might at first mistake sotol (a member of the lily family) with the yucca, but its sawtooth-shaped leaves and tall stalk with tight clusters of tiny white flowers are unique. The Apaches roasted the "heart" of the sotol plant in stone-lined pits, made a fermented drink from the sap and wove the tough, flexible leaves into baskets and mats. Lechuguilla, with its collection of foot-long, sword-like leaves (and, in some years, a 6- to 10-foot-tall flower stalk), provided fiber, food and drink, while the tall, palm-shaped soaptree yucca gave rope, food and a soapy cleanser that could be squeezed from the plant's roots. Though some people confuse the yucca with the agave, the yucca has white fibers curling back from the edges of its leaves.

Our trail continues around this thumb of rock, the land opening up with each step. By 0.3 mile you'll have gained a sweeping view of the sharply eroded lands to the southwest. This area has a rugged, untamed look to it, as if desperados might still be holed up in the stony side pockets of Rattlesnake Canyon, plotting an evening bust of the Butterfield Stage.

John Butterfield's mail stage ran just to the south of here, twisting along the soaring Guadalupe Ridge. Butterfield was a mail-stage operator from the East, and in 1857 he was awarded a post office plum worth more than half-a-million dollars a year to construct a stage system that could deliver mail between St. Louis and San Francisco. The 2,800-mile run was to be made twice a week, and each trip was to take no longer than five days to complete. Remarkably, Butterfield was able to get the entire system up and running within the single year that the government

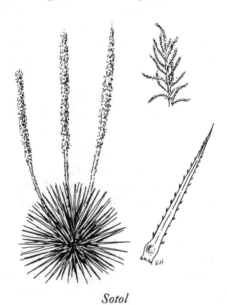

Sotol

Cholla

had allotted him. While for the most part, the mail rode east and west no worse for the wear, the same could not be said for Butterfield's passengers. Most found the ride through these vast spaces to be a bone-shaking horror of dust and heat; more than a few decided to abandon the trip long before their stage ever rolled onto California soil. Unfortunately, the Overland Mail Line had hardly settled into a comfortable routine when Texas seceded from the Union, and no longer allowed passage of the U.S. Mail. The operation was moved north, and sold in 1862.

Our turnaround point is reached in 0.5 mile, just before the path begins a zig-zag plunge into the drainage below. Those who wish to make this descent will find themselves wrapped in a thick blanket of wash vegetation, reaching in another 0.5 mile a fine amphitheater formed by the intersection of two canyon systems. This is a particularly good place to see a variety of desert bird and animal life. As you head back from our turnaround point, keep your eyes open along this open stretch for ocotillo and Engelmann prickly pear. Ocotillo is a strange-looking collection of spiny, spindly branches, typically growing 5 to 10 feet high. If you see tiny green leaves running up and down the ocotillo's branches, it has rained here in the not-too-distant past. As the soil dries these will wither and fall off, helping the plant to avoid a loss of moisture from water escaping through the leaf pores.

WALK #80—GUANO ROAD

DISTANCE: 2.5 miles
ENVIRONMENT: Desert
LOCATION: Carlsbad Caverns National Park. Northeast of the visitor center. The walk heads east along the old entrance road to the park, which is adjacent to the current entrance. Alternatively, you can take the nature trail near the cavern entrance and come out on our walking road just a short distance to the east; you would take a right onto this road. (Those beginning near the main cave entrance may have to tell the ranger where they are headed, since this is a holding area for cave tours.)

You may be surprised at how you can meander a couple hundred yards from the spot where most of Carlsbad Caverns' 800,000 yearly visitors gather, and suddenly find yourself wrapped in the peace and quiet of the Chihuahuan Desert. The ravine you'll be following (Bat Cave Draw) derives its name from the fantastic explosion of Mexican free-tail bats that pour out of the cavern entrance most evenings from May to October. Hundreds of thousands of these nimble fliers spin out of the cave like a small cyclone, always flying out counterclockwise, then pour down this dry land bound for the insect-laden banks of the Black and Pecos rivers. The amphitheater on your left at the beginning of our walk is devoted to this spectacle. Each evening, except during inclement weather, a short, interpretive talk is given before the bats rise out of the cavern to begin their all-night forays. Mexican free-tail bats live at the highest population density of any mammal in the world; adults typically form cozy roost packs of 1,800 animals to the square yard!

It was these bats, incidentally, or more correctly the feces, or *guano*, they produce, that brought the first Europeans into this largest of North American caves. Guano is a valuable, nitrate-rich fertilizer, and collections here during the first two decades of this century ended up on farm crops throughout the country, especially on the citrus crops of southern California. The road you're walking on is the route that miners used to haul guano from the cave into the town of Carlsbad.

It wasn't until almost 1920 that tourists began coming here in earnest; the earliest were lowered two at a time into the cavern in large metal buckets. Though this cavern system has been thoroughly explored since it became part of the national park system in 1923, new discoveries continue to be made both in Carlsbad Caverns as well as in the park's other backcountry caves, which now number 77.

The faint tracks you're following run through a fine mat of Chihuahuan Desert vegetation. You'll see plenty of soaptree yucca, recognizable from the curled white fibers on the edges of its leaves. Also here is a small evergreen tree known as one-seed juniper, as well as snakeweed, algerita, catclaw acacia (watch out for the thorns!) and Engelmann prickly pear. The large purple fruits visible on the prickly pear during late summer are known as "tunas," hence the common name of tuna cactus. They are quite tasty, though over the last hundred years they have shifted from the mainstay of desert Native Americans into a substance for making novelty candy and jelly. (Collecting of fruits is not permitted in national parks except for personal consumption; plants, rocks or artifacts may not be removed.) An abundance of prickly

Black-tailed Jackrabbit

pear, along with snakeweed and Russian thistle, can be an indication that the land has been overgrazed. Because in many areas outside these parklands overgrazing is the rule rather than the exception, prickly pear continues to claim new territory each year. At about 0.5 mile the path branches left, marked by a sign and a series of rock cairns (small rock piles used as trail markers). From here you'll follow a shallow ravine, with a ridge of land on your right that will drop away as you reach the 1-mile point.

From the flat ridgetop at 1 mile, high on a 400-mile-long ancient ocean reef, you'll be afforded an expansive view of a vast, dry tableland, with only the mighty Guadalupe Mountains checking the long drift of desert far to the southwest. Not far from here the Overland Mail Stage bounced its way west from St. Louis to California, the desert dust licking at its wooden wheels. Here also were outlaws, some lurking in the caves that dot this reef, and some, like Blackjack Ketchum, riding fast on lathered, thirsty horses in mad dashes for the Mexican border.

To the north and east of where you now stand was also the domain of one Henry McCarty, or, as his gravestone in the old Fort Sumner cemetery declares, "alias Billy the Kid." By the time

Mexican Free-tail Bat

sheriff Pat Garrett gunned the Kid down in a dark room at the tender age of 22, he had amassed an amazing reputation. At least one eastern newspaper painted him as a dashing outlaw dressed in black buckskin and silver bells, sporting $300 jewel-bedecked hats. But, as a newspaper correspondent in Lamy, New Mexico, related after the Kid's death in 1881, "He needs no bogus silver spurs stuck on his heels by a Philadelphia scribbler to send him galloping down to a bloody and dare-devilish immortality in the annals of this strange, wild territory. The simple story of his hideous career would fill a volume written in letters of fire and blood, and give a better idea than all the inventions of pen-and-ink extravaganzas of a thousand correspondents, of the desperadoism that has for years cursed New Mexico and retarded the development of the richest region on the continent."

Though I chose to turn around at the 1.25-mile mark, you can continue to follow the Guano Road for another 2.25 miles.

WALK #81—RATTLESNAKE SPRINGS

DISTANCE:	0.3 mile
ENVIRONMENT:	Desert
LOCATION:	Carlsbad Caverns National Park. Head south out of Carlsbad, New Mexico, on U.S. Highway 62/180 for approximately 25 miles to County Road 418. Turn right and follow signs to Rattlesnake Springs Picnic Area, 3 miles to the west. Park in the space provided adjacent to the restrooms.

Whether you've never seen a true desert oasis before or have spent half your life rambling from one water hole to the next, you'll find Rattlesnake Springs to be one of the finest, most enchanting places ever born along a cool trickle of water. The distance to be covered barely qualifies this as a walk at all. But there is so much to be seen here, such a rich, tightly woven tapestry of life, that making even a hundred yards can take the better part of an hour.

In particular, this is a place for birds of all feathers. The small unit of land surrounding the spring, as well as the picnic area where you parked, forms a small subunit of Carlsbad Caverns National Park. This 80-acre tract is co-managed with a 14-acre parcel immediately to the south owned by the Nature Conservancy; together they provide critical habitat for several of the 273 species that have been sighted in the immediate area. This is the only breeding area in the entire state for eastern bluebirds and orchard orioles; the latter can sometimes be seen in the branches of the plains cottonwoods. Perhaps new to your New Mexico bird list will be the Bell's vireo, usually quite willing to entertain your curiosity, as well as the varied bunting, either of which may be seen in the mesquite thickets surrounding the oasis.

From the parking area, walk west on the dirt road and pass through a Park Service gate at the far end of the picnic ground. The land to your left contains a lush mix of plains cottonwoods, black willow and, in late summer, a virtual jungle of sunflowers. To the right is a beautiful grove of Russian olives. This was a tree frequently planted throughout the Southwest as a windbreak, which ultimately escaped the civilized life and has since done quite well on its own. Just beyond this grove to the north, as if an invisible climate line had been drawn, lie the northern reaches of the Chihuahuan Desert. Here is a much more measured collection

Globemallow

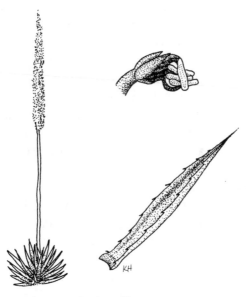

Lechuguilla

of life which includes mesquite, prince's plume, little leaf desert sumac, feather dahlia, western soapberry and catclaw acacia.

Because the Chihuahuan Desert experiences slightly greater precipitation and cooler temperatures than other deserts of the Southwest, you'll find more grasses here than you might expect (at least in areas where they haven't been grazed out of existence). There are also more agaves, particularly the lechuguilla. This plant, practically the trademark of the Chihuahuan Desert, was used by early desert peoples to make sandals, mats and baskets. Because it may take more than 15 years for a lechuguilla to store enough food to launch its towering 6- to 10-foot flower stalk, you'll never see all the plants in one area flying their beautiful lemon-colored blossoms in the same season. Lovely as it is during bloom, this is not a plant to tangle with; its pointed leaves can easily puncture an automobile tire.

Visible to the north through the thick line of vegetation is towering Capitan Reef. This is a massive, 400-mile-long precipice made up of billions of marine plant and animal skeletons deposited here by ancient oceans more than 200 million years ago, then cemented together by a thick crust of lime. Soaring on the desert thermals that rise along this wall are turkey vultures, those insufferably homely, but tremendously graceful, birds that make a most sensible living off of what is already dead. Rattlesnake Springs is an important stopover for turkey vultures migrating south in the fall.

Soon you'll come to a Park Service residence on the right, just past which is Rattlesnake Springs itself—a beautiful rock-lined pool built by workers in the 1930s, fringed on the south and east by thick curtains of Johnson grass. These springs, by the way, provide all of the 28,000 gallons of water used each day in Carlsbad Caverns National Park.

Return to the picnic area the way you came. If you're interested in getting to know more of the feathered residents of Rattlesnake Springs, take a right past the Park Service gate at the west end of the picnic ground, and then another right on a small trail near the park boundary. You can stroll for about 60 yards along the Nature Conservancy wetlands—a wonderful spot to see long-billed marsh wrens, vireos, vermilion flycatchers and perhaps even a green heron. If you do cross the fence into this area, do not in any way disturb the marsh. Sitting along this path in the cool shade of a plains cottonwood, the air thick with bird song and the flash of colored feathers, is a rare, delicious treat—one more of the Chihuahuan Desert's many surprises.

· Suggested Reading ·

Benyus, Janine M. *The Field Guide to Wildlife Habitats of the Western United States*. New York: Fireside, 1989.

Buchholtz, C. W. *Rocky Mountain National Park—A History*. Boulder: Colorado Associated University Press, 1983.

Christiansen, Paige, and Frank Kottlowski, eds. *Mosaic of New Mexico's Scenery, Rocks, and History*. Socorro: New Mexico Bureau of Mines and Mineral Resources, 1972.

Costello, David. *The Prairie World*. Minneapolis: University of Minnesota Press, 1981.

Dobelis, Inge N., ed. *The Magic and Medicine of Plants*. Pleasantville, N.Y.: The Reader's Digest Association, Inc., 1986.

Dodge, Natt N. *Flowers of the Southwest Deserts*. Tucson, Ariz.: Southwest Parks and Monuments Association, 1985.

Elmore, Francis H. *Shrubs and Trees of the Southwest Uplands*. Tucson, Ariz.: Southwest Parks and Monuments Association, 1976.

Haines, Aubrey. *The Yellowstone Story*. 2 vols. Yellowstone National Park, Wyo.: Yellowstone Library and Museum Association, 1977.

Howard, Joseph Kinsey. *Montana: High, Wide, and Handsome*. New Haven, Conn.: Yale University Press, 1959.

Larson, T. A. *Wyoming: A History*. New York: W. W. Norton & Company, 1984.

Lavender, David. *The Rockies*. Lincoln: University of Nebraska Press, 1968.

Mutel, Cornelia Fleischer, and John C. Emerick. *From Grassland to Glacier: The Natural History of Colorado*. Boulder, Colo.: Johnson Books, 1984.

Peattie, Donald Culross. *A Natural History of Western Trees*. Lincoln: University of Nebraska Press, 1953.

Roadside Geology Series. Missoula, Mont.: Mountain Press Publishing. (This series includes books on New Mexico, Wyoming, Colorado, Montana and the Yellowstone country.)

Ubbelohde, Carl, Maxine Benson, and Duane A. Smith, eds. *A Colorado History*. Boulder, Colo.: Pruett Publishing, 1982.

Vandenbusche, Duane, and Duane A. Smith. *A Land Alone: Colorado's Western Slope*. Boulder, Colo.: Pruett Publishing, 1982.

Zwinger, Ann, and Beatrice Willard. *Land Above the Trees*. New York: Harper & Row, 1972.

· Index ·

Index

Index

Index

Washburn, Mount, 51
Water birch, 178
Water lily, 126
Water ouzel. *See* Dipper
Waters, E. C., 52–53
Waterton Canyon Recreation Area, 173–75
Wavyleaf oak, 243
Weasel, xiv, 90, 160
Weber sandstone, 108
Weminuche Wilderness, 130
West Fork Trail, 230
West Glacier, Montana, 16
West Mesa, 196, 198
West Needle Mountains, 127
West Yellowstone, Montana, 33
Western bluebird, 169
Western coneflower, 76
Western Hemlock, *5*
Western kingbird, *181*, 182
Western larch tree, 17, 28
Western meadowlark, *181*, 182, 246, 252
Western soapberry, 261
Western tanager, *24*, 223
Western wheatgrass, 95, 180, 183
Western white pine, 5
Westport, Missouri, 184
Wheatgrass, xvii, 45, 46, 84, 85, 87. *See also*
    Western wheatgrass
Whiptail lizard, 252
Whirlpool Canyon, 105, 108
Whirlpool Canyon Overlook, 103–5
White clover, 34
White fir, 124, 215, 216, 221, 228
White Mountains (California), 136
White Sands National Monument, 249–52
White swan, 28
Whitebark pine, 51
White-breasted nuthatch, 98
White-crowned sparrow, xiv, 129, *151*, 152
White's City, New Mexico, 253
White-tailed deer, 23, 42, 45, 57, 99
White-tailed ptarmigan, xv, *142*
Whortleberry, 51, 164, 171
Wijiji, 201–4
Wijiji Mesa, 202
Wild ginger, 5, 9
Wild horse, 78
Wild lettuce. *See* Monkeyflower
Wild lily-of-the-valley, 178
Wild plum, 99
Wild prairie rose, 189
Wild rose, *35*, 36, 46, 59, 172, 178, 232
Wildflower, 111, 128, 155
    alpine, 133
Williamson's sapsucker, xxi
Willow, 36, 62, 89, 121, 126, 128, 150, 152, 154,
    163, 180, 189, 232, 233
    Anasazi use of, 196
    Montana Indians use of, 31
    Native American use of, 128–29, 229
Wilson, Mount, 132

Wilson Peak, 134
Wind River Range, 64, 82
Windy Ridge Bristelcone Pine Scenic Area, 140
Wingate Sandstone, 113
Winsor trail, 222–23
Wintergreen, 155
"Witches' thimble." *See* Harebell
Wolf currant, 209
Womac, "Crazy" Bob, 177
Wood duck, 42
Wood nymph, 155
Wood pewee, 98
Woodpecker, 165
Woodrats, 234
Wormwood. *See* Big sagebrush
Wyoming, xi, *50*, 51–99
Wyoming, Great Basin, walks, 77–85
    Emigrant Trail, South Pass, 80–82
    Honeycomb Buttes, 83–85
    Killpecker Dunes, 77–80
Wyoming, northeastern, walks, 87–99
    Joyner Ridge, 97–99
    Rochelle Hills, 87–89
    School Creek, 89–94
    Thunder Basin Flats, 94–96
Wyoming, northwestern, walks, 51–99
    Blackwater Creek, 57–60
    Dog Creek, 71–73
    Elephant Back Loop Trail, 51–53
    Elk Fork Creek, 60–62
    Granite Creek, 74–76
    Gros Ventre Slide, 64–67
    Pahaska Sunlight Trail, 53–57
    Shadow Mountain, 63–64
    Snow King Nature Trail, 67–71
Wyoming, southwest. *See* Wyoming, Great Basin

Yampa River, 108
Yampa River (walk), 109–11
Yarrow, 64, 67, 70, 72, 116, 117, 119, 128, 146,
    157, 163, 174, 178, 225, *226*, 230, 239
    medicinal uses, 72–73, 205–6
Yellow bell, xx
Yellow-bellied Marmot, xv, *65*
Yellow columbine, 19
Yellow dock. *See* Curly dock
Yellow pine. *See* Ponderosa pine
Yellow pond lily, use by Native Americans, 126
Yellow-rumped warbler, 99, 126, 172, *172*
Yellow warbler, 99, 126
Yellowstone Lake, 52
Yellowstone National Park, 34, 38, 97
    Elephant Back Loop Trail, 51–53
    Quake Lake, 66
Yellowstone River, 41, 44, 151, 152
    Clarks Fork, xiii, 38
Yucca, xvi, 45, 113, 178, 183, 188, 208, 213, 220,
    243
    Native Americans use of, 168

Zuni Indians, 231

· About the Author ·

Gary Ferguson is a freelance writer whose travel and outdoor recreation articles have appeared in more than a hundred magazines, including *Field and Stream, Outside* and *Sierra*. He is the author of 10 books on travel, science and medicine, including *Walks of the Pacific Northwest, Walks of New England* and the forthcoming *Walking Down the Wild,* a study of natural and cultural issues in the Yellowstone Rockies. For four years,  he was an interpretive naturalist for the U.S. Forest Service and won a 1990 National Association for Interpretation Award for Excellence in Communication. He lives in Red Lodge, Montana, with his wife, Jane.